Living by Inches

For Miss Nelle,

Thanks for supporting
my work! Hope you enjoy.

Best,
Evan Kutzler

CIVIL WAR AMERICA

Peter S. Carmichael, Caroline E. Janney, and Aaron Sheehan-Dean, editors

This landmark series interprets broadly the history and culture of the Civil War era through the long nineteenth century and beyond. Drawing on diverse approaches and methods, the series publishes historical works that explore all aspects of the war, biographies of leading commanders, and tactical and campaign studies, along with select editions of primary sources. Together, these books shed new light on an era that remains central to our understanding of American and world history.

Living by Inches

The Smells, Sounds, Tastes, and Feeling of Captivity in Civil War Prisons

Evan A. Kutzler

The University of North Carolina Press CHAPEL HILL

© 2019 The University of North Carolina Press
All rights reserved
Set in Merope Basic by Westchester Publishing Services
Manufactured in the United States of America

The University of North Carolina Press has been a member of the
Green Press Initiative since 2003.

Library of Congress Cataloging-in-Publication Data
Names: Kutzler, Evan, author.
Title: Living by inches : the smells, sounds, tastes, and feeling of captivity in
    Civil War prisons / Evan A. Kutzler.
Other titles: Civil War America (Series)
Description: University of North Carolina Press : Chapel Hill, [2019] |
    Series: Civil War America | Includes bibliographical references and index.
Identifiers: LCCN 2019012191 | ISBN 9781469653778 (cloth : alk. paper) |
    ISBN 9781469653785 (pbk : alk. paper) | ISBN 9781469653792 (ebook)
Subjects: LCSH: United States—History—Civil War, 1861–1865—
    Prisoners and prisons. | Military prisons—United States—History—
    19th century. | Military prisons—Confederate States of America—History. |
    Prisoners of war—Psychology. | Senses and sensation.
Classification: LCC E615 .K88 2019 | DDC 973.7—dc23 LC record available at
    https://lccn.loc.gov/2019012191

Cover illustration: Henry Van der Weyde's sketch of a fellow prisoner in
Danville, Virginia, from Henry Van der Weyde Sketchbook, 1864–1865.
Courtesy of the Library of Virginia, James I. Robertson Jr. Civil War
Sesquicentennial Legacy Collection.

For Amanda

Contents

Figures

Acknowledgments

Finishing this book has been a humbling experience that calls for more than a moment of reflection. As more experienced writers than I can confirm, every project takes on a life of its own, with a corresponding social web that extends far beyond the final pages and citations. I am so grateful for the mentorship of Mark Smith and Walter Edgar, both of whom have shared much wisdom over the years. I am also thankful to have learned much from Don Doyle, Larry Glickman, Ann Johnson, Lauren Sklaroff, Tracy Power, Bob Weyeneth, Saskia Coenen Snyder, Tom Brown, Kenneth Kelly, Adam Schor, and Dave Roediger. The Friends of Andersonville, the Kentucky Historical Society, the Virginia Historical Society, and Georgia Southwestern State University funded many short-term research trips over the years. Keeping a running list of each archivist's hint, each public historian's insight, or every random act of kindness by a fellow historian is easier kept in notes than transformed into formal acknowledgments. I have learned a great deal from talking with Chris Barr, Mike Gray, Angela Riotto, John McClure, John Coski, Patrick Lewis, Brian Cuthrell, John LeJeune, and Susan Bragg—to name just a few.

It is customary to share credit but none of the potential blame with readers—and time will tell if it is wise for me to continue in that tradition. In addition to several of the names above, Aaron Sheehan-Dean, Lorien Foote, Joan Cashin, Megan Kate Nelson, Kathryn Shively Meier, James Beeby, Barbara Gannon, Christopher Graham, Jennifer Hopkins, Tim Minella, Robert Greene, and Andrew Kettler read specific chapters from earlier versions of this book. I am especially grateful to Lacy Ford, Stephen Berry, Amanda Noll Kutzler, Mitch Oxford, Glenn Robins, Tim Williams, and the anonymous readers for the University of North Carolina Press who read the full manuscript and offered insight at critical points. Bob Ellis, in addition to being a good friend over the years, can index a book. Roger Pickenpaugh not only read chapters but also shared his personal research files. Pete Carmichael has been a key and consistent supporter from our first conversation in the fall of 2014 through the final manuscript. At the outset, this journey had promised to lead down a lonely road. I never would have predicted that I would make so many new friends and rack up so much social and professional debt along the way.

Not all forms of support are measured in dollars given or pages read. Roger and Marion Pickenpaugh, as well as Fern Pickenpaugh, opened their homes to me during my penultimate research trip in 2014. I also met a warm welcome in Plains and Americus, Georgia. Jill Stuckey gave me a furnished room when circumstances meant that I arrived in the state with one carload of possessions. Perhaps Jimmy and Rosalynn Carter regret asking about my work at our first dinner together at Jill's house; however, they did not recoil in horror during the conversation about odors and lice. The extended Carter family and friends, as well as the local public history community, have all supported this project in subtle but meaningful ways. Finally, my colleagues at GSW as well as my friends at Café Campesino, Habitat for Humanity, and the Americus community have been more than encouraging. I do not know what I would do without their drinks, humor, and fellowship.

More than anyone else, my family has sustained me through the ups and downs of research, writing, and rewriting. My mother has read more of my writing than anyone else, and my stepmother, father, and stepfather have all entertained strange historical ideas for decades—as has the rest of my family. My Noll in-laws, all of whom are teachers and/or historians, have shown great patience as I scurry off to work at early hours and on important holidays. Amanda and the cats—Billy and Jasper—never doubted me even when I doubted myself (well, maybe the cats did). Amanda nudged me to begin working when I felt that I could not start and reminded me to take breaks when I feared that I could not stop.

Introduction

For Samuel Gibson, a thirty-year-old carpenter from Armstrong County, Pennsylvania, captivity was agonizing before he ever reached a prison. It took only five days for him to romanticize the battlefield death he had escaped at Plymouth, North Carolina, where his whole regiment and garrison had surrendered. "I would prefer to be killed," he wrote along the railroad, "than be captured & killed by inches, and starved to death." What he then called "slim living" resulted not from spectacular abuse but the ordinary, even mundane, details of day-to-day life. Perhaps reconsidering his death wish the next day, Gibson concluded with a coda that expressed his longing to be home: "I wish I was my Fathers dog."[1] For twelve days the train was stop and go along the rails, and the men were often so crowded in boxcars that Gibson could not sit or lie down, let alone sleep. Above everything else on those early days, Gibson felt the heat. Moving from a covered railcar to an open one at Charleston, South Carolina, was "a leap, out of the pot [and] into the fire."[2]

Gibson's metaphors served as shorthand for his experience. Being "killed by inches" was an expression that dated back to at least the eighteenth century, when it was also used to describe agonizing experiences.[3] In both the American Revolutionary War and the Civil War it meant suffering on a different scale than on a battlefield and applied to prisons and hospitals where men wasted away over weeks and months. Yet for most captives, dying by inches was more about lived experience than death. Each prisoner was a casualty, and captivity was a prolonged state of limbo, uncertainty, and day-to-day suffering. One did not need to perish to experience this "dying" or, more accurately, "living" by inches.

Captivity overwhelmed Gibson's senses. In his first prison, he found the other men "literally rotten with dirt & vermin, & dying like sheep." Gibson considered himself a gentleman. At first he blamed the men around him for their apparent lack of hygiene; however, he soon adopted a bleaker environmental explanation, describing their circumstances as helpless. A week before messmate John Foster died of dysentery and a lung ailment, Gibson discovered that his friend had weakened from a man to something "as helpless as a child."[4] Gibson became numb to these surroundings, and

1

this made him feel more like what other soldiers called a "rough" than a gentleman. "I used to consider myself a man of *feeling* & some *principal*," he confessed the day before Foster died, but the hardships of captivity "have made me selfish & more like a Devil than a man." He reasoned that if hunger could make "the Hind forsake its calf," it must certainly make men "desperate" and quarrelsome.[5]

He was right. After hardly writing about rations at Plymouth, Gibson became fixated on food. During his third week of captivity, he promised to never again complain of "U.S. grub," and that night he "suffered a great deal with cramp in stomach, caused by the miserable corn bread we have to eat." Longing for the taste of coffee, Gibson steeped burnt cornmeal in hot water as a substitute for the beverage. Unseasoned observers might have considered this a waste of food, but Gibson knew better. The meat was "not fit for the stomach of an alligator" and the coarse meal was unfit for the stomachs of civilized men.[6]

Gibson's ears became attuned to the reverberations of captivity in places where each day sounded much like the one before it. The constant hum of rumors contributed to a feeling of timelessness; and while Gibson claimed the rumors were "not worth the breath that tells it," he still listened to them, wrote them down, and participated in their circulation. His listening paralleled the ups and downs of hope and despair. In songbirds, Gibson heard an echo of his own longing for freedom. "The birds sing as gayly as if all was well," he wrote. "How much I envy their happiness!" He daydreamed about breathing the fresh, free air outside of prison. "If I were metamorphosed into a bird," he longed, "I would not be long in this 'Bull Pen,' this Hell upon Earth."[7] The sounds of birds clarified Gibson's wish. He wanted to grow wings, fly over the north wall, and never look south.

Unable to take flight, Gibson drew inspiration from a successful escape in his dreams. Sleep did not come easily during the rainy days of June or the hot days of July, and night brought other discomforts and dangers. When Gibson rested in July, he had a recurring nightmare. Finding himself aboard a sinking steamboat on "a deep & *muddy* river," Gibson escaped by leaping from the upper deck of his vessel to the deck of another. Only then did he realize the second vessel was also sinking; he saved himself again by jumping to the broken pieces of a third ship and then moved across more boat wreckage to land. He survived while many others had drowned. Weeks later, the recurring dream still spoke to him when he vowed "to keep my head '*above water*.'" Yet, he admitted, "I am seeing my dream verified every day."[8] Comparing daily life to living by inches on a deep and muddy river, Gibson struggled to express meanings that resisted easy description. Near drowning was an apt metaphor for the daily bombardment of his senses at Andersonville, Charleston, and Florence.

Living by inches extracted a heavy toll. Gibson emerged from prison so "thin & shattered" seven months later that he could hardly stand the winter temperatures at Camp Parole, Maryland.[9] Men and women who thought themselves accustomed to the sights, sounds, and smells of camps, battle-fields, and hospitals were shocked at the condition of returning Union prisoners in 1864 and 1865. Walt Whitman thought the sight of exchanged prisoners at Annapolis the worst he had ever seen. Captivity had disabled strong men: it had stripped them of their physique, their color, their humanity, and at the time of his observation still threatened to claim their lives. Thinking about the disabled men brought off the boat on stretchers, Whitman asked, "Can those be *men* — those little livid brown, ash-streak'd, monkey-looking dwarfs? — are they really not mummied, dwindled corpses?" Even if they lived, Whitman predicted, "many of them are mentally imbecile, and will never recuperate." Far from the able-bodied Union men then routing Southern armies across the Confederacy, these ex-prisoners were something else. To Whitman they were the undead, the subhuman, and the evidence pointing to an unforgivable crime. Whitman's reaction spoke to the shock of seeing released prisoners, but it revealed little about how those men who had hung on for months thought about themselves.[10]

Prisoners shared with Whitman the belief that captivity could disable and dehumanize men. While Whitman could not believe his eyes at Annapolis, those returning explained their conditions most clearly in patterns of sounds, smells, tastes, and feeling. Whereas Whitman and many postwar memoirists interpreted returning prisoners as evidence of barbaric mistreatment — torture and murder — wartime diarists were more likely to record the inch-by-inch enervation of daily life. At times, living by inches pushed prisoners into cooperative agreements with one another against seen and unseen dangers; at other times, those same forces individualized experience and pulled prisoners against one another. Surviving captivity meant understanding the more subtle dangers of the sensory environment that came from passive neglect rather than active punishment.

Samuel Gibson's writing is compelling because all of us navigate the world through the eyes, ears, nose, palate, and skin. The senses not only provide orientation to time, place, and condition but also enable us to make decisions in a complicated world. In solo and in concert, the senses hide in everyday language and provide meaning in the unintentional sensory pun. Something that "makes sense" is communicable in the written or spoken word. To "see eye-to-eye" is to agree on an interpretation or, at the very least, agree on a set of facts. Getting a whiff, a taste, or a sense of something is a step toward grasping a broader topic or truth. Understanding the world through the five senses is part of being human.[11]

Studying history through the senses humanizes the past by exploring how people perceived their world. This is not because the senses are infallible; rather, it is their subjectivity that makes them valuable. Confederate civilians and soldiers prided themselves that Southern men could fight on cornmeal and a little bacon; Union prisoners believed that abrasive cornmeal ravaged their intestines and gave them the pervasive diarrhea that wore men down. If sensation connects humans across time and place in a neat uniformity, close attention to perception shatters that homogeneity. Gibson was no universal soldier. Cataloguing sensations is a start, but sensory perception holds the marrow of human experience. What—or who—smells foul and what that means to an individual may reveal as much about the person behind the nose as it does about the odor. The same goes for the other senses: what tastes wholesome; what laws and customs reflect the social norms of touch; what sounds like music, or noise, or humor, or harassment depends on time, place, and culture. From the individual to the society, perception reveals perspective and the patterns of experiencing the world.[12]

Prisoners and Their Senses

Prisoners, this book argues, feared that captivity had a disabling and decivilizing effect on men. From Gibson's degradation—wishing he was his father's dog, feeling like a rough instead of a gentleman, and watching his helpless, childlike friend die—to Whitman's zombies, the belief that captivity could tear men down is key to understanding their experiences. Sometimes this withering was literal. Many went into captivity as what their officers and physicians would have called able-bodied men. Exchanged prisoners, especially those coming from Southern prisons, often returned unfit for service. The unfitness of returning prisoners was one of the reasons the U.S. government refused to reopen the prisoner exchange in 1864 and began measured retaliation against Confederate prisoners. When special exchanges took place, men unfit for service came home on stretchers.

What accounted for these worn-down men was controversial in Whitman's time and remains so in our own. Postwar writings focused on acute suffering such as the hunger pangs of vindictive starvation, the shootings by bloodthirsty guards, and slave catchers running down men with blood-hounds. While wartime records contained these accusations as well, more persistent was the idea that the chronic details of prison life made captivity an inner struggle for prisoners. Fleeting and persistent sensations—the inches of lived experience—were how men perceived captivity as disabling and decivilizing. For this reason, *Living by Inches* breaks from the usual de-bates about intentional mistreatment and whose prisons were more wretched. It does not dwell on mortality rates. Most prisoners, Union and Confederate, survived imprisonment. Had the United States or the Confed-eracy wanted to kill their captured foe, even Andersonville and Elmira could have been more efficient in completing the task. Searching for an explana-tion as to *why* so many men died and who was responsible overlooks the human question of *how* so many lived.[13]

In recovering the totality of prison experience through fresh and foul air, familiar and foreign sounds, the tastes of ordinary meals, and other features of daily life, this book prioritizes imprisoned voices. Taking these men seri-ously requires avoiding the stereotype of pure victim and pure villain. It also requires recognizing the ability of prisoners to adapt in myriad ways to pre-serve their bodies, their minds, and their conceptions of themselves as civi-lized men. Night, for example, blinded the eyes and amplified the nonvisual senses in ways that ushered in prison's decivilizing realities. Some men felt disconnected from their past lives and alienated from other prisoners by the sounds and smells and feeling of night in captivity; others reached for com-radery, warmth, and emotional intimacy from men beside them. Darkness also affected power relations by blinding the guards and offering cover for small acts of resistance. Still, this was a deadly game. If night emboldened defiance, it also meant that guards turned to lethal force more quickly than in the daylight. While a few men found escape in fooling the eyes and ears of guards, many more found safer relief in their dreams of civilized home-lands and reunited families.

The same acute sensations at night were chronic during the day. Sanita-tion was an olfactory problem in the modernizing era of the mid-nineteenth century. Prison smells weakened men with every breath in places unfit for animals. Breathing fresh air and/or foul air became olfactory metonyms for imprisonment and freedom. Anosmia, a temporary loss of the sense of smell, could be a blessing or a sign of complacency, laziness, or neglect. The effect was similar: over time, prison wore down the nose, neutralizing the body's perceived defense against airborne disease. This was not mere hyperbole for people who upheld the civilized nose as the body's arbitrator between fresh air and foul air, healthy landscapes and sickly ones. Nor were lice simply annoying. As symbols of moral inferiority and uncleanliness in the antebellum era, these tiny prison tricksters pushed prisoners to reassess what it meant to be a clean man in a filthy place. Ultimately, many prisoners found relief by adjusting the rules of self-care—and exchanging disgust for humor.

Living by inches also meant adjusting to new sounds and tastes, including the endless prison cacophony and restricted choices in the quantity, quality, and supplementation of rations. Attention to patterns of listening reveals the cycles of hope and despair as prisoners tuned their ears to captivity. The absence of certain sounds, such as church bells, heightened the sense of isolation away from homes, families, and familiar places of worship. Hunger altered the palate, making men think, taste, and behave in ways that troubled them and their fellow prisoners. Still, the lonely and the hungry were not powerless. Prisoners chose what sounds to listen *for*, and they found temporary reassurance in rumors, singing, and sounds that came from beyond prison walls. Hungry prisoners also used, to varying degrees, external and internal supply lines that enabled them to preserve choice, an essential element in exercising taste. The language of disability and decivilization, though not necessarily physical or permanent, pervaded the thoughts of imprisoned men and those who interacted with them.

As an exercise in contextualizing experience, *Living by Inches* is not representative of all experiences. Black Union soldiers made up less than 1 percent of all those captured during the Civil War; however, in a war to preserve the Union and destroy slavery, the significance of African American prisoners cannot be underestimated. As U.S. Secretary of War Edwin Stanton explained to Major General Benjamin Butler in November 1863, Confederate officials "will exchange man for man and officer for officer, except blacks and officers in command of black troops." The issue of black prisoners and white officers, Stanton wrote, "is the point on which the whole matter hinges." From Stanton's perspective, consenting to the Confederate double standard of humanitarianism would abandon these prisoners, and the result "would be a shameful dishonor to the Government bound to protect them."[14] Despite the importance of black prisoners, the scarcity of wartime testimony means that recovering those experiences will require a different kind of book that more fully explores the postwar world.[15]

This book takes interpretive risks. By juxtaposing the sensory experiences of Union prisoners at Andersonville or Libby and Confederate prisoners at Johnson's Island or Elmira, there is the danger of implying parity of experience or a dubious brotherhood of blue and gray. That is not something I wish to convey. Rather, *Living by Inches* presents subjective and emotional experiences in a way that leads to a greater understanding of what wartime imprisonment meant to those who lived it. Instead of burying subjective experiences for the sake of appearing objective, the following pages excavate the difficult stuff of prison life: the smells, sounds, tastes, and feelings. Doing so recovers patterns of individual experience and the small terrors and small victories of daily life that are missed by keeping the senses—especially the nonvisual ones—in the background.

The Senses and the Civil War

The study of the senses in the Civil War era to which this book contributes has the potential to teach us a great deal about how Americans experienced the war. From battlefield to prison and across the entangled home front, the Civil War battered the senses day and night. As Mark M. Smith demonstrates in *The Smell of Battle, the Taste of Siege*, Americans believed in a sensory progressivism on the eve of the Civil War. The sanitarian movement fought smell and disease by promoting new underground sewers, and more Americans were bathing with soap and wearing intentionally clean clothing than ever before. Although the slaveholding South was stereotyped as exceptionally violent, there were social customs and legal codes surrounding touch in all regions of the United States. The Market Revolution had increased access to imported food across the urbanizing North as well as Southern cities from Richmond to Vicksburg and beyond. Americans across regional boundaries carefully ordered urban and rural soundscapes. The American officer class believed in the power of reason and vision to solve military problems.[16]

From camp to battlefield, hospital, and prison, the Civil War shook this confidence, and many experienced the war as a sensory revolution—or devolution. Having "smelled the gunpowder" became the olfactory equivalent of "seeing the elephant." Both expressions captured some essence of being amid the sulfurous smoke of rifled muskets and cannon. The human, nonhuman, and inhuman sounds of battle overwhelmed the ears. Shouting, whether the famous "Rebel yell" or not, stabilized the nerves of the yeller while intimidating the enemy. A volley of rifle fire produced a ripping sound; bullets and shells hummed, hissed, zipped through the air, and ripped through trees. Listeners turned to metaphors to familiarize the discord. The roar of cannons sounded like a thunderstorm. Lead projectiles and iron fragments rained down like hailstones.[17]

The results were more like a tornado. When striking bodies, the sound of destructive contact ranged from the "sharp crack" of broken bone to a "thud, a sickening, dull cracking sound." Lead and iron shattered men, animals, and landscapes in ghastly new ways. The animate sounds and smells of the aftermath affected the men and women involved in helping the wounded and collecting the bodies and the pieces of men from battlefields.[18]

Yet the sensory tumult of the Civil War was not limited to the battlefield. The physical distance separating families pushed men and women to write, and this resulted in a glut of new archival voices. When death occurred, advances in the preservation of corpses increased the possibility of family reunification. New music and national airs abounded. The sounds and feeling of slavery, so central to the experience of slaves, planters, travelers, and abolitionists, ended with the triumph of an alliance between enslaved African Americans, the Union army, and the U.S. government. By the end of Reconstruction, the voices of African American men became known in American politics and society, even if it took another century of struggle before the basic spirit of the era's constitutional amendments had secure footing.[19]

Scholars of Civil War soldiering have long used the senses implicitly to add texture to their sources. These sensory experiences often hid in plain sight. Few soldiers escaped encounters with spoiled food and bad water, whether in Union or Confederate armies. Sleeping arrangements were uncomfortable, and soldiers—especially prisoners—dreamed of the comforts of home. Soldiers read newspapers from around the country both silently and out loud to one another and sometimes published their own. Camp life spawned its own world of sound that was neither entirely new nor entirely old: instrumental music, glee clubs, minstrel troupes, political debate, jokes, and endless rumor. Soldiers protected their health by managing smell and taste: soldiers washed and bathed; they also foraged for food to supplement their rations. The senses, explicitly or implicitly, were everywhere in the American Civil War.[20]

Sensory history can help Civil War history move beyond stereotypes about soldiers and restore individuality without neglecting the big picture. Jason Phillips argues that Civil War soldiers have been typecast as the "heroes, victims, villains, race warriors, and citizens at war." Each of these categories can shed light on the conflict, but each also inevitably falls short of encompassing the full range of human experience. Phillips writes that Civil War soldiers "were individuals from diverse places who formed enormous armies bursting with local colors and scents, myriad accents, and internal rivalries."[21] Experience then was both collective and individual. For example, hundreds of thousands of men received ghastly wounds, but pain was individualized and, in some ways, inexpressible. "The moment a soldier got hit," Stephen Berry writes, "he and his wound were alone in the world, and they would walk the road to recovery alone too."[22] What was true for men in armies and field hospitals was similar for those in the hands of the enemy. Attention to the senses, to emotion, or to the hybridity between people and nature humanizes the individual experience that warfare, time, and stereotypes have blunted.[23]

An Overview of Civil War Prisons

Capture as much made one a casualty as a bullet wound. Like the wounded in a makeshift hospital, imprisonment was a collective and an individual experience. More than 400,000 soldiers and thousands of civilians fell into the hands of their enemies, and about 56,000 died in captivity.[24] For many individuals, captivity was more than just one chapter in their wartime lives; rather, it overshadowed other wartime experiences. In the decades after the Civil War, scores of postwar diaries and memoirs were published and hundreds more went unpublished. Yet this outflow is not reflected in academic literature. Civil War histories have traditionally favored soldiers who were not captured. Before the twenty-first century, there were a handful of articles and monographs on individual prisons, but only two general studies of Civil War prisons.[25] Since then there has been an uptick in scholarship on prison management, government policies, life inside prisons, and historical memory. *Living by Inches* brings focus back to the experience of captivity.[26]

If the language of disability and decivilization helps explain sensory experience, mobility is also key. The flow of prisoners from one place to another individualized experience and negates the necessity of focusing on a single prison. Every prison had its own unique qualities, but captivity was felt by the imprisoned person and not imprisoned populations. When Confederates placed Hiram Eddy, a Congregational minister and a regimental chaplain captured at Bull Run, in an abandoned tobacco factory in Richmond on July 28, 1861, it was just the start of his journey. He spent three nights in September on a prison train to Charleston, South Carolina, where he was moved back and forth between the Charleston City Jail and Castle Pinckney, a coastal fortification in Charleston Harbor. On January 1, 1862, he left for Columbia, South Carolina, remaining there for two months before returning to the original tobacco factory and then Libby Prison. With a Union army moving up the peninsula between the James and York Rivers in late spring, Confederates moved him to Salisbury, North Carolina, where a stockade surrounded a cotton factory and barracks. Finally, in July 1862, after twelve months, three states, six prisons, and fourteen hundred miles, the chaplain returned to Washington, D.C. Eddy's captivity was not at one place or the other; it encompassed each of these points and all the miles and railroad ties between them.[27]

The sheer number and diversity of makeshift prisons—at least 150—makes generalization difficult. Lonnie Speer divides these spaces into seven categories: there were preexisting jails ranging from the county and city level to state penitentiaries; preexisting fortifications along the Atlantic Ocean; large urban warehouses and abandoned factories converted into prisons; a gridded system of barracks, usually a converted training camp for U.S. volunteers, surrounded by a high wall; a gridded system of tents surrounded by a high wall or some other barrier; a simple stockade in which prisoners brought or made their own shelter; and barren ground in which a perimeter of guards stood around captured men. These prison types varied from one region to another. Most Confederate prisoners in the North lived in barracks at prison camps, though an important minority lived in tents, within or alongside coastal fortifications, and in formerly non-carceral buildings. In contrast, most Union prisoners in the South experienced the bottom tiers of this hierarchy. Many Union prisoners saw the inside of an old warehouse or scraped together shelter in barren stockades or open fields. Some Union prisoners late in the war saw all three. The diversity of prisons has led to a number of useful micro-histories on individual prisons, especially Northern prisons that were more organized and had longer operational lives than those in the Confederacy.[28]

These individual prisons were not isolatable parts of a rational, organized system of prison keeping. Union and Confederate governments responded to the unprecedented number of prisoners with different degrees of organization, but all prisons were improvised spaces. Prisons were established, expanded, and abandoned in response to changing military and political needs. Captivity for some began before the firing on Fort Sumter in April 1861 and ended after the surrenders of Confederate armies in the spring of 1865. Within these nebulous end points, ad hoc sites of captivity went well beyond Speer's typologies: battlefields were also places of captivity; major roads, railroads, rivers, and the eastern coast were routes of captivity; and makeshift spaces included open fields, railroad cuts, slave pens, jails, churches, abandoned houses, and outbuildings. At these points and along these routes, captives moved like flotsam from capture to prison and then often from one type of prison to another.[29]

Timing affected the construction of prisons, the mobility of prisoners, and the duration of captivity. There were two phases of prison expansion separated by a yearlong interlude. The first phase of expansion took place in 1861 through early summer 1862. For much of this time, it was uncertain whether the United States would exchange prisoners with an unrecognized Confederate government. Early prisons included many coastal fortifications. Along the Atlantic Coast, Fort McHenry, Fort Lafayette, and Fort Warren became early prisons for Confederate soldiers and political prisoners from the Border States. Confederates used Castle Pinckney in Charleston Harbor. In Midwestern states, U.S. officials established prisons at McDowell Medical College in St. Louis, the Illinois state prison at Alton, and built what became an officers' prison at Johnson's Island. After the fall of forts Henry and Donelson in February 1862, U.S. officials converted training camps at Camp Douglas (Chicago), Camp Butler (Springfield), Camp Morton (Indianapolis), and Camp Chase (Columbus). In the South, Confederate officials converted buildings into prisons in Tuscaloosa, Alabama; Macon, Georgia; Columbia, South Carolina; Salisbury, North Carolina; and, especially, Richmond, Virginia.[30]

A general exchange of prisoners, beginning in July 1862, lowered captive populations and put prison expansion on hold. The agreement, signed by Major General John A. Dix (Union) and Major General Daniel Harvey Hill (Confederate), was between U.S. and Confederate armies, not governments, for an important legal reason: the U.S. government worried about bestowing international legitimacy on the Confederate States of America. The "Dix-Hill Cartel" mirrored exchange systems of past American wars by exchanging prisoners on a man-to-man basis by rank. Designed to avoid prolonged detention, the agreement stipulated that prisoners must be paroled within ten days of capture after promising not to take up arms until they were formally exchanged.[31]

The short-lived agreement showed signs of weakness almost as soon as it was signed. Government officials and exchange agents on both sides of the divide bickered about technicalities, declared certain exchanges illegal and certain men outlaws, and came to different calculations about the number of prisoners owed to them. The United States had never been eager to enter into a prisoner exchange, but it soon lost one of its incentives when exchange did not improve soldier morale. Instead of reassuring soldiers that their country had their backs, the policy seemed ripe for exploitation by homesick soldiers. If capture meant being quickly paroled on an oath not to fight again until being formally exchanged, it amounted to a ticket away from the front line. However, race was the most important factor. By mid-1863, African American men were fighting in the Union army, and a new Confederate policy stipulated that black prisoners would be enslaved and white officers commanding black soldiers could be executed for inciting slave rebellions. In contrast, the United States had just bound itself to General Orders No. 100, stipulating treatment of prisoners without regard to race and institutionalizing proportional retaliation for abuses to prisoners. By July 1863, the Dix-Hill Cartel had all but collapsed.[32]

Scholars of prisoner policy have looked at the same records and come to different conclusions. Without suggesting moral equivalency between the United States and the Confederacy, prisoner exchange broke down because — for both sides — exchanging prisoners and humanitarianism were a possible means to an end but not the goal itself. While U.S. and Confederate intentions are still debatable, the effect on prisoners was more certain. The simultaneous surrender of Vicksburg and the Battle of Gettysburg reflected changing policy and experience. General Ulysses S. Grant paroled Vicksburg prisoners; many Union and Confederate prisoners taken at Gettysburg remained in captivity until 1865. Limited exchanges continued throughout the war, but the absence of a general exchange meant that prison populations surged.[33]

As exchange broke down, the impasse rerouted the current of captured soldiers into existing prisons and prompted a second wave of prison construction. In the North, these included Point Lookout, Maryland, in the summer of 1863; Rock Island, Illinois, in the late fall of 1863; and Elmira, New York, in July 1864. Instead of heading to points of exchange within ten days, prisoners now faced indefinite captivity in the circuitous network of Civil War prisons. Wash Nelson, a Confederate officer captured in northern Virginia, faced a journey similar to that of Hiram Eddy in 1861. Nelson traveled through Harper's Ferry to Camp Chase and Johnson's Island in Ohio. In late spring 1864, while hoping to be exchanged, he began a winding route of captivity: Point Lookout, Maryland; Fort Delaware; Morris Island, South Carolina; Fort Pulaski, Georgia. In the spring of 1865, he traveled back to Fort Delaware before taking the oath of allegiance to the United States and becoming free in the summer of 1865. While spanning more miles and months than most, his circuitous journey was common.[34]

The impasse created a similar effect in the Confederacy, and Union soldiers had similar odysseys. Confederate officials established prisons at Danville, Virginia, and Andersonville, Georgia. Union officers and enlisted men captured at the Battle of Chickamauga faced transportation from Georgia to Virginia to spend the winter. In the spring of 1864, instead of the exchange prisoners had anticipated all winter, the majority found themselves on trains bound for Macon and Andersonville. From the late summer of 1864 until the end of the war, Confederates deftly moved prisoners out of reach of Union armies through a series of makeshift prisons built by enslaved labor in parts of eastern Georgia and South Carolina. Special exchanges of prisoners became more common in late 1864 and early 1865, but many remained in captivity for the duration of the war.[35]

The Prison Archive

The smells, sounds, tastes, feeling, and sights of captivity are recoverable because prisoners left a vast archival record. This collective and decentralized prison archive consists of five broad types of sources, each of which has its own biases. Eight volumes of *The War of the Rebellion* provide the perspective of Union and Confederate captors, who were not necessarily disposed to look upon prisoners with sympathy. Wartime newspapers and government publications in the North and South during the war offered accusations of cruelty across the lines while defending prisons in their respective regions. Historians have been slower to recognize the subjectivity of the former than of the latter. The remaining three categories of the prison archive were produced by prisoners. Special collections repositories across the country contain letters, wartime diaries, and postwar memoirs. Letters from prisoners to family and friends are abundant, but these collections have unique limitations. Regulations limited letter size and content, restricting incoming and outgoing letters to one page and forbidding political or military invective. While some censors took bribes for longer letters and some prisoners smuggled private letters out, these were rare exceptions.[36]

Letter regulations, in effect, proscribed detailed descriptions of daily life. On June 12, 1864, Samuel Gibson bemoaned daily life at Andersonville in his diary. He wrote, "O Liberty; Law & Order! Thou canst not be appreciated till thou art once lost." A letter that left the stockade unsealed and reached Rachel Gibson bore the same date and came as close as any prison letter to being explicit about conditions. He stated that his circumstances were not enviable but "might be a great deal worse," adding a miniature, parenthetical question mark that the censor allowed to pass. Samuel maintained a cheerful tone, with the caveat that he did not know if she was receiving his letters. He instructed her to have "no uneasiness concerning *me*; I can live where any other man can."[37] Perhaps Rachel read fear into her Samuel's closing line when he reminded her that he was her loving husband until death. But this message, whether intended or perceived, went unstated. Neither the Gibsons nor anyone who wrote or read typical prison letters would have considered them private thoughts.

A great gap exists between the reputation of prison diaries and postwar memoirs in the prison archive. Here, disability—or at least the rhetoric of disability—has been used to discredit prisoner testimony. This idea became infused in scholarly literature with William Hesseltine's *Civil War Prisons: A Study in War Psychology* (1930). Hesseltine argued that prison conditions in the South were simply the consequence of losing a war; in the North, a "war psychosis" in the press and the public spurred an official policy of retaliation. This also poisoned the prison archive. According to Hesseltine, the "physical and mental wrecks" returning from Confederate prisons were untrustworthy and bitter. From Hesseltine's view, prisoner psychosis led to the execution of Henry Wirz, and ulterior motives led ex-prisoners to publish tales of suffering. This included writing for posterity, for economic necessity, and for retribution against Confederate leaders. Hesseltine also inferred two political purposes. Union prisoners, especially those who escaped and were aided by African Americans in reaching Union lines, were biased, according to Hesseltine, because they favored extending voting rights to black men. There was also pension legislation. "Prisoners came to the opinion," Hesseltine wrote, "that the mere fact of having spent the summer of 1864 at Andersonville should be adequate evidence of permanent disability." Hesseltine never explained why "war psychosis" afflicted the victor but not the defeated. Moreover, he simultaneously used the rhetoric of psychosis to discredit prisoners while denying that captivity disabled men.[38]

The handling of complicated sources has come a long way since Hesseltine. Postwar prison narratives represent the reality that Americans have never reconciled conflicting memories about captivity. The creation and preservation of the prison archive was itself a product of historical forces and the bitter debates about the treatment of prisoners and the meaning of the war. Nor is the distinction between unedited wartime diary and polished public memoir a fair dichotomy. As historian Ann Fabian notes, prisoners understood the world of reading, writing, and publishing. These writers knew that authenticity mattered to readers and sought to prove their prison narratives were the real deal. However, in manufacturing authenticity, wartime and postwar writers reproduced the narrative qualities of a captivity genre that echoed back to early American colonies.[39]

That concerns about audience are found even in wartime diaries further muddies the distinction of wartime truth and postwar fiction. Prisoners often wrote diaries as if speaking to a family member, usually a wife.[40] Sometimes the audience was broader. Samuel Gibson knew someone would read his work because on at least one occasion he spoke directly to the "reader." He also showed editorial concerns in the occasional revision. In October 1864, on a day Gibson received no food and watched Union men take the oath of allegiance to the Confederacy, he penned something he must have regretted. He wrote, "I always regarded *Slavery* as a great evil; but Abolitionism, as a far greater evil; & since I have seen the effects of Abolitionism, I *hate* the very name of it, & if I ever come out of this scrape, I will teach my children to hate it." At some point, Gibson changed his mind, inserting "war" in the place of "abolitionism" and blotting out the promise to teach his children to hate abolitionists. That Gibson could hate slavery and abolitionism and war and write for multiple audiences adds to rather than detracts from his historical value. His second thoughts betrayed the complexity of his experience. Gibson knew he was not a stereotype.[41]

The prison archive requires careful handling and a methodological approach that appreciates complexity and subjectivity. *Living by Inches* cuts through the tired debates over whose prisons were more wretched or whose prisoners were liars and replaces invective with empathy. For the sake of caution and deference to tradition, this book relies heavily on wartime diaries, but also considers the *Official Records*, letter collections, and, on a limited basis, wartime newspapers and postwar memoirs. Wartime diaries are not more "authentic" than the later sources; however, as subjectivity goes, it is preferable in a study on lived experience to prioritize wartime biases over postwar biases.

In exploring Civil War prisons from dark nights to the unbolted cornmeal, *Living by Inches* recovers how imprisoned men perceived their world. It is not necessarily a book on gender, though it recognizes that the vast majority of prisoners experienced captivity as men and analyzes manhood and honor where applicable; nor is it singularly focused on class, race, or religion, even though first-person Civil War sources skew toward educated white Protestant Christians. Instead, this book is about experience, which means it considers these cultural ideas in relation to daily life. Prisoners thought of themselves as soldiers and citizens and men, but they were also individuals in a liminal space between and beyond tidy categories. Learning from and adapting to unfamiliar sensory environments was not an academic exercise. For imprisoned men, it was essential to survival.

CHAPTER ONE

Dusk

Leveling the Senses

At sundown, Robert Bingham felt most alone in his captivity.

This was not for a lack of company at night nor of loneliness during the day. While most of the Army of Northern Virginia invaded Pennsylvania, his regiment had stayed behind to guard railroad bridges near Hanover Junction, a distance of about twenty miles from Richmond. There Union cavalry attacked on June 26, 1863, burning the bridge and capturing Bingham along with most of his company. Sailing down the Pamunkey and York Rivers as a prisoner, Bingham fell into "a sort of comatose state" that felt like perpetual twilight. "I am a good deal of a sun worshipper," he admitted, "and there was no gleam of sunlight across the water and no light and shade on the hill & the broad valley." Weeks later, from Johnson's Island, Bingham's days seemed to improve. "The first days of my captivity were sunless," he reflected as a now-seasoned prisoner, "the clouds hung low & dark — & the first month was dark."[1] As his mood improved the days seemed sunnier, but his isolation returned at dusk.

Bingham was a standoffish man who resisted losing what he perceived as a masculine individuality. This may not have been unusual. As historian Stephen Berry writes, "Men kept each other at a distance; that was the point — the distance was the measure of the other man's respect, and in consequence the measure of one's own self-respect."[2] Still, the other officers from whom Bingham kept his distance were quite different men and their comradery suggests a range of emotional intimacy among Southern men in prison. These were the "rabble" officers, who Bingham believed lacked his manly quietude, an essential part of how he defined being a gentleman and a patriot. Regulations kept officers in the barracks after sunset, making his avoidance of the rabble impossible, and Bingham contemplated the contradiction. He wrote, "one can't be alone, with so many noisy men around him, — & yet I am never more alone & lonely than during the twilight hours." He found comfort in writing to his wife, Della, using the diary as an extended monologue to her. The noise of other men reminded him of days "when I did *not* spend the twilight alone." Bingham required his wife's love to sustain him in prison, even though as the form of writing indicates, he could survive emotionally by journaling his thoughts to her. The noise, the crowd, and the loneliness spurred him to contrast his present captivity with memories of home and family. The gulf between past and present pained Bingham and contributed to what he called "this half-living life."[3]

Focusing on night and darkness reveals elements of captivity that are taken for granted in studies about prison policies and living conditions. Bingham's twilight ushered in contrasts important to the ambiguity of half-living: overcrowding and isolation, sleep and restlessness, resistance and domination, dreams and reality. Bingham may have wished he was invulnerable, but dimming the lights revealed his emotional fragility. He was alone and isolated in his captivity no matter how many crowded around him. Acting as the boundary of "daily life," darkness disoriented and reoriented the perceptions, expectations, and relationships of imprisoned men.

Night made up a disorienting interval in the already tumultuous Civil War era. The predictable retreat of light reminded those enmeshed in "a people's contest" of the sovereignty of natural time, which ended battles and provided a mantle for rest and tactical movements. Temporarily disabling the eyes, darkness increased one's reliance on moonlight, artificial light, as well as the nonvisual senses to understand the environment and ward off danger. Night mattered to soldiers and civilians, who recorded their nocturnal experiences, including the quality of their rest, with almost as much regularity as remarks about the weather. It also put armies on edge and stiffened discipline, exemplified by the Forty-Sixth Article of War, which made sleeping while on sentry duty a capital offense. In recovering a sensory history of Civil War prisons, night makes a fitting place to begin for two reasons. First, Union and Confederate prisoners often remarked on the timelessness of captivity by which they meant that the passage of days blended together into a muddy humdrum. Darkness not only bounded those indistinguishable days but also contributed to the sensory bewilderment. Second, night elevated the nonvisual senses, revealing the singular importance of—and interplay between— sight, sound, smell, taste, and touch. The disorientation of night serves as a primer for the enduring importance of these senses during the day.[4]

In the Shadows of Antebellum Night

Nights in Civil War America were more than just a time for dreams, sleepless guards, and a backdrop for the social life of soldiering. The evening infused the antebellum cycle of natural time into the war and affected the perception, if not always the reality, of power relationships in cities, on plantations, in camps, and in prisons. White soldiers and civilians shared common cultural fears about literal and metaphorical darkness. Night seemed to offer the weak cover to shed some constraints, even if it shielded the actions of the powerful as well. In places of undemocratic and concentrated power, night had the potential to erode supervision as discipline. From colonial America to the antebellum decades, night seemed to empower somebody, but whether it was the devil, wild animals, witches, Indians, thieves, slaves, or the mob depended on time, place, and perception.[5]

By the eve of the Civil War, powerful Americans in rural and urban environments treated nighttime as a conquerable frontier and a social problem to solve. Street lamps, a symbol of modernity in the nineteenth century, combined elements of "luxury and control" to appropriate night. Chasing darkness with streetlights extended social control and carved out leisure space in the parts of cities where refined, civilized people and the dangerous masses overlapped.[6] Noise ordinances, which served as a deputy to street lighting, reflected a shift in tolerance for sound between day and night. Sounds of business endurable in the daytime, such as horses and draymen, became noise at night, at least for those whose livelihoods were not relegated to those hours.[7] Emerging in the eighteenth century, noise ordinances became widespread toward the end of the nineteenth century. By the time buildings began competing with steeples for city skylines, even the sound of church bells, once resonant with power, came under scrutiny because they awoke more than just the members of their denomination.[8]

Street lamps and noise ordinances of the nineteenth century were part of a larger movement to tame darkness and discipline people. By at least the mid-eighteenth century, Southern white men passed laws and developed customs that restricted African American mobility, assembly, keeping of weapons, and the use of "drums, horns, or other loud instruments," especially at night.[9] Masters forbade slaves from leaving their quarters or the plantation after dark because enslaved people used night to suit their individual and collective interests. James Henry Hammond advised overseers to visit the slave quarters "after horn blow at night to see that all are in."[10] Such measures reflected the knowledge that enslaved people took advantage of darkness to conceal activities ranging from the practical, such as hunting, to the economic, political, and spiritual. While masters may or may not have considered daily resistance a serious threat to social order, nighttime resistance gave them cause for concern.[11]

For white men and women in the South, real and imagined slave revolts justified vigilant night patrols. Describing a supposed plot in South Carolina on the night of July 4, 1816, Rachel Blanding wrote that the slaves planned to take advantage of nighttime and white drunkenness, setting fire to the town as a diversion and then seizing the arsenal. Afterward the slaves would murder the men and hold as prisoners the women "for their own purposes."[12] As Blanding's fears suggest, insurrection scares assumed slaves would militarize darkness. Mary Boykin Chesnut reflected on an 1861 murder—a smothering—inside a plantation house while the rest of the white family slept. The South Carolinian wrote, "If they want to kill us, they can do it when they please, they are [as] noiseless as panthers." For Chesnut the timing of enslaved people's resistance was as important as the soundlessness. If the dreaded revolution occurred, white men and women knew it would begin silently at night. Civil War soldiers carried these antebellum perspectives about night with them into camp and prison.[13]

As much as long days characterized the Civil War era, Americans also witnessed the period as a series of restless nights. Sleeping accommodations varied by season, location, and rank, ranging from commandeered houses, outbuildings, and elaborate wooden huts to lying exposed on the open ground with or without a blanket or ground cloth. As historian Jonathan White points out, environmental factors including the weather, rodents, and insects affected the availability and quality of rest, as did important circumstantial factors such as proximity to the enemy and active fighting. For soldiers and civilians, the war was one long night.[14]

Darkness dulled vision but sharpened nonvisual senses. Five days before his capture at Brentwood, Tennessee, in March 1863, Union soldier Charles Prentiss listened to the discordant martial and natural sounds of night. From his picket station he heard drums and the bugle call "tattoo" eight miles south at Franklin. Prentiss also perceived the sounds of spring: a clashing symphony of singing toads, braying mules, and clacking frogs, peacocks, and guinea hens.[15] With Confederate cavalry in the area, Prentiss's attention to human and nonhuman sound was an essential part of vigilance. In Virginia in 1864, George Albee considered it a strange sensation to walk along the picket line in the moonlight with "the Rebs within hearing distance."[16] Even within the safety of camp, creatures howled louder and bit harder in the darkness. Illinoisan John Follett described nature as piercing both ears and skin. The fauna preventing "peace or quiet" ranged from lice to alligators and "all creeping things keep up such an ever lasting hissing and noise it is almost impossible to sleep." He saved particular ire for the mosquitoes that "present their bills for liquidation" and the fleas that "play backgammon on my anatomy."[17] The conflict seemed to enter a new dimension after dark that was both intimate and troubling. Prisoners transferred this acuity with them into captivity.

Prison Nights

Prison nights were a far cry from the idealized slumbers of antebellum America. As John Gunn wrote in *Gunn's Domestic Medicine*, "When we lie down to sleep, we voluntarily exclude the operation of the senses; in other words, we see nothing, hear nothing, feel nothing, smell nothing, and taste nothing; and endeavor to think nothing."[18] For Civil War prisoners, the experience was almost the complete opposite. While night blinded the eyes, the nonvisual senses from feeling to smelling were most acute in hours of darkness.

No two captivities were exactly the same, but the relentless cycle of natural time ensured that all prisoners shared early, formative experiences in hours of darkness. Some were captured at night. Confederate Colonel Virgil Murphey fell into Union hands during the Battle of Franklin on November 30, 1864. The battle subsided around 9 P.M., and the reality of Murphey's situation rolled over him, producing "a sense of loneliness and despondency" during his march that night with the Union army to Nashville.[19] Union men also described sundown as the moment captivity felt real. James Bell, a U.S. government clerk, fell into Confederate hands along with fifty-eight other Washington citizens who rode out to Manassas to assist in caring for men wounded during the Second Battle of Bull Run. Bell recalled the week after his release an abrupt change in emotions at a temporary bivouac near Gainesville. "As long as day lasted, we were cheerful," he wrote, "but when night spread her sable mantel over us and the cold night air pierced our thin apparel, then, we realized to the fullest extent the misery in store for us." Even though Bell had not slept in days, the cold air and the wet grass prevented him from sleeping until he arrived in Richmond. He continued, "In silent but bitter mental anguish, we watched through the tedious hours of darkness, till at last nature rebelled against inactivity, and we got up and paced about the ground." The next evening a thunderstorm struck, further reminding the prisoners of the helplessness of their condition. Unable to shield themselves, they stood "like dumb beasts with backs to the gale" until the storm ended.[20]

For wounded men, nighttime captivity added to the powerlessness and isolation of living with a disabled body. Jacob Heffelfinger, a Pennsylvanian in his early twenties, fell into Confederate hands three times, twice with disabling leg wounds. On his first capture, Heffelfinger received a bullet through the thigh at Gaines's Mill and spent an immobilized first night "compelled to lie on the bare floor, unable to turn myself, or change position." The anonymous noise of wounded prisoners—all of whom were a second priority to the injured Confederates—affected him more than his disabled state. "The house is crowded with wounded," he wrote, "and their cries and groans cause me more suffering than my own pain." For weeks, Heffelfinger recorded the timing of each journal entry, preferring to write at sunrise or sunset and focusing on environmental assaults to his senses.

Most of Heffelfinger's nighttime complaints involved space. The wounded took up every room in the house, the porch and the ground beneath it, all the outbuildings, and the yard. A fellow Pennsylvanian, who lay so close to Heffelfinger they were "almost touching," died on the seventh night. Odor from the dead took up its own space and encroached on the air of the living. On the second night, Heffelfinger wrote, "The stench arising from the dead bodies in the adjacent fields is sickening." Like the smell of death, the sounds of suffering took up space and amplified the hospital's close quarters. An anonymous man called throughout one night for two women: a mother and a wife, "Lizzie." When that man died the next morning, pungent odors from inside the house had overpowered the inconsolable pleading. "The house is very filthy," Heffelfinger wrote, and "the blood on the floors [is] causing a sickening stench." By sunset on July 9, a growing population of lice and maggots added to the competition for space and the feel of captivity. When the wounded prisoners finally left the hospital for the railroad on July 14, Heffelfinger worried about the jolt of "rough, baggage wagons." A few hours later, he confided that he would never forget "the shrieks and groans" of those who made the journey with "shattered bones" that night.[21]

Heffelfinger's first captivity was relatively short, lasting only a few weeks. For those who endured longer imprisonments, sleeping arrangements varied from barracks, casements, and tents in the North to warehouses, rotten tents, earthen burrows, and—very rarely—barracks in the South. As they had in army camps, imprisoned men lay close together and often complained about sleeping arrangements. Enoch George McKnight, a printer by trade who composed many poems at Johnson's Island under the pseudonym Aza Hartz, juxtaposed the feeling of his lover's bed to his own at Johnson's Island in the poem, "My Love and I." The woman was not his wife, Elizabeth, who had died two months before his capture. The mystery woman, perhaps his future second wife, Isabel Taylor, fell asleep quickly on a soft mattress while he lay sleepless on a bunk with a straw mattress:

My love reposes on a rosewood frame —
A "bunk" have I;
A couch of feathery down fills up the same —
Mine's straw, but dry;
She sinks to sleep at night with scarce a sigh —
With waking eyes I watch the hours creep by.[22]

Union prisoners may have envied McKnight's bunk and straw mattress. At Camp Lawton, Georgia, George Shearer and three others spent four dollars to purchase materials for a hut of timber and pine boughs.[23] Men burrowed into the ground to take advantage of thermal heating and cooling. These small caves, hardly larger than a grave, created new problems. A Christmas downpour at Andersonville drove men into their caves, but at least two men near George Clarkson suffocated when the hole they crawled into caved in.[24]

Sleeping arrangements translated into longtime restlessness inside wooden, brick, or stone walls. Twenty-one-year-old Franklin Krause, the son of a Massachusetts mother and a German father, reflected on sleep at Andersonville forty times in June, July, and August 1864.[25] Although rain and the dampness of the ground corresponded most directly to sleep quality, other factors included air temperature and health. During the rainy month of June, Krause recorded four nights of good sleep and nine nights of poor sleep. On the night of June 12 it rained, and neither the blanket nor the tent provided much protection. In the drier month of July, his rest improved, with eight nights of good sleep, five of poor sleep, and one of mixed sleep. Although Krause reflected more on nights of poor sleep, dreams, such as one in which he visited home and saw his sister, improved the quality of rest. The worst came in August with five nights of good sleep and twelve restless ones. While the weather continued to play a role in his sleep, Krause now attributed discomfort to insects and disease. Increasingly sore from scurvy by the end of August, he reflected, "It goes pretty hard and tough to have to lie on the hard ground now." Still, Krause believed he had stood the nights better than he would have predicted.[26]

Whether stepping into barracks or crawling into tents, huts, or holes in the ground, it was common for prisoners to sleep close together as they had in Civil War armies. Michael Dougherty wrote that men in the open rooms of Libby Prison "wormed and dove-tailed together like so many fish in a basket."[27] Those captured with army friends bunked together; others "messed" together by unit, hometown, state, nationality, or other social factors. Robert Bingham knew none of the nine men in his mess before captivity, but they shared a similar temperament, preferring to avoid the rest of the "rabble" about the prison.[28] Having long-term messmates was common, but changes were not uncommon. At the onset of cooler weather at Fort Delaware, Francis Boyle swapped messmates when he found a man with a straw mattress and extra blankets "so that we shall sleep warm."[29] Sleeping arrangements were in part choices about group cohesion and comfort.

Prison sleeping arrangements made individual sickness a collective problem. In September 1864, Samuel Gibson worried about a messmate and brother-in-law, Cyrus McKee, who was "sinking fast" in their tent shelter. Weighing the options about what to do, Gibson wrote, "To lie in camp & be sick is but to die," but "a Reb. Hos. is only another name for a 'Dead House.'" Chronic diarrhea took McKee's life, but it took another seventy days for the disease to run its course.[30] At Fort Delaware, Francis Boyle took notice when a prisoner in the adjoining bunk came down with smallpox. He felt unmoved by earlier cases, but he and the afflicted young man lay so close at night that their bodies touched. "This summer it has made its appearance all around me," he acknowledged, "but never quite so close before."[31]

Most accounts of illness came from survivors, but men like Samuel Foust recorded their own slow decline. Beginning in July 1864, coughing, soreness, sweating, shivering, and diarrhea interrupted his sleep. That same month, a messmate dug a hole for him "to use as a sink," indicating that his illness and waning mobility also put a strain on his companions. By mid-September Foust could no longer walk without assistance. It took four men to carry Foust to the newly constructed barracks to aid him and possibly to rid themselves of a disabled man with scurvy and chronic diarrhea. Foust spent his final weeks crippled, blind, and shivering, first in those barracks and then in the prison hospital. Upon entering the latter he became "completely discouraged," with the one consolation that he "found a partner with a blanket." Foust then stopped writing, and a fellow prisoner finished the diary for him four weeks later. Foust had "talked often about death" and died "sensible of his condition."[32]

Few dying prisoners wrote about their final weeks, and it was more common for messmates to trace out a friend's decline. George Clarkson, Corwin Kenney, and two other men shared two blankets, one of which served as a tent. Early on January 11, 1865, Kenney woke Clarkson up "saying he was sick." Kenney soon became "out of his head" and died before sunrise. "I shall feel more lonesome now," Clarkson admitted, "for we have slept together for most seven months."[33] While Kenney sought comfort from friends in his final hours, Robert Shellito did not. Officially, he died of chronic diarrhea, but a fellow prisoner told a darker story. From William Seeley's viewpoint, Shellito must have lain awake while the others slept. Fastening one end of his suspenders to a beam in the hut and making a slipknot with the other end, Shellito hanged himself in the dark. His messmates awoke to the body of a man who chose death at his own hands as opposed to one by inches.[34]

Close sleeping offered little protection from thieves, who were more active in the dark hours. Thomas Jones, a member of William Dolphin's prison squad, used his pants as a pillow until February 1864 when someone removed them "from under his head" in the middle of the night.[35] Basic necessities such as pants, blankets, hats, eating utensils, and food were the most common articles to go missing. A tin cup, for example, could be worth as much as a dozen eggs or a pound of meat because of its versatility when cooking. When someone stole Thomas Springer's tin cup at Belle Isle, it threatened his chances for survival. Three days later, he rose "before daylight and stole a tin bucket" so that he and a messmate could boil their meat, bread, and soup together.[36] Near Charleston, South Carolina, "some Scamp" stole the meat issued to James Burton's mess. "I hope it will choke him," he wrote.[37]

Union prisoners generally complained of organized theft more frequently than Confederate prisoners, for two reasons. First, Union prisoners experienced greater desperation for basic provisions, and the lack of internal barriers such as barracks gave thieves greater mobility. Organized theft focused on money and valuables, such as watches and jewelry that could easily be turned into cash in the informal prison marketplace. From late 1863 through mid-1864, nighttime theft became both violent and increasingly systematized. Describing gangs at the Pemberton warehouse as the "roughs," Robert Sneden recalled how men would "prowl about at night like hyenas, three or four in a gang," attacking those weakened by illness, and if a victim resisted "they club him into a state of insensibility."[38] Competing gangs at Belle Isle and Andersonville, known collectively as "raiders," operated mostly at night and necessitated vigilance within prison squads. Effective resistance to organized crime developed only after gangs became so bold that they no longer attacked only at night. This boldness in late spring and early summer 1864 turned out to be their undoing at Andersonville. Daytime assaults galvanized effective resistance from within the prison population that ended in the public execution of six "raiders." It also led to the creation of the "regulators," a police force of prisoners supported by Confederate officials. Despite concerns among fellow prisoners that the regulators were also roughs, the police force meant Andersonville prisoners could rest easier at night.[39]

Despite the sensationalism of theft at places like Andersonville, the most pervasive nighttime threats came from other creatures. When prisoners crawled into bunks, tents, or earthen holes, bedbugs, fleas, and lice (often used interchangeably) were more active and prisoners were more sensitive to them. At the Charleston jail in 1862, Frank Bennett bought blankets from another prisoner, but night was far from comfortable. The next day he described the haptic experience of lying on the floor as being left "to the tender mercies of hosts of vermin, which appeared to hold a Saturnalia last night. Mice, bugs, roaches, horrid crawling things. Ugh! My flesh creeps at the remembrance."[40] Stephen Weld, a prisoner in the Columbia city jail in 1864, could not sleep at all. "The bedbugs & other vermin crawled over me in thousands," he wrote. "I looked like a man with small pox from the number of my bites." He attempted to sleep on top of a table, but he could find no space free of the vermin.[41] Likewise, George Gill, captured at Murfreesboro and taken to Richmond, described having "plenty of company in the shape of Grey Backs," which "bite like Hell at night and therefore Disturb our repose."[42] When Confederate physician Joseph Jones visited Andersonville for his medical report, he remarked on the mosquitoes' "everlasting buzzing" and their "troublesome bites" which "peppered" his skin. Mosquitoes made his sleep nearly impossible and he speculated "that the immense amount of filth generated by the prisoners may have had much to do with the development and multiplication of these insects."[43]

The vermin that crawled on the floors, walls, clothes, and skin were enduring features of restlessness. The "singular concomitants" of diarrhea and lice kept Alonzo Keeler up at night fighting with vermin and visiting the sink.[44] Jacob Heffelfinger thought the Charleston jail provided his best shelter in months, even though he shared a close cell with five prisoners and innumerable insects and rodents. "Mice, rats, cock-roaches, lice, fleas, and 'kindred Cattle' infested our beds," he wrote. "While the stench was anything but pleasant, still it was better than out in the drenching rain." The next day, he admitted that his "slumbers were disturbed during the night by a pair of mice trying to build a nest in my hair."[45] Robert Sneden described the effect of high water in the James River for the rat and human population in Pemberton warehouse. The flood drove in rats seeking higher ground and they scurried over prisoners in the warehouse at night.[46]

The inability to prevent incursions by insects and rodents had a humbling and desensitizing effect on prisoners. At Johnson's Island, E. John Ellis described the "Chintzes" or bedbugs in ways others referred to lice. According to Ellis, "a battalion" first attempted to capture his nose. "I repulsed them with great slaughter," he wrote. "They then attacked along the lines. I held my ground for an hour and killed many, but they bring in constant receipt of reinforcements." Ellis retreated from the bunk to the ground, where he "was annoyed by a few skirmishers but no serious demonstration was made against my position." Three of his five friends also traded their bunks for the floor, and Ellis satirized that only the "ugly and hideous" snoring of the remaining man kept the insects off him. Ellis also inferred a moral from the relationship between insects and humans. Rather than being "stinking and insignificant little things," as a fellow prisoner lamented, Ellis mused that while humans think the world was made for them, "the chintz might say, 'man sleeps to feed me, night to hide me comes.'"[47] Night revealed an important lesson about power dynamics within the prison ecosystem. Men were not the uncontested masters over the nonhuman world.

Alongside vermin, the olfactory landscape of prison environments also prevented sleep and precipitated disgust and fear. Damp air increased pungency, making "night air" more noticeable and odor more inescapable. Fears about night air had deep roots. During the American Revolution, John Adams and Benjamin Franklin quarreled over night air while traveling together through New Jersey. Adams wanted the windows closed for fear of night air; Franklin believed that without open windows the men would suffocate for want of proper ventilation. For more than a century thereafter, it was common, especially in sickly seasons, to retire at night inside a sealed house regardless of the weather. At issue was whether damp, odorous air from outside was more harmful than rebreathing the exhalations of self and family. This made intuitive sense in an era when odor was equated to the manifestation of disease.[48] By the 1850s sanitarians favored ventilation, even night air, over stale air. Social reformer Florence Nightingale downplayed fears of night air. She asked, "What air can we breathe at night but night air? The choice is between pure night air from without and foul night air from within."[49] Yet there was not a consensus. Night air was dangerous whether it came from the inside or outside.

Prisoners continued in this tradition and those who wrote the most about smell considered night air more potent and dangerous than day air. William Wilkins described the night air of a Richmond warehouse as suffocating. He wrote, "Last night I was literally almost suffocated with the noisome vapors that filled the room, and had to wrap my head in my blanket in order to breathe."[50] James Franklin spent an early night in captivity aboard a boxcar parked a few miles from Westminster, Maryland. "Here we remained all night," he recalled, "our misery being increased by the sentinels insisting upon closing both doors, which shut out not only the light, but what little air there was."[51] Franklin faced a similar night in the dark hold of a steamer bound for Fort Delaware packed "so close that we could scarcely breathe" and with only a hatchway "to let in the much-needed air." Like Wilkins, Franklin feared suffocating amid the foul night air.[52]

The natural ventilation of an open-air prison offered little respite. On one of his first nights in Andersonville, Samuel Grosvenor wrote that "the stench was horrible & a black cloud of smoke & steam hung over us like a pall, shutting out the very stars from our sight." An ex-prisoner reflected that "during the day the sun drank up the most noxious of these vapors, but in the night the terrible miasma and stench pervaded the atmosphere almost to suffocation."[53] Confederate prisoners, especially those in enclosed spaces such as fortresses or brick buildings, drew similar conclusions about night air. Griffin Frost described his room in a college-turned-prison in Springfield, Missouri, as "eighteen feet square" and occupied by twenty-eight prisoners. Frost acquired a bunk, but most of the prisoners slept on a floor that Frost compared unfavorably to a hog pen. He wrote, "The *night buckets* are kept in one corner of the room, and persons are up and down all through the night answering the calls of nature, which renders our quarters very unpleasant indeed."[54] These experiences during the hours of rest were a far cry from the antebellum ideal as prisoners discovered the impossibility of hearing, smelling, or thinking nothing.

The senses, both individually and in concert, also had a long staying power in prisoner memory. John Flinn, a Mississippian by birth who studied theology at Columbia Theological Seminary in South Carolina and the University of Edinburgh, recalled in 1893 the sound and feeling of winter nights at Point Lookout. The title of his unpublished account, "A Southern Soldier Boy's Story of Some Things He Saw and Heard & Felt in a Northern Prison," gestured to the synesthesia of prison sensations that were clearest at night. Prisoners rubbed their hands, climbed, jumped, and stamped their feet on sleepless cold nights to keep warm. Two sounds predominated. The first "were rhythmic, as if one throb from 10000 hearts, like a muffled drum-beat, had instantly passed from man to man, causing their feet to beat in unison the measure of a common voiceless woe!" The second resonance "was a weird wailing sound, like the far away voice of the sea moaning in a storm." Flinn attributed this to chattering teeth. Searching for metaphors to describe the strange feeling and sensation, he first compared it to the sound of an organ and then like "a huge animal in pain yet trying to hush the voice of its pangs!"[55] The nonvisual senses reached their full expression individually and in concert at night.

Controlling Darkness

Night also posed a security risk for prison officials. For this reason, officials sought to manage the night through stricter rules that controlled the use of light and sound. The nighttime sounds of captivity meant suffering to Flinn; it just as easily sounded like dangerous disorder to guards. The guards' preference, though rarely in such clear terms, was a form of quietude suggesting order and stability. The link between order and sound had its roots not just in Union and Confederate armies but also in antebellum prisons, plantations, and factories. Plantation overseers and factory owners used horns, whistles, and bells. In place of corporal punishment, the modernizing justice system put quiet penance to work in the new penitentiaries to reform the mind and soul. The overlap between the antebellum penitentiaries and wartime prisons had its limits; after all, Civil War prisons emphasized controlling the body, not reforming the mind. Still, both types of prisons shared an interest in control, especially during the night hours.[56]

Guards tried to regulate night by controlling light and sound. By the end of 1862, Camp Chase had lights "of the same character as the ordinary street lights" at each corner inside and outside of the prison wall. According to an inspector, this put the "whole prison at all times under the surveillance of the guard."[57] Other Northern prisons in the fall of 1863 used a combination of coal oil and gas lamps at St. Louis, Alton, Cincinnati, Columbus, and Point Lookout.[58] Almost as soon as Elmira opened as a prison in the summer of 1864, prison guards installed dozens of kerosene lamps aided by reflectors that lit up the night.[59] The sounds of prison guards aided the lamps and reflectors in projecting control over the nightscape. Predetermined alarms provided the most immediate way to alert the entire guard of an emergency. Confederate regulations in Richmond defined the meaning of gunshots: "The firing of one gun at night, or two during the day, will be the signal for the immediate assembling of the guard."[60] Union and Confederate guards used the sound of their own voices to mark the passage of time. By identifying their post number and yelling out the hour, guards projected their alertness to captives and their fellow guards.

Rules during the dark hours were less forgiving than during daylight hours. At Camp Morton in 1862, the prison commandant stipulated that "prisoners will carefully avoid interrupting sentinels in the discharge of their duty, and especially will not curse them, use abusive language or climb onto fences or trees." The guards were instructed to fire after three warnings in the daytime but after only one at night.[61] At Camp Chase in 1864, the rules forbade guards from speaking to prisoners or conversing with each other day or night, but the sound of taps ushered in stricter vigilance in which prisoners could not burn lights or collect in groups.[62] Regulations for prisons in Richmond called for "lights-out" at 9:00 P.M. and instructed the guards to ensure darkness and quietude. A prison hospital in Richmond required patients to retire at 9:00 P.M. "with as little noise as possible," and regulations forbade "heavy walking and loud talking," at all times.[63]

Darkness and quietude mattered because guards connected disorder, noise, and, after taps, lights with resistance. Night seemed to scare guards, and nervous guards were quicker to shoot prisoners. In 1862, Clarence Wicks, a seventeen-year-old guard at Camp Randall, Wisconsin, shot a prisoner in the early morning for threatening and insulting him. Wicks had attempted to dissuade a prisoner from creating an olfactory "nuisance" by relieving his bowels on the ground near the guard's post instead of at the sinks. When the offender refused to move, Wicks hit the man in the face with a rock. In response, six or seven angry prisoners emerged from the barracks. George Washington Spears called Wicks a "damned son of a bitch!" and charged him with an improvised weapon. Explaining his decision to shoot, Wicks told investigators, "I had orders to shoot rebels insulting me and did shoot him." Guards at nearby posts corroborated the insulting language, and one reported that the insult had come after a night of prisoners hurling words as well as sticks, bones, and rocks at the guards from the cover of darkness. Other prisoners had made a game of defecating in the yard near the guards, calling them names, and inviting them to "kiss their arses." Officials did not indict or discipline Wicks for shooting, but they documented the narrative of contributing causes that led to the homicide. Two years later, Wicks fell wounded into the hands of Confederates at Cold Harbor and died a prisoner.[64]

The death of Spears at Camp Randall, a remote Northern prison, paralleled controversial but quite common shootings across Northern and Southern prisons. Darkness, aural resistance, and fear were recurring factors. The Camp Chase guards had orders to first warn and then fire upon prisoners who came within ten feet of the wall, collected in large numbers, or had lights in their barracks after taps. There in November 1862, "after the hour of extinguishing lights," prisoners loudly rushed out of their barracks. The sentinel gave half a dozen "loud and determined" warnings before firing into the crowd and killing one prisoner.[65] Likewise, Frank Wilkeson, a guard at Elmira, feared that the "ugly-tempered and rebellious" Confederate prisoners were testing the poorly trained guards at night by raising the "charging-yell," and he inferred that a breakout would follow. In response, guards fired at a prisoner barracks, making the darkness as "silent as death." No one was seriously injured, but Wilkeson wrote that the Confederates never again made "night hideous by their yells and howls."[66]

Gunfire in the night reinforced the belief among Union and Confederate prisoners that guards killed men out of spite. This belief was not without reason; after all, prisoners did what they could to infuriate the guards. When the sentinels at Andersonville called out the 2 A.M. mark on the Fourth of July, a Union man yelled back from the darkness, "you son of a bitch!" The guard fired in the direction of the voice but struck a different man in the knee.[67] But even just the sound of guns had a practical effect on the nerves of prisoners. Ten nights after this shooting, Confederate artillerymen fired blanks. The sound reminded Henry H. Stone of warnings issued the same day by the prison commander claiming he could stop a breakout by spraying grapeshot indiscriminately into the prison. The sound "made all our number jump" and demonstrated the effectiveness of using sound to inspire fear. For the masses of prisoners, a gunshot need not hit a target to be effective. Each time a gun sounded, it reminded imprisoned men that the guards could fire into the camp at any moment and that cannons could annihilate the prisoners.[68]

Prison officials believed that darkness, noise, and prisoner silence abetted escapes by blinding and deafening the guards. Only one day after capturing Fort Donelson in February 1862, Ulysses S. Grant reported that during the night many animals and prisoners had run off.[69] At Johnson's Island that same spring, Commissary-General of Prisoners William Hoffman noted that with the ill-trained recruits who guarded Confederate officers, "there will be little difficulty in a prisoner escaping on a dark, stormy night."[70] Another official had similar concerns the next year. "It does not do to rely on hearing at all," he warned, "as the noise of the waves [on Lake Erie] overcomes every other."[71] He ordered the installation of more lamps so that the sentinels could see in any weather conditions. Still, security was never complete. Eighteen Confederates used the cover of darkness and a storm to break out of jail in Springfield, Missouri, in May 1862. They cut a hole under the stove, descended into the cellar, and left through an unlocked door. In addition to the prison's laxity, one guard inferred that the prisoners "took advantage of the noise and darkness of the heavy rain."[72] Union prisoner Frank Hughes, imprisoned at Macon in the summer of 1862, noted that "Yankees begin to leak out at dusk," and for that reason, the guards tripled their number.[73]

When prisoners controlled sound, it had the potential to translate into freedom. The combination of natural darkness and intentional silence helped prisoners "leak out" of even the more secure prisons. At the Ohio Penitentiary, where Confederate cavalryman John Hunt Morgan silently escaped, guards walked around the building to see that prisoners were still in their cells and to hear that they were quiet. Jesse Watson testified during an inquiry that there was no indication of an escape because he "heard no noise or disturbance of any sort." The escape baffled guards, who thought they were experts in interpreting the sounds of prisoner activity. "Entire stillness almost always prevails," Watson testified, "and the least noise or jar is immediately and distinctly heard anywhere in the hall, and it would be impossible, I think, for any prisoner or convict to cut, saw, dig, pound, scrape, or attempt anything of that kind without being immediately heard and discovered by the night watch."[74] This nighttime silence at the Ohio Penitentiary was not common elsewhere. Though guards trusted their ears to detect escaping prisoners, incidents such as these indicated the ability of prisoners to fool the guards' sense of hearing.

While guards listened to infer discipline, they were not alone in perceiving disruptive noise. Noise clashed with how some prisoners thought night should sound. At Johnson's Island, Confederate James Mayo wrote that "the crickets' shrill cries coupled with the *monotonous* snoring of the sleepers around me," and the somber, howling winds clashed in discord with the hourly "all is well" call coming from the prison guards.[75] At Libby Prison, George Albee listened to the footfalls of prisoners without blankets upstairs "walking the floor this whole night long to keep warm."[76] Vying interpretations of merriment and noise revealed class differences among men. Griffin Frost described the din of a college turned into a prison at Springfield, Missouri. He wrote, "It is midnight, the hour when everything should be quiet, no sound heard except the tread of the sentinel." Yet instead of quietude, the sounds of agony, prayers, songs, swearing, and playing cards filled the rooms. Frost asked rhetorically, "How can a man think, or write, or hope to sleep?" Transferred by Union guards to Gratiot Street prison in St. Louis, Frost listened to the "hideous" roar beneath his feet coming from other prisoners. He heard "coughing, swearing, singing, and praying" in addition to the "almost unearthly noises, issuing from uproarious gangs, laughing, shouting, stamping and howling." The "unnatural clang" coming from other prisoners made night sound like "hell on earth."[77] Prisons could be loud at any hour, but noise became more offensive to sensitive ears at night.

While some men interpreted noise as unnatural and disruptive, other men clearly interpreted the sounds as uplifting. At Camp Douglas, Thomas Beadles wrote in early 1864, "Hilarity prevails with some of the prisoners whilst others look rather gloomy. Some nights they will get an old violin & fiddle & dance until lights out. Seemingly with all [the] happiness of a crowd at a country grocery."[78] In spring the following year, the Camp Douglas prison string band held a concert in his barracks, which also recalled pleasant memories of home. At Point Lookout, Confederate prisoners at the very end of the war mimicked animals' calls to remind themselves of home. William Haigh wrote, "Many of the men are gifted with the faculty of mimicking all kinds of birds, dogs, cats, coons &c," and the sound of a whip-poor-will carried him "to my once happy home in the Sand Hills," at least until discovering it was an imitation.[79]

Prisoners also expressed patriotic and partisan sentiments by singing, yelling, and howling at night. After several weeks at Libby Prison, William Wilkins recorded nighttime singing as the room's new amusement. Each evening a choir of fifteen to twenty prisoners gathered near a window to make "the indignant Streets of Richmond ring with the 'Star Spangled Banner', 'Red, White, & Blue' & 'We'll hang Jeff Davis on a Sour Apple tree.'" The singing provoked the guards, who were "hugely annoyed at this, but [they] cannot stop it without gagging every man; & the crosser they look, the louder swells the chorus."[80] Chanting and singing became a nightly occupation for prisoners in Richmond for the rest of the war. At Libby Prison in October 1863, John Kay and other prisoners sang "John Brown's Body" and "Hang Jeff Davis" in the evening hours. For Alonzo Keeler, it was a carnivalesque atmosphere of men not only singing and dancing but also "crowing, barking, [and] braying" like animals in the dimly lit, multistory warehouse. Confederate guards loathed "John Brown's Body" more than most songs, which made singing it especially satisfying to prisoners. In silent pauses, prisoners listened for the effect, hoping to catch the swearing that sounded like "music to our ears" and encouraged the prisoners to keep up the noise.[81]

While music, cheering, and singing were important modes of resistance during the day and during holidays, prisoners learned from the reaction of the prison guards that noise was a better weapon after dark. At Point Lookout, Confederate prisoners reacted to the sound of gunshots in the same way they had at Petersburg, giving a "precautionary cry to their fellows, 'lie down.'" However, in the context of white prisoners and black guards, Confederates used the cover of darkness to ridicule the masculinity of the guards from the safety of anonymity. One skilled imitator of bird calls, "mimicking a distressed woman's voice," cried out, "'lie down, children, daddy's coming home drunk again.'"[82] In January 1864, Lewis Bisbee wrote that a hundred officers in Libby Prison began "promenading in the dining room singing

John Brown and other songs when the officials pounced upon them and made them stand in line until 9:30."[83] A few months later, Jacob Heffelfinger admitted that he and the prisoners at Libby had been "very noisy, singing the Star Spangled Banner, John Brown &c.," and in response, "the Provost Marshall has just now forbidden us to sing."[84] After their first week at Andersonville, many of the Connecticut prisoners captured at Plymouth, North Carolina, gathered in the evening to sing a little after sunset. Robert Kellogg described it as a way to express their resilience. He wrote, "we vented our enthusiasm by singing 'America,' 'Star Spangled Banner,' and 'Red, White, and Blue' at the top of our voices, much to the edification of the Confederate guards, probably."[85] Kellogg's qualification indicated they could not control how their captors interpreted their singing. They sang, however, not only to raise their own spirits but in hopes of affecting the guards as well.

Fears of revolt were not unwarranted, but leveraging silence might have been a better tool than noise. In November 1863, John Kay wrote an imaginative plan for how he and other Union prisoners would revolt and escape from the Pemberton prison. The most able-bodied men would sneak up and gag a night watchman. From there they would fall upon the room where the relief guard slept with "the greatest possible silence" and without "shouting or noise of any kind." After swapping clothes with the guard, the plotters would first free the officers at Libby Prison and then the enlisted men on Belle Isle. The plan, more an imaginative dream than a serious plot, ended with the capture of Richmond and the arrest of Jefferson Davis. The key was making tactical use of darkness and silence. Butchering the guards, however agreeable to the prisoners, would make too much noise. While the Pemberton prisoners never put the plan into effect, the proposal said much about how they imagined a revolt might take place. It would have to be undertaken as quietly as an antebellum slave uprising.[86]

Dreams as Escape

The most common escape, albeit temporary, came in the form of a sensory illusion—dreaming. Perhaps John Kay's plan to overthrow the Confederate government came to him while sleeping. He certainly had a broader range of dreams than most soldiers or prisoners recorded. Early in his captivity, he had pleasant dreams of home almost every night. Yet by early 1864, Kay admitted, "I do not sleep well nights, my dreams are troubled."[87] This last part was unusual, for despite the environment, most prisoners recorded positive dreams. Virgil Murphey described his first dream in captivity as a "dim land, where floats, mans unfulfilled aspirations." Those aspirations amounted to the visual, auditory, and haptic illusion of being home combined with an effusion of positive emotion. In Murphey's dreams laughter, "a soft touching hand," and "kisses of devoted affection" replaced "the fetters of captivity" and produced a feeling of "ecstasy." The voice of a guard snatched Murphey from this "bright" place and returned him to the darkness of early morning and a continuation of a forced march from Franklin to Nashville.[88]

As with Civil War soldiers more broadly, prisoners like Murphey tended to have multisensory dreams of friends, loved ones, and home. On Robert Bingham's birthday, he wrote to his wife through his diary, "I dreamed of you last night—that you met me with a smile, such a smile—& sat on my knee clinging to my neck & kissing me. I could hardly dismiss it when I woke."[89] In November that year he noted, "I woke often last night & was always dreaming of you—I never sleep a moment or night without dreaming of you." The settings of his dreams varied from a walk in the woods or along a stream to "gliding along over a smooth, still lake" to sitting on her sofa together before they were married.[90]

Others dreamed of time travel and childhood. An Irish immigrant to Brooklyn, Hoboken, and later Savannah, George Bell returned to New York harbor as a prisoner after the capture of Fort Pulaski in 1862. From Governor's Island, Bell dreamed he was back in Ireland visiting his mother, uncle, and boyhood home.[91] At Florence, South Carolina, Eugene Sly admitted that reading novels and Lord Byron helped pass the time, but dreaming provided the only true pleasure for prisoners "amid the Dying Groans of the destitute & Starving." Sly dreamed of home, including the "old haunts of his Childhood" and wandering through a grove of trees with "a fair young Damsel at his side." More than anything else, these dreams offered moments of escape.[92]

While pleasant dreams produced such a rush of excitement, the prisoner's dream came full circle when the individual awoke to rediscover his surroundings. In Tuscaloosa, Alabama, Elisha Reed composed a short poem "during the noise and tumult" that conveyed the full cycle of pleasure and despair that came from dreaming in prison:

On Tuscaloosa's Prison Floor
A Prisoner sleeping lay
And dreaming of his distant home
Some Thousand Miles away

He dreamed he reached his distant home
But ere the door he gained

His mother ran in haste to meet
Her son with joy unfeigned

One fond embrace with tears of joy
Alas the spell is riven
He widely gazed about the room
Oh! God! He's *Back in Prison*.[93]

As Reed's poem underscores, dreams were ephemeral and provided only a reprieve from captivity. Perhaps for this reason, those who recorded dreams sometimes found it difficult to trust reality. William Tillson described release as being "like awakening from an awful dream."[94] After reaching Union lines in October 1862, paroled prisoner Milton Woodford told his sister, "In jail, I used to dream of being at home, and, it would seem so *natural*. I would think, this *must be real*. But I would wake up and find it all a dream, and it seems now, almost as though I should find *this* all a dream, but I guess this is a 'sure thing,' if I had been asleep *before*."[95] Dreams taught prisoners not to always trust what their senses declared real.

The narrative of Reed's dream paralleled the most famous, albeit fictional, captivity dream of the Civil War era. This was the dream of Peyton Farquhar, the main character in Ambrose Bierce's short story, "An Occurrence at Owl Creek Bridge." Bierce imagined the final sensations of Farquhar, a Confederate sentenced to hang for plotting to burn a railroad bridge. In the dream, the hangman's rope breaks and Farquhar falls into the river below. By seemingly good fortune Farquhar evades the soldiers and makes his way downstream and through the countryside to his wife standing on the porch. Reality intrudes as he approaches the house and before he can embrace his wife. At that moment he feels "a stunning blow" to the neck, hears "a sound like the shock of a cannon," and sees a blinding white light. These are the last sensations before "all is darkness and silence!"[96] Farquhar's dream has a flow similar to those described by Elisha Reed and other prisoners. The delusions of real prisoners vanished from their eyes, ears, and hands as they awoke. For the fictional Farquhar, the sound of his own neck breaking jerks him back into reality at the moment his eternal darkness and silence begins. Yet for both the spell was broken.

Nights that disoriented men's senses also reoriented them to captivity. While disabling the eyes, darkness enabled the nonvisual senses and brought a multisensory experience to the forefront of prison life. By listening, smelling, and feeling, men engaged in an interpretive process that gave meaning to the phenomena around them and taught them what to expect in the future.

This included the loneliness and social entanglements that came from sleeping in overcrowded warehouses, barracks, prison pens, tents, and huts alongside the accompanying sounds, feelings, and odors.

Under cover of darkness, prisoners also engaged in small acts of defiance. The guards' control of prisons was never complete, in part because prisoners enlisted darkness and sound for their own purposes. Prisoners' music, singing, and noise tested the boundaries of captivity and selective silence helped facilitate escape plots. Yet if night softened the one-sided power of prison environments, it made resistance an even more lethal game. Safer escape came in the form of dreams, in which prisoners traded the lice and odor and noise of prison for illusions of familiar sights and sounds of home. The disappointment came in waking up. Daylight brought a continuation of challenges that were most acute at night.

CHAPTER TWO

Anosmia

The Disabled Nose

William Wilkins once had a good nose.

Born in Pennsylvania in 1826, Wilkins served in the Mexican-American War before becoming a lawyer in Michigan. As a writer he conveyed sharp sensory analysis and reflection. When he was captured at the Battle of Cedar Mountain on August 9, 1862, Confederates not only searched but also "stripped" Wilkins of his possessions; while passing the Orange County Court House, Southern civilians "hooted" and "jeered" him; the "scorching sun" blasted his skin; and his only food was "raw rancid bacon & hard crackers." In captivity, Wilkins's nose served as his best bodyguard against less-visible dangers. The dirt in the dark train car, for instance, was not earth but manure from the car's previous cargo of cattle. At Libby Prison, Wilkins's nose, aided by the eyes, helped form his understanding of the dangers of the place.[1]

On the first floor of Libby Prison, where he lived for about six weeks, Wilkins discovered an inch-thick layer of "black greasy slime" on the floor that prisoners had been unable to remedy. One wall contained the room's three open windows, which meant air could not circulate through the building. "Slops" and other "excretions" from enlisted men imprisoned on the floors above his quarters covered the walls. Located ten feet from his bed, a privy "exhaling most dreadful smells" befouled the confined air as if it were a living thing. These fumes, in addition to the walls and two hundred men, took up physical, though invisible, space. "A horrible odor," Wilkins wrote, "pervades the apartment." On his third day at Libby, his nose detected another fearsome odor coming through a crevice in the floor beneath his bed. Peering through cracks into the basement, Wilkins eyes confirmed what his nose must have suspected. On one side of the basement lay the bodies of men awaiting burial—a makeshift "dead house." The other side contained "a swamp filled with fetid matter, the exhalations from which ascend around my bed and mingle with those of the room." Without exaggeration, each inhalation warned Wilkins of invisible dangers—the building's deadly breath—lurking in the air. His nose told him that some awful disease could spontaneously generate at any moment.[2]

The personified privy that exhaled those invisible, lurking dangers also threatened to disable Wilkins's nose. After starting a journal on August 12, he discussed olfaction on six of his first seven days in prison. Gendering his nose—or at least pointing out his refinement—and making up his own word, Wilkins confessed on day four, "I used to have a womanish fondness for perfumes. But I fear my nostrils will become deodored by the horrid smells I am continually inhaling that I never will be able to relish a sweet scent again."[3] Libby Prison threatened either to make him unable to appreciate pleasant scents or perhaps lose his sophisticated sense of smell altogether.

Although rarely articulated with such clarity, Wilkins was not alone in his fear. Nearby prisoner James Bell, a captured government clerk, also found a "sickening, gloomy, loathsome, Stygian Den" at Libby Prison. That same "oozy compound of filth" covered the floor, emitting "a stench more intolerable than I ever before inhaled." At first Bell thought it was impossible to breathe the odor and live. At night the "damp exhalations" and the accumulations of filth poisoned every breath. A leaking privy saturated everything in the room "with its disgusting odor." The stench remained inescapable as long as Wilkins and Bell continued to breathe and retained their sense of smell. The uncompromising nature of breathing—it was a necessary part of living—meant prisoners had no choice but to inhale the combined odors of privy effluvia, rotting food, smoke, and the bodies of sick and unwashed men. Bell pointed out that in time, "as it could not be escaped, continual breathing accustomed our olfactories, until we became in a degree insensible to its presence." The nose only took so much before the sense of smell withered. The smells of prison produced anosmia, an olfactory equivalent of temporary blindness or deafness that came from familiar smells.[4]

Alongside Bell's, Wilkins's writings make it possible to uncover how the nose became "insensible." In his forty-four days at Libby, Wilkins referenced olfaction on at least twenty-five days in three ways: primary, explicit descriptions of odor; secondary, implicit descriptions of fresh air, foul air, night air, or a noisome atmosphere; and tertiary visual cues—such as the "filthy" and "wretched" space—or animalistic comparisons to hogs and cattle. During the first three weeks at Libby, Wilkins referenced smell explicitly or implicitly an average of five times a week. During the last three weeks, he only referenced smell between two and three times each week. Moreover, nearly all of Wilkins's analytic forays into odor took place during his first week at Libby Prison; afterward, his descriptions became shorter and shifted from the explicit to the implicit to the tertiary. His writings trended toward the anosmia he feared.

Wilkins, like Bell, never experienced permanent or total anosmia. The duration of imprisonment, coupled with his consciousness of the peril of losing the sense of smell, allowed him to preserve olfaction. Smoke from the stove and tobacco served as a makeshift prison perfume. "The constant fumes & odors of the stove (which is in continual use)," Wilkins wrote, "somewhat counteract denser smells of a much more odious kind." When Wilkins had a rare opportunity to "stretch my limbs" outside of prison walls, he also stretched his nose. "I had a breath of fresh air," he wrote that day, and "the sensation was most delicious & inspiring." Upon returning to the "noisome hole," he sought to preserve his body by smoking a pipe. Still, he worried that "close confinement" was "gradually sapping the mind, as well as enfeebling the body."[5] Hours after leaving Libby Prison for good in late September, Wilkins remarked that "fresh air tastes delicious" in comparison to a filthy place already passing from sight and smell.[6]

It is worth following the ideas of prisoners like Bell and Wilkins who linked antebellum ideas about sanitation to the smells of captivity. Historicizing prison olfaction in this way means considering how people used sensory knowledge to understand their environment before the bacteriological revolution of the late nineteenth century. Despite stereotypes of the Civil War era as a medical dark age, close attention to the language of sanitation reveals the nuances of olfaction in everyday life. Prisoners used smell to understand the landscape of captivity. Breathing "pure" and "foul" air became an olfactory metonym that differentiated freedom and captivity. Prisoners' thoughts on smell were also consistent with sanitarian views that foul air threatened the nose, body, and mind.

The partially "deodored" or "insensible" nose that affected prisoners, prison officials, sanitarians, and governments in the sensory tumult of Civil War America was a mixed blessing. Becoming insensible to a foul environment mitigated a terror of captivity for Bell and Wilkins, but it also enfeebled what nineteenth-century Americans considered the body's best sentinel against disease. The perspective of outsiders was also important. Prison officials, sanitarians, and civilians were often appalled by prison smells, but they could also exhibit a form of anosmia. This problem connected prisons to the larger issue of sanitation reform. Sanitation and cleanliness, measured through the eyes and nose, were two parts of the same problem: the former was increasingly a public, environmental issue in the nineteenth century; the latter remained a private, personal one. Outsiders were concerned about prison smells, but they also showed willful anosmia by turning a blind eye — or nose — to prison odor.[7]

Anosmia complicates its own recovery because the phenomenon cannot be inferred simply from a lack of olfactory evidence. However, as in the case of Wilkins and Bell, men who remarked on prison odor most often in their captivity also remarked on the sense's decline. The constant inflow and out-flow of prisoners guaranteed a constant introduction of new noses to old en-vironments; therefore, references to smell are abundant. Careful use of tertiary references to smell—references to visual cleanliness, filthiness, the specter of disease, and so on—also mitigates the challenge of locating odor in the prison archive and points to the interconnection of smell and vision. Foregrounding olfaction while not losing sight of vision allows historians to take the former seriously without forgetting that the senses work together. Sanitation was multisensory. Exposing and exploring cooperation between smell and vision allows for informed inferences about one sense through the other. If it was possible to "see" disease through the nose, there was equal potential to "smell" sanitary and unsanitary landscapes through the eyes.[8]

Fresh Air, Foul Air

Far from being blank slates, prisoners brought ideas with them into captiv-ity, including understandings about the role of the nose and eyes. Only five years before the Civil War, a writer for *Harper's New Monthly Magazine* argued that smell was the least appreciated but one of the most important senses. The nose modulated the voice, aided in respiration, drained moisture from the eyes, and assessed air quality. According to popular belief, the nose—like the eyes—also projected a man's strength and character: the short, thick nose meant sensual indulgence; a "turned-up nose," vanity; big nostrils, strength. "The strong man," according the essayist, "breathes fully and freely, and opens his nostrils, as his lungs, widely and largely." The nose also came with certain weaknesses. First, lacking the olfactory equivalent of eyelids or lips, humans had to cease breathing to prevent a "nauseous current" from entering the body. However, one might benefit from this defect by utilizing one strong smell, such as tobacco, to shield the nose from another, such as the stench of a corpse. Second, the nose could become exhausted. Prefigur-ing the partial anosmia of Civil War hospitals and prisons, the author pointed out that because "habit diminishes the power of the sense," those who worked with "putrid substances" became insensitive to the noxious fumes. Finally, individual smells evaded precise description. Places and things that were foul, putrid, stale, or musty were more difficult to describe and identify than colors, musical notes, or even tastes.[9]

Despite widening sectional differences on issues relating to slavery, antebellum Americans held a baseline understanding about human bodies and healthy landscapes. Sanitarians in the United States and Europe, nurses and physicians, city dwellers, Southern planters, and Western settlers along the frontier believed healthy landscapes shared at least four basic features: sufficient drainage, air ventilation, visual cleanliness, and the absence of offensive odors. Turning to statistics and mapping, sanitarians showed the connection between environmental factors—drainage, air, cleanliness, odor—and health. Following the 1853 outbreak of yellow fever in New Orleans, sanitarians mapped "nuisances" and thereby visualized the antebellum smellscape of New Orleans. In addition to the "undrained swamps," the Mississippi River, and streets, their map depicted soil disturbances and specific nuisances, including "Cemeteries," "Slaughterhouses," and "Livery stables," as well as "Manufactories of soap, tallow, bone, Open basins & unfilled lots, Canals, Drains, Gas works, Fever nests, [and] Crowded boarding houses." As the report went to the printer, a "noisome odor" presaged the next year's outbreak. While humanity's olfactory capacity exceeded the capacity of its language, the nose linked vision, odor, and disease.[10]

Prisoners were more likely to comment on foul odors early in captivity and in certain types of prisons. Spaces of confinement were diverse, but can be generalized as closed-air prisons and open-air camps. Closed-air prisons often smelled worse and included city jails, coastal fortifications, and state penitentiaries; abandoned buildings such as hotels, college buildings, warehouses, and factories; and temporary spaces including boats and train cars. Open-air camps consisted of fields surrounded by barriers: wooden walls, earthen embankments, water, or just sentries. While Confederate prisoners in Northern open-air camps usually lived in wooden barracks, some lived in tents provided by the U.S. government. Union prisoners in the South often lived in open-air prison camps and improvised their own shelter from old tents, blankets, wood, and mud.

Olfaction helped prisoners map the parameters of their confinement. Whether in closed-air or open-air prisons, prisoners experienced foul air and longed to breathe pure or free air. Odor also warned of worse dangers than discomfort. Physicians and sanitarians feared "zymotic diseases" that spawned in warm, filthy environments.[11] When Randal McGavock entered open-air Camp Chase at Columbus, Ohio, and smelled the "intolerable" sinks, he anticipated it would generate disease. "I predict that if these men are kept here until warm weather," he wrote, "they will die like sheep with the rots."[12] In Richmond's closed-air Libby Prison, William Wilkins drew a direct connection between those "noisome vapors" and the prospect that "Typhus fever must soon appear." It was common knowledge that foul air was lethal.[13]

Closed-air prisons, such as the casemates of Union coastal fortifications and Confederate warehouses, magnified the realization that odor occupied its own physical space. Imprisoned in a casemate at Fort Warren, Baltimore mayor George Brown wrote, "There is one invading evil which as yet has defied all the efforts to correct it—a very bad smell which comes from the sewer of cesspool."[14] The odor affected the prison quarters unequally, "for strangely enough the rooms on one side of each passage are worse than those on the other. We suppose that this is the consequence of greater or less proximity to the water closet." While some prisoners made room for the odor by changing quarters, Brown considered himself lucky because his room was "on the less nasty side." Atmospheric factors affected the location and intensity of the odor. An eastwardly wind blew the smell off, "but a westwardly wind brings it up through the wainscots & down the ventilators."[15] Confederate prisoner William Davis characterized his enclosure at Fort McHenry in Baltimore as "well supplied" with vermin and filth and more fit for horses than humans. He wrote, "Our stable smells very bad for Some of the Boys lay with their heads in the Trough."[16] Making the best of a bad odor, Charles B. Stone joked that the fumes radiating from Libby Prison's water closet substituted for his lack of cologne.[17]

There were strategies to alleviate offensive odors. In George Brown's cell in Fort Warren, prisoners applied disinfectants, such as lime, but had mixed results. Frank Bennett, imprisoned at two South Carolina city jails in 1862, found relief in tobacco and whitewash. At Charleston, Bennett and other prisoners lit cigars and surrounded themselves "in the soft and pleasant tobacco smoke which lay heavily around us." Later at Columbia, the prisoners cleaned and whitewashed their living spaces. "It now looks much more cheerful and smells less offensively," he wrote.[18] In a letter smuggled out of a Richmond tobacco warehouse, Hiram Eddy relayed to his wife how tobacco eased a hellish scene. Plumbing from an upstairs water closet had been leaking for some time, but as Eddy wrote in his secret letter, "the pipe from the upper closets burst, & discharged the excrement of 400 men upon us, filling the room with the villainous odor. It fell within 15 feet of where I was writing, & within a few feet of our dining table." In response, "every man lit his pipe, & smoked for his life." Despite their fumigation efforts, "the awful stench" was more powerful.[19]

In small rooms, tobacco smoke filled the air and some men doubted that the benefit of tobacco fumigation outweighed the cost. Captured in

October 1861 at the Battle of Ball's Bluff, Jonathan Stowe of Massachusetts described the noxious clouds of smoke in a Richmond prison. He wrote, "It is all smoke here and the smell of tobacco, will I hope, keep off the vermin; but I fear for our health." Stowe linked smoking to health and morality, an equivalent to drinking or gambling. Other prisoners received his protests "with jibes and jest," and the smoking never abated: "I suffer from the want of pure air—the continual smoking—oh dear!" The debate continued throughout the war. In late 1863, "Gerold" complained in a prison-produced newspaper, the *Libby Chronicle*, that "at least four hundred stinking pipes pollute the air most villainously." While the writer admitted that the smell reduced "the noxious and sickening effluvia from the sinks," he maintained that "the remedy is worse than the disease." Like other odors, tobacco smoke was "choking" and "permeates every nook and corner of the prison." It even contaminated the food. For some men tobacco protected the nose, but for others it simply added to the suffocating atmosphere.[20]

Smell occupied considerable space in open-air prisons, especially as they became overcrowded and drainage systems failed. A large section of Andersonville was uninhabitable, an olfactory reality documented in wartime photographs (see figure 3). Prisoners chose to live in more crowded parts of the stockade, leaving swaths of vacant space on both sides of a stream designed to meet all the prisoners' drinking, washing, and excretory needs. Winds affected the smell of the prison as well. Although John Ransom's Andersonville "diary" was no such thing, his memory of prison odor had the ring of truth. While other prisoners described crowding windward or pressing their noses to the ground, Ransom recalled that the walls and, beyond those, trees seemed to keep a foul atmosphere hovering over the prisoners.[21]

New arrivals at Andersonville blamed odor not only on the guards but also on the condition and habits of other men. Samuel Gibson found "the condition of many of them is horrible in the extreme," but he placed blame for the "Monstrum Horiendum" on the prisoners because they seemed "to be to[o] lazy to do anything for themselves."[22] In describing the "Horrors-of-horrors" at Andersonville, John Hoster pointed out that some of the sick prisoners "do their business just outside their tents in small holes and some have been seen to do it in small holes made with the heel inside the tent, while some do it on the surface outside." Others used the steep slope that led to the sinks, "creating an awful stench and rendering the water unfit to wash in."[23] William Tritt characterized two categories of men suffering from chronic diarrhea: those who washed their clothes on a regular basis and the lazy. "Some [are] standing at the brook washing their trousers," he observed. "Others [are] standing with the dung running down their legs into their shoes." The effect was to make Andersonville an olfactory nightmare.[24]

Whether in closed- or open-air prisons, confined men desired to breathe freer, fresher, or purer air. Confined in the Old Capitol Prison in Washington after his capture at Fort Harrison, William Burgwyn calculated that fourteen men occupied a 300-square-foot room with no windows and a closed door, which made the air "very close and suffocating."[25] When Randal McGavock had the privilege of walking around the island at Fort Warren in the spring of 1862, he took the opportunity and "inhaled the fresh air from the sea."[26] Prisoners at Libby Prison crowded by the windows, and expressed outrage when guards shot at them from the streets for trying to breathe pure air.[27] Andersonville prisoner Alonzo Decker wrote in loose pages of his diary a poem entitled "The Prisoners Dream." Rather than the recounting of a literal dream, Decker used poetry to express the feeling of suffocation at Andersonville and the wish to breathe unsullied air:

> Oh give me a breath of air
> At the rose morning dawn
> When dew drops like Jewels rare
> Brightly Sparkle on the Lawn
> To live on some mountain top
> Where the Breeze sweeps from the Sea
> In vain I cherish the Hope
> For life has few Days for me
>
> . . .
>
> I am going with each breath
> Despite my wishes and tears
> Now the lone foot falls of Death
> Are echoing in my ears
> Toward home I turn my face
> Where my wife and children Dear
> Gather round the bright fireplace

In Decker's poem, the air in Andersonville sapped "robust and strong" men of health and strength one breath at a time until they were "wasted and weak."[28]

Opportunities to leave suffocating environments gave men a literal breath of fresh air. When Charles Lee went from the prison at Andersonville to the hospital outside the main stockade, he thought the "nice fresh breath of air" was better for his health than the castor oil he received from a Confederate physician. After carrying the corpse of an anonymous man to the cemetery a few days later, Lee reiterated the lesson that "the fresh air and the green fields and forests made me feel almost like one risen from the dead."[29] Collecting wood, Samuel Grosvenor noticed that breathing outside air had an invigorating and restorative effect on his health and spirits. He wrote, "Went out & breathed once more the free air of heaven uncontaminated by the thousands within."[30] Availing himself of a similar opportunity "just to breathe pure air once more," Robert Kellogg described "how good it seemed to get out in the woods, among the trees & flowers. The world seemed almost like a new world to me." After being transferred from Andersonville, Kellogg described a "splendid" atmosphere at the Washington Race Course prison in Charleston and he predicted it would benefit prisoner health.[31]

As even brief respites suggest, breathing free air served as an olfactory metonym for freedom. John Ward wrote to a Confederate senator from Camp Chase hoping he would intercede on his behalf for a release and allow him to "again breathe the free air of our sunny south."[32] When Randal McGavock stepped off the exchange boat at Aikin's landing downstream of Richmond, he noted that every man "seemed to draw a long breath."[33] Griffin Frost in Missouri wrote, "God knows we all long to breathe the pure air of Dixie once more, free from the tyrant rule we are now under."[34] After Henry L. Stone, a cavalryman who rode with John Hunt Morgan, made a successful escape from prison, he fled north to find free air in Canada. There he wrote, "I'm now no longer under the accursed dominion of Yankeedom. I can here breathe free, much freer, Cousin, than I could in Mt. Sterling Dungeon. Here the air is cool, pure & invigorating, especially to one who has been a prisoner."[35] If captivity meant breathing foul, noxious air, freedom was a long breath of pure, free air.

Breathing fresh air mattered because foul air degraded men's sense of smell over time. Florence Nightingale, an internationally renowned nurse and sanitarian, had warned of this in *Notes on Nursing* (1859), remarking that nurses needed scientific instruments—a mechanical nose of sorts—to measure the concentrations of organic matter in the air. Otherwise the nose would eventually fail. "The senses of nurses and mothers become so dulled to foul air," Nightingale wrote, "that they are perfectly unconscious of what an atmosphere they have let their children, patients, or charges, sleep in." There was good reason to fear losing the sense of smell.[36]

In war and captivity, noses underwent a similar seasoning. When war broke out, James Higginson, a wine merchant in Great Britain and Germany, entered the war in the service of the United States Sanitary Commission

(USSC) before becoming an officer in a Massachusetts regiment. As with many sanitarians, he had a discriminating nose. Near Fairfax, Virginia, Higginson spent a miserable night in "a nasty little tavern," sleeping in the same bed with a sutler "who smelt badly."[37] After his capture at the Battle of Aldie, Virginia, in June 1863, Higginson's nose became less sensitive. Five months into captivity, he noted that men were becoming used to the smell of prison and "no longer shudder at the unpleasant smells from the dirty sinks nor from the numerous *lice* with which everything is infested."[38] Higginson did not mourn this fate like Wilkins or Nightingale. From his perspective, anosmia was a blessing. A paroled Union prisoner recalled that when he entered Castle Thunder in Richmond a "curious, disagreeable smell" accosted his nose. Over time it decreased. "A persistent detention, however, as I found, has a remarkable effect on blunting one's olfactory sensibilities, and I owe nature for this wise provision of hers a heavy bill of thanks."[39] In contrast to Wilkins and Nightingale, some thought the blunting of smell was olfactory mercy. By the time the nose began to fail, prisoners were well aware of the dangers of their environments.

Amid partial anosmia, olfactory experience lived on through metaphors that intertwined human and animal landscapes. After predicting prisoners would die like sheep at Camp Chase in the warm months, Randal McGavock asserted that no respectable Tennessee farmer would allow their hogs or cattle to live in such a "dirty and loathsome" place.[40] James Dennison, captured by Nathan Bedford Forrest's cavalry at Brice's Crossroads, Mississippi, wrote that he had no shelter at Andersonville and the "place stinks as bad as a hog pen."[41] Two days after his capture at Brentwood, Tennessee, Charles Prentiss stayed briefly in the Columbia, Tennessee, courthouse, which he described as a place bad for hogs and worse for men.[42] Prisoners invoked hog metaphors to indicate the presence of filth, disease, and degradation.

For Civil War prisoners, hog pens were living metaphors that required serious consideration. Illinoisan Eugene Sly frequently drew on the nonhuman imagery to describe the conditions from Danville, Virginia, to prisons farther south. Only at Andersonville did Sly regularly compare the prison to a hog pen. The lack of proper shelter added to the mud and smells of the prison and made Sly think that "we are used with no more respect than a lot of hogs." One month after entering Andersonville, Sly used the metaphor a final time, writing that "fathers hog pen is a paradise to this place." Growing up on a farm, Sly used a familiar farm scene to explain the extraordinary— Andersonville. When Sly retired the metaphor, he suggested it was out of exhaustion. Perhaps it slandered his family's hog pen to link it to Andersonville.[43]

Sanitation and Willful Anosmia

Prison conditions were the consequences of assumptions and choices about the environment, human health, and the responsibility of prison keepers. In the North, prison officials and sanitarians hoped to improve prison sanitation in ways that foreshadowed the large-scale sanitation of urban areas by the late nineteenth century. This model stressed dry, ventilated, deodorized environments on the spatial configuration of a city. The USSC, through at least part of the conflict, took a bold stance in favor of bettering the prison environment. The Confederacy, in contrast, had no semiautonomous organization equivalent to the USSC, and prison sanitation was never a high priority. To be sure, neither the Union nor the Confederacy designed their prisons to exterminate prisoners. However, to different degrees, Union and Confederate officials also exhibited what might be called willful anosmia, a neglect of responsibility to ensure sanitation, especially late in the war.

Northern officials expressed confidence they could design healthy landscapes with the right spatial layout and the proper regulation of humans and nature. This reflected a shared assumption held by European and American reformers in the mid-nineteenth century that humans could rein in odor and disease by rationalizing and disciplining human environments. Nightingale had propagated a certain mode of sensing and, especially, smelling. She emphasized the role of smell in the environmental origin of disease, reasoning that if 25,000 children sickened and died in London the culprit was "want of cleanliness, want of ventilation, want of whitewashing; in one word, defective *household* hygiene." Although Nightingale's emphasis on nursing was multisensory, nothing was more critical than the origin, movement, and perceived freshness of air. Alongside other sanitarians, she believed the nose cautioned against disease like a bell warned of fire. She cautioned against complacency, writing that "although we 'nose' the murderers, in the musty unaired[,] unsunned room, the scarlet fever which is behind the door, or the fever and hospital gangrene which are stalking among the crowded beds of a hospital ward, we say, 'It's all right.'"[44]

The USSC provided the most direct channel for antebellum sanitarian beliefs into Civil War camps, hospitals, and prisons. Although deeply committed to the Union cause, the USSC often criticized military sanitation.[45] First within U.S. military camps and later in Northern prisons, USSC officials took the principles of sanitation seriously. Inspectors asked questions about drainage, soil, the arrangement and cleanliness of streets and tents, bathing habits, "odors of decay," and waste management. Foul smells were not just unpleasant, they were lethal; and sanitation provided to cities, camps, and prisons what nursing offered to patients.[46]

Northern prison officials responded to odor in ways that mirrored sanitary officials. After an influx of prisoners in 1862, Union Commissary-General of Prisons William Hoffman placed Confederate officers at Johnson's Island, and in Illinois, Indiana, and Ohio he converted military training camps into long-term prisons for enlisted men. Later that spring, Hoffman sent Captain Henry Lazelle to investigate training camps in New York that might also be converted into prisons. Lazelle, a prisoner himself in 1861 and 1862, had a sanitarian's nose for environmental detail. Camp Rathbun near Elmira sat west of the city on "gravely soil covered with greensward which does not during the most violent storms become soft." The air was free from the foul air of decomposition. "There is not in its vicinity either marsh or standing water nor dense forest or shrubbery which could generate malaria or disease," he wrote, "and the whole country about Elmira is exceedingly healthful and no forms of low fever prevail." The barracks inside the camp were "well ventilated by square windows placed sufficiently near each other." Only one attribute, the "insufficient, incomplete, and filthy" sinks, spoiled the tranquil air. After inspecting six other training camps, Lazelle deemed Camp Rathbun the most practical. Although the sinks were "filthy," the buildings were structurally sound and the ground drained and odor free.[47]

Neither Lazelle nor Hoffman had any way of knowing that Elmira would become home to the deadliest Northern prison two years later. For the time being, they worried more about prison camps west of the Appalachian Mountains. At Camp Douglas, near Chicago, USSC president Henry Bellows feared only "special providence or some peculiar efficacy of the lake winds" would prevent the generation of pestilence. He wrote, "The amount of standing water, of unpoliced grounds, of foul sinks, of unventilated and crowded barracks, of general disorder, of soil reeking with miasmatic accretions, of rotten bones and the emptyings of camp-kettles is enough to drive a sanitarian to despair."[48] The only sure way to purify Camp Douglas, Bellows advised, would be to burn it down, and he urged Hoffman to abandon the camp and start again with ridge ventilation in the barracks and sufficient ground drainage.

While historians have criticized Hoffman as stingy at best or cruel at worst, he took the sanitarian's warning seriously. While he floated the idea of abandoning Camp Douglas to Quartermaster General Montgomery C. Meigs, Hoffman also proposed a solution that mirrored urban sanitary reforms. He suggested building an underground sewer, connected to water pipes and the sinks, around all sides of the prison that would empty into Lake Michigan. In addition to supplying the camp with water, the pipes would help "float out the filth of all kinds." The subterranean sewer would have the benefit of relieving whole prison environs "from the stench which now pollutes the air" and threatened the health of the place.[49] This suggestion paralleled ongoing proposals in the United States and Europe to move from a "private system" of cesspools and vaults to a "public system" of subterranean sewers. Brooklyn and Chicago had already built sections of underground sewers in the 1850s, and other Northern cities such as Boston, Cincinnati, and Indianapolis followed in the 1870s. Quartermaster General Meigs rejected the expenditure, arguing that the prisoners "should certainly be able to keep this camp clean, and the United States has other uses for its money than to build water-works to save them the labor necessary to their health." Meigs's response echoed calls for the older, private system, arguing that individuals, not the government, were responsible for sanitation.[50]

The quartermaster general's decision was not surprising given the ongoing resistance to public sewer systems. While Hoffman backed down on the sewer project until the next year, when it was finally approved, he directed Colonel J. H. Tucker, commanding Camp Douglas, to fill in old sinks and dig "new ones large and deep, with good shed houses over them. Have a thorough police of all the grounds daily and carry off the refuse trash of all kinds in carts; use lime plentifully everywhere."[51] He also stressed that there needed to be better enforcement of personal cleanliness among prisoners. Hoffman wrote, "The quarters must be well aired and policed by removing all bedding and clothing from them once a week and there must be a free use of lime everywhere to neutralize all impurities. There can be no excuse for non-compliance with this order."[52]

Prison officials made similar decisions elsewhere. At the largest of three prisons at Camp Chase, Ohio, Henry Lazelle reported that "the air of the camp, and more particularly of the prison, is polluted and the stench is horrible." In contrast to Camp Rathbun's orderly grid, Camp Chase's largest prison had only irregular clusters of barracks obstructing proper ventilation. The barracks and the spaces between the buildings were in poor condition. Stoves begrimed prisoners with smoke, grease, and cooking debris. Barracks had not been whitewashed in months, lacked brooms, and let in water where prisoners had bored holes to ventilate the hot buildings. The outside ground held surface water and the prison's main drain emptied into the sinks: holes in the ground over which a single rail was placed lengthwise. While the drain did not provide enough water to remove filth, there was enough water "to insure rapid decomposition and load the air of the prison with the most nauseating and disgusting stench." The result was "overpowering [to] the nostrils and stomach" of men whose noses had not become "impermeated" and, therefore, desensitized to the environment.

Lazelle's criticism and his detailed instructions highlighted a sanitarian's faith in purifying landscapes by draining, ventilating, and deodorizing the land. Responsibility for these collective improvements fell not on the Confederate prisoners, whom he described as quiet and eager to improve their living conditions, but on the prison administration. Lazelle instructed officials to excavate ten-foot-deep vaults lined with planks and surrounded at the surface by sloped ground to keep out surface water. On top of these excavations, Lazelle ordered "substantial privies with air chimneys and bench seats." In conjunction with the liberal use of deodorizing lime, this structural improvement would diminish the smell of privies throughout the camp. The use of lime linked the efforts at the privies with the general sanitation of the camp, particularly in the barracks. To improve the smell of the barracks, Lazelle called for "lime and whitewash brushes in sufficient abundance for rapidly whitewashing all the quarters in all the prisons." Every twenty prisoners should have a twenty-gallon tub of whitewash. Lime-fortified whitewash on wood deterred decomposition and helped deodorize the air. Lazelle also instructed that the barracks be raised above the ground with the side coverings removed below the floor to limit moisture and allow better air circulation. Finally, Lazelle had drains constructed to move water away from the barracks, improved streets with side drains, and graded open areas to prevent standing water.[53]

When Lazelle returned to Camp Chase later that summer, he breathed fresher air. He found the prison barracks whitewashed and the regular application of lime in the prison. Lazelle wrote that the changes "render the atmosphere of the prisons comparatively pure."[54] Exterior improvements, including the drainage and privies, had greatly improved the smell of the place. "I need not add that the health and comfort of not only the prisoners," Lazelle wrote, "but the whole camp, have been materially increased, and the stench, before so intolerable, almost removed."[55] His confidence in improving health through deodorization reflected the same sanitary impulse as the USSC and antebellum sanitarians.

Variations on this theme—earth, air, water, and smell—echoed in other reports within the Union prison system in the summer of 1862 and continued throughout the war. Whitewash, in particular, was a cure-all in Northern prisons (figure 1). The substance had been widely used to clean privies

FIGURE 1 Manfred M. Griswold's photograph of Camp Chase depicts elements of sanitary reform: drainage, ventilation, and a coat of whitewash. Photograph of Camp Chase, National Archives and Records Administration.

and paint throughout the nineteenth century. Advertisements promised that lime would absorb "disagreeable and unhealthful gases and odors" in "cellars, privies, stables, and gutters of the streets." When mixed with water, lime-fortified whitewash evoked purified air both to the nose and eyes.[56] Following the sanitarian lead, prison officials applied whitewash on outside walls and inside walls, floors, and ceilings at prisons across the North. At Camp Douglas, prisoner Curtis Burke was detailed to whitewash the hospital in September 1863. There he found several other prisoners "smearing the white wash over everything. They had the floor about half an inch deep in white wash."[57] A medical inspector at Fort Delaware suggested whitewashing the insides of barracks every six weeks as well as applying Ridgewood Disinfecting Powder and chloride of lime.[58] Officials at Rock Island praised the effect of whitewashing barracks formerly occupied by smallpox patients, which had rendered these spaces "measurably free from smell."[59] Whitewash produced temporary deodorization, and it left unmistakable visual evidence of how sanitary spaces should look to the eyes.

The focus on whitewash, drainage, and improved sinks indicated a commitment to sanitarian principles, but the scale of imprisonment stretched the effectiveness of these efforts to their limits. These approaches worked when prison populations were small in late 1862 and early 1863, but by that summer the problems associated with securing equal treatment for African American prisoners and the subsequent breakdown of the exchange cartel began filling prisons once again. Then the same olfactory problems resurfaced. Dr. Thomas Hun and Dr. Mason Cogswell visited Camp Douglas at Chicago and Gratiot Street Prison in St. Louis and found both places reeking of filth and disease. At Gratiot Street Prison, they wrote in a letter that reached Secretary of War Edwin M. Stanton, "the small yard of the prison is scarcely sufficient to contain a foul and stinking privy," adding "it is difficult to conceive how human beings can continue to live in such an atmosphere as must be generated when the windows are closed at night or in stormy weather."[60]

When the foul smells of unsanitary prisons returned, however, the USSC also became more critical of Confederate prisoners, painting these men as the source, not the victims, of the foul air. Dr. William F. Swalm, a former prisoner of war himself, inspected Point Lookout, Maryland, for the USSC in 1864, and commented that the prisoners "seem to abhor soap and water," paid no attention to the location of the sinks, and preferred to sit on the ground and "roll into it as a hog will wallow in the mire."[61] While Swalm did not completely absolve prison officials of the duty to maintain cleanliness, he implied that the "mire" was the fault of the "hogs." The report was also one of the last USSC reports on Northern prisons. Afterward, the USSC focused their efforts on publishing accounts of privation and suffering among Union prisoners in Confederate prisons while downplaying the nuisances of Northern prisons. It was anosmia all over again, but this time there was a willful quality to it.[62]

Sanitary problems in the North reached their zenith when Camp Rathbun received its second life as Elmira Prison in 1864. The transformation enhanced the gridded camp by adding several streets. As with other large-scale prison camps in the North and South, Elmira was a self-contained unit like a simplified, walled city or a living organism (figure 2). Water flowed through the enclosure, which provided water for bathing, washing, and drinking. Prisons also centralized necessities such as a cookhouse, and a series of sinks was designed to remove prison waste. Hospital barracks, represented in a prisoner's map, were separated from the barracks by the "Gardens," as well as a network of sentry boxes and walkways. From the sanitarian perspective, the position of the hospital at the western end of the prison environment allowed for ventilation of fresh air. The hospital's separation from the prisoner barracks by a garden placed pleasant smells between the sick and the rest of the prison population.[63]

Despite the city-like order, drainage, and ventilation, the pure air turned foul when Elmira Prison opened in 1864. From a sanitarian's standpoint, the problem was clear from the very beginning. Several weeks after the first Confederates arrived, head surgeon Eugene Sanger reported that the sinks were polluting the entire prison. Seven thousand Confederate prisoners produced 2,600 gallons of urine per day. "A portion is absorbed by the earth," Sanger wrote, but "a large amount decomposes on the top of the earth" or drained into Foster's Pond within the stockade. Sanger suggested many of the same actions that prison officials had deployed against odor in the preceding years, but he was more skeptical about the panacea of disinfectants. Rather than destroying the odor, Sanger argued, the disinfectants might just be masking it. He questioned "whether disinfectants exert any chemical changes upon miasmata, or whether the obnoxious odors are merely displaced and overpowered by the stronger, less disgusting, and more rapidly evolved gasses of the disinfectants." If the latter were true, Sanger reasoned, "we have two deleterious gases in the atmosphere instead of one." Moreover, chemical disinfectants were expensive, and Sanger suggested creating a current through the canal and pond that would remove the source of the odor.[64]

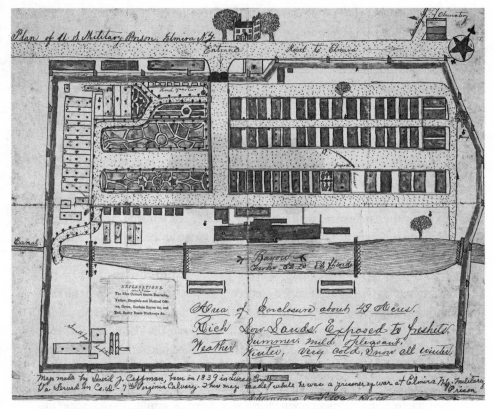

FIGURE 2 Confederate prisoner David Coffman's map of Elmira reveals both sanitarian thought and an oversight: a garden separates the prison barracks (upper right) from the hospital (upper left); the pond became the main olfactory nuisance in the fall of 1864. Map of Elmira, ca. 1865, Library of Virginia.

It took months for improvements at Elmira to begin. The landowner who leased the prison site to the U.S. government complained that an open sewer violated the terms of their agreement. To make matters worse, Union officials were also slow to respond. Benjamin Tracy, Elmira's commander, brought the "stagnant pond of water" to the attention of William Hoffman in October and recommended constructing a subterranean sewer. The solution was not unlike the sewer Hoffman had suggested at Camp Douglas two years earlier, though he suggested using prison labor to lower the price. By November, the work was underway, but Sanger described the pond as still "green with putrescence, filling the air with its messengers of disease and death, the vaults give out their sickly odors, and the hospitals are crowded with victims for the grave." The sluice was completed by early 1865, but not before more than 1,200 prisoners had died. Over twelve months, Elmira claimed the lives of a quarter of its prisoners. It was the only Union prison with a hospital recovery rate below that of the Chimborazo Hospital for Confederate soldiers at Richmond, Virginia. In other words, Elmira prison was the only place in the North where men who entered the hospital would have stood a better chance of surviving in a Southern hospital.[65]

Northern prisons were more organized than those in the Confederacy, but Southern prison officials, soldiers, and civilians shared an understanding of the same sanitarian principles of the time. Confederate newspapers complained about the deleterious effect of Richmond's prisons on both civilians and prisoners. In July 1862, the *Richmond Enquirer* sympathized with city residents living between two sources of foul air: a Union prison and a candle factory. In a gesture to the antebellum sensory norms and nuisance laws, the paper suggested the removal of both sources to less populous locations outside "the average range of the sense of smell."[66] Later that year, the *Richmond Examiner* reported that Belle Isle had "undergone a fumigation for purification purposes." This purification benefited the residents, but because it took place at the height of prison exchange, Union captives had already left the island.[67] The *Enquirer* displayed more concern for the prisoners in early 1864, criticizing the "unwholesome atmospheric diet" of Libby Prison and comparing the place to a tin of sardines. The paper stated, "It is truly surprising that some pestilence has not already been the result of this indiscriminate herding together of human beings, who are thus forced constantly to breathe an impure air."[68] Recommending fresh air and sunshine, the newspaper projected common understandings of fresh and foul air.

Confederate officials prioritized their resources toward the Confederate army and away from their prisoners. Infrequent reviews of Richmond prisons in 1863 and 1864 focused on drainage, ventilation, and odor less than the USSC or Hoffman. When surgeon John Wilkins inspected Libby Prison in 1863, his report would have surprised the men inside. "The prevailing wind (south)," Wilkins wrote, "unobstructed by adjacent buildings, secures thorough ventilation." Other inspections at Richmond prisons that fall found sufficient attention to prison water closets and general cleanliness.[69] In stark contrast, when surgeon G. William Semple inspected nearby Belle Isle a few months later, he found ten thousand men forbidden from using the sinks at night because their location at the river could aid escapes. This prohibition, combined with the prevalence of chronic diarrhea, meant that "the whole surface of the camp has thus been saturated with putrid animal matter."[70] Richmond medical director William Carrington, who had declared Richmond prisons clean four months earlier, hinted a powerful reason for willful anosmia. "I lost no occasion to make known to the proper authorities the violation of ordinary hygienic laws," Carrington asserted, but he also claimed he was "deterred from further remonstrance by a feeling that it was supererogatory, and might be understood as disrespectful."[71] Concern about reception led inspectors to hold their noses.

Supply shortages and security concerns, as well as civilian complaints about the strong odors emanating from prisons, led to the removal of prisoners to other locations farther south in 1864 and 1865. Wherever large numbers of prisoners went, civilian complaints about foul odors and fears of disease soon followed. At Danville, Virginia, the town mayor and the leaders of the town council petitioned Confederate secretary of war James A. Seddon for the removal of Union prisoners from the area or, at the very least, from buildings in town to somewhere outside the city limits. Smallpox had broken out, and the civilians complained that disease-laden air from the prisoners would infect the town: "The stench from the hospitals even now (in winter) is almost unsupportable, and is offensive at the distance of several hundred yards." The town had no waterworks to aid in cleaning the streets, into which the filth of the prison and prison hospitals drained.[72]

Andersonville emerged as a place to relocate Union prisoners away from Richmond and populated areas. The prison had the outward shell of a Northern prison camp, but it lacked much of the interior infrastructure: barracks; wide, drained streets; or an effective water and sink system. Sanitary reports were more candid than in Richmond. In May 1864, barely two months after the first prisoners arrived, surgeon E. J. Eldridge complained about the unsanitary conditions of the prison. Already overcrowded with 12,000 prisoners, Andersonville had no separation between prison and hospital, and the Union men even lacked enough space to bathe in the stream that bisected the prison. Prison officials supplied two squads of twenty-five prisoners with shovels and told them to collect and burn "all offal" and throw the remainder at the lower end of the stream.[73]

Medical officials recognized that Andersonville stank, but they came to different conclusions about the meaning of the odor. Throughout the spring and summer of 1864, prison surgeon Isaiah H. White recommended sanitary improvements that would deodorize the prison. He criticized the placement of the hospitals within the prison because of the "contaminating effluvia" entering the hospital from the camp.[74] The hospital was eventually removed. White later pointed to drainage, ventilation, and odor to explain the high mortality rate. The water and drainage system generated pestilence because it exposed "a large surface covered with decomposing vegetable matter" to the sun. Overcrowding and the irregularity of the prison tents and streets created ventilation problems.[75] By August, White lamented the failure of sanitary regulations. There were feces everywhere, "among the very shelters [and] under their very noses." Summer thunderstorms caused the lower end of the steam to rise and recede rapidly, leaving "a solution of human excrement" on the banks to dry under the sun, which, he wrote, "produces an intolerable stench."[76] White's recommendations to drain, ventilate, and deodorize the prison were never implemented.

The failure to improve the sanitary conditions at Andersonville had at least two causes. It is generally accepted that Andersonville was both mismanaged and lacked sufficient tools and enslaved men to build up defense systems and improve sanitary conditions at the same time.[77] However, Captain Henry Wirz, in charge of the prisoners, also dismissed criticism about the sanitary conditions. When Daniel T. Chandler reported to Richmond officials in September that the lack of attention to sanitation made Andersonville a close approximation of hell, Wirz ridiculed his manhood and loyalty, called him "the plaything of cute Yankees," and asserted that another inspector confided to him that Andersonville was as "on par with the Federal prison at Johnson's Island."[78] Direct comparisons are fraught with danger, but not here. When Wirz wrote those words there were 10,507 prisoners at Andersonville and ninety-two prisoners—a typical figure for July, August, and September— died that same day. Johnson's Island, which held prisoners from April 1862 until after the end of the war, lost 235 men over the course of the war. In contrast to Hoffman's efforts to drain, ventilate, and deodorize Northern prisons, Wirz seemed to display some form of willful anosmia.[79]

Outside investigations into sickness at Andersonville underscored the subjectivity of smelling. Dr. Joseph Jones and his secretary, Louis Manigault, received permission from the Confederate surgeon general to visit Andersonville and study disease at the camp. Jones examined the passage of water through the prison stockade and found it remarkably pure upstream of the prison and the natural topography of the surrounding land healthier than parts of Georgia to the south and southeast. Yet the volume of water in the creek was not sufficient to remove excrement and scraps from the prison. "The action of the hot sun upon this putrefying mass of fragments of bread and meat and bones," Jones explained, "excited most rapid fermentation, and developed a horrible stench." Downstream from the prison Jones found a swamp, "filled with trees and reeds coated with a filthy deposit" and "emit[ing] an intolerable and most sickening stench."[80] Within the prison stockade,

Jones also remarked on the close confinement of prisoners, with less than thirty-six square feet for each man.

While Jones emphasized smell and disease, he also blamed the olfactory environment on sick and lazy prisoners. The men left filth "at the very tent doors and around the little vessels in which they were cooking their food. Small pits not more than a foot or two deep, nearly filled with soft offensive feces, were everywhere seen, and emitted, under a hot sun, a strong and disgusting odor."[81] Louis Manigault came to a more extreme conclusion. In a private letter to his wife, Manigault conceded the camp was worse than what he had found in a Shanghai prison or a cholera hospital in northern China: "The dirt, filth, and stench in and around the stockade is awful." But the smell did not otherwise move him. "I feel no pity for them," he told her, "and behold a dead Yankee in a far different light from a dead Confederate killed in fighting for all that is dear to him."[82] The interpretation of odor highlighted not only the connection between smell and disease, but also the partisanship of the person behind the nose.

The olfactory environment at Andersonville left a visual imprint. Andrew Jackson Riddle, a semiofficial Confederate photographer, visited Andersonville in August 1864, the deadliest month in the prison. Perhaps surprisingly, Riddle's photographs captured the sinks and the stream that ran through the center of the camp (figure 3). What he intended to portray with the images was unclear. However, there is no reason to believe that Riddle desired to capture a more sympathetic view of the prisoners than Jones or Manigault. If he had expressed a desire to do so, it is reasonable to assume that he would not have been welcome at the prison. The photographs suggest prison order and disorder: tents are arranged in rows, especially on high ground away from the sinks. They also convey one of the sanitary problems of the prison. Prisoners may be seen defecating in two places: at the prison-supplied sinks in the foreground and, faintly, on the side of the hill in the background. The timing was also significant. One week before Riddle's arrival, a flash flood had swept away parts of the stockade wall and some of the accumulated filth. Riddle's photographs may convey not the foulest Andersonville but the most orderly depiction that camera perspective and timing could provide.[83]

The human catastrophe of Andersonville, downplayed or ignored by Confederate officials, was noticeable to civilians in the region. These effects lingered long after the prison population rapidly declined from its peak in the summer of 1864. Remembering the experience of passing Andersonville on a train in January 1865, Eliza Frances Andrews compared the "seething mass

FIGURE 3 In this photo taken one week after a flash flood, Andrew Jackson Riddle caught the most favorable view of the prison sinks and sanitary conditions. "Andersonville Prison, Ga., August 17, 1864, Bird's Eye View," Library of Congress, Prints and Photographs Division, https://www.loc.gov/resource/ppmsca.33769/.

of humanity" to "a swarm of blue flies crawling over a grave." In conversation with a paroled Union soldier from France, Andrews learned that prisoners had burrowed into the ground and the subterranean huts "were alive with vermin and stank like charnel houses."[84] Ambrose Spencer, a resident of nearby Americus, Georgia, testified before the U.S. congressional committee on the treatment of Union prisoners. Spencer remarked, "The condition of the stockade perhaps can be expressed most aptly by saying that in passing up and down the railroad, if the wind was favorable, the odor from the stockade could be detected at least two miles."[85] Spencer was a Union man, Andrews a Southern female writer, but they both framed their concerns in relation to odor and the environment.

The specific charges that led to the conviction and execution of Henry Wirz had an olfactory dimension, including conspiracy to destroy the lives of prisoners by subjecting them to an unhealthy landscape. Guards' testimony indicated they shared the common understanding of the nose as the arbiter of healthy landscapes. "The stench arising from the camp was very bad," Nazareth Allen stated, noting that even the guards had little relief from it. "We soldiers preferred doing picket duty to sentry duty" because the air was fresher, even though from the distance of a mile he could detect the stench. More than merely unpleasant, the odor sickened guards. "The stench was so bad," Allen testified, "that it kept me sick pretty nearly all the time I was around the stockade." William Dillard, another Confederate guard, stated that a very bad smell came from the prison that he could smell from the depot at Andersonville about a mile away.[86] The testimony of the guards highlighted not only the widespread belief that foul odor was disease but also the notable absence of Confederate officials attempting to ameliorate the unwholesome air.

THE WIDESPREAD BELIEF in nineteenth-century Europe and America that foul odor threatened public health necessitated a sharp nose among sanitarians, soldiers, prisoners, and prison keepers. For prisoners, odor became an element of their captivity, and the inability to escape foul air exemplified inhuman suffering. As a way of conceptualizing the essence of prison, odor symbolized the disabling and dehumanizing process of captivity, and, at the same time, breathing fresh air symbolized freedom and the promise of survival. These same odors posed a problem for officials whose goal was containment, not punishment or extermination, of their prisoners. Sanitation and military officials drew on the same international sanitary movement to understand prisons, but implementation was difficult. If rendering prisons orderly and deodorized with city-like grids, drainage, and ventilation was a losing battle in the North, it was hardly fought at all in the Confederacy. Civilians and medical officers complained to varying degrees about the dangers of prison odor. Those who could do something about it had other priorities.

At the practical level, it mattered little whether anosmia came organically through overuse of the nose or willfully through neglect. When prisoners became sick, "lazy," or gave up hope, it worsened the condition of men around them. The same thing happened when sanitarians gave up on Confederate prisoners or Confederate officials held their noses against the smells emanating from their prisons. For sanitarians, prisoners, and prison keepers, anosmia meant complacency. This inaction, as Nightingale had warned, courted disabling and deadly disease.

CHAPTER THREE

Bite and Be Damned!

William Haigh surrendered with one pair of pants and thin skin.

Still a prisoner at Point Lookout one month after the surrender of Generals Robert E. Lee and Joseph E. Johnston, though, Haigh recorded a grim memory of his first days of captivity. "I don't believe that I ever pre meditated suicide before," he admitted, "but if such a thought be ever pardonable, it would be under such circumstances as I then found myself." Haigh started keeping a journal, written in the form of an unsent letter to his wife, about four months after his capture at Fort Fisher near Wilmington, North Carolina, in January 1865. He told her about sleeping as a prisoner on the cold beach and in the dark cargo hold of the *North Point*, a ship that brought prisoners to Maryland. Taking Haigh at his word, he wanted to kill himself for a more specific reason. When Haigh first awoke in prison, he found himself among tent mates "of the unwashed, unclean order," whose filthiness had spread to him in the night. But there was more. "A feeling of something, that I never felt before, startled me, something creeping & *crawling* next to my skin," he wrote, "and then, for the first time in my experience, I found that I was *lousy*. Oh horror of horrors! And no change of garments!" Haigh's first encounter with the lice and the unwashed men made him ill.[1]

In his disgust, Haigh signaled to his wife several important ideas that could have been written by any number of Northern or Southern men who considered themselves part of the "washed" gentlemen class. As historian Lorien Foote has observed among Union soldiers, "For some proponents of gentility, cleanliness was one of the essential marks of the gentleman."[2] Haigh, a Confederate soldier, had also internalized this conception of honor. He was a forty-two-year-old lawyer, an alumnus of the University of North Carolina, and part of an extended slaveholding family. As a member of the washed class, Haigh was not the sort of person, or so he thought, whose status and habits invited lice even as a private in the Confederate army. Maintaining his self-image and reputation required his depiction of fellow prisoners as part of an unwashed class whom he had the grave misfortune of encountering. Those men, not he, were the proper habitat of lice. Finally, the disgust, the sickness, the longing for a change of clothes, and the thoughts of suicide all reinforced the same message: despite his company and his affliction, he would preserve his standards of manly cleanliness as best as possible.[3]

Self-preservation for Haigh required learning to remain clean among other men who ranged from "noble and generous fellows" to "penitentiary scape goats and off scourings of creation." He praised the work of the prison "police," the men who cleaned the ditches, swept the streets, and threw refuse into the Chesapeake Bay. He also learned how to wash his own clothes. "One thing may be of service to us now that the negroes are free," he wrote, "we have all learned how to cook and wash, and are very easily made contented." Finally, there was also a subtle but important change in how Haigh thought about lice. "There is no mock modesty or sentimentality allowed," he wrote, when a "reb strips for a battle with his tormenters the 'gray backs.'"[4] The same encounter that had inspired revulsion had turned into a normal, even honorable, task by the time he sat down to confess the difficult transition to prison life. This transformation, deeply personal for Haigh and other men, was one way lice affected the feeling of war and captivity. It was also how men bent the social rules for touch, cleanliness, and loathsome vermin.

Lice played an outsized role in the prison ecosystem. It is worth imagining the louse as a participant in wartime prisons, a trickster of sorts who first made prisoners cringe, then laugh, and should make historians think about what was lost and gained in the process. Stripping down to the skin and hunting lice became how members of Haigh's "washed" class preserved a sense of civility in filthy environments and among their fellow "unwashed" prisoners. Lousing become an inside joke for prisoners told through the "battles" with "graybacks," the common nickname adopted by both Union and Confederate soldiers. Lice transformed the feeling of prison life by pushing men to accept different measures of cleanliness.

The relationship between lice and men was one of the deeply haptic—or felt—experiences of Civil War prisons. For men like Haigh who learned to exercise the power of their senses, attention to detail could save lives. The same *Harper's New Monthly Magazine* writer who described the nose as a sentinel began an essay on touch with a curious comparison: a silkworm and a monarch's firstborn son. While the former "greets the light of day" in a "warm, cozy nest" and "finds silk and thread in his own body, which he weaves into clothes and wrappings for his season of rest," the latter "comes into the world naked and helpless, amidst tears and loud complaints, to lead a life ever threatened by others, and yet ever depending on the assistance of others." From the unflattering comparison of an heir apparent to an insect, the writer argued that the senses "are but so many sources of suffering, until we have learned to guide and protect them."[5] Just as olfaction warned men of invisible dangers lurking in the air, changing the rules of touch empowered civilized men in war and prison to maintain some degree of cleanliness by washing clothing, bathing the skin, and—most importantly—keeping the lice in check.

Threats to skin in Civil War prisons came from all directions. While lice, men, and changing standards of cleanliness represent just one way to explore the feeling of captivity, it is part of an underdeveloped aspect of the war that acknowledges that nature was a key participant. Recovering the power of lice serves as a reminder that while much of the violence in the Civil War era came from the hands of humans, nonhuman participants also played their parts in the forefront of this human drama.[6] Prison environments were neither the first nor the only place in Civil War America that lice crossed paths with humans. The host-specific body louse, joined with humans since before agriculture, is unable to feed on most other mammal hosts and so has never left. The Civil War era was a great boon for lice, and nowhere did lice play a larger role in shaping human experience than in places of captivity.[7]

Lice encapsulated the feeling of living by inches. There was no better environment for lice and fewer worse places for men. Prisoners adapted to this situation in two ways. Men fell back on existing methods of self-care they had learned as civilians and soldiers. Self-care was for the individual what sanitation had been for cities, armies, and prisons. Second, prisoners reconsidered what the sight and feel of lice meant, carving out a scenario in which a few lice were not the sine qua non of filthy people and dishonorable men, as they had been in the antebellum era. Preserving civility meant tempering the cultural instinct of revulsion and resisting private shame with public action. The louse was the trickster of Civil War prisons who could outwit the best nitpicker. As long as a prisoner remained in the fight with lice—so long as he did not become overrun by them—he was in on the joke and therefore remained a clean gentleman making the best of an uncivilized place.

Lice before Captivity

Prejudices against lice in Civil War America were part of the larger struggle between humans and nature in armies, hospitals, contraband camps, and prisons. Within each of these spaces there developed a give-and-take relationship between humans and nature, with no single participant or group controlling the outcome. Insects made up the smallest visible contributors. Flies, mosquitoes, ticks, and plenty of other insects came near the skin, but it was vermin—bedbugs, fleas, and lice—that carried connotations of poverty, impurity, and inferiority. Civilians and soldiers reacted with similar disgust when their skin came into physical contact with vermin, especially lice. A female nurse working in Washington, D.C., warned her daughter to stay home in Boston instead of joining her. The reason was that the mother's "needle-woman" had just "found nine body lice inside of her flannel waistcoat." Even worse, the mother confessed, "I caught two inside the binding of my drawers!"[8] Plenty of men and women felt eaten alive by flies and mosquitoes, but few reacted with the shame and disgust reserved for contact with a louse. In its wretchedness and its symbolism, the louse was a pest above the rest.

By the time of secession and Civil War, a centuries-long shift in hygienic standards had taken place, emphasizing bathing and fresh clothing while stressing the avoidance of dirt and vermin. Cultural undertones of impurity, rather than fear of specific disease-causing microbes, made vermin physically and emotionally important for soldiers and civilians who practiced what historian Kathryn Shively Meier calls "self-care," a set of adaptations seasoned men and women in the Civil War era learned to protect the body. Self-care could be endless, but early adaptations included learning how to forage for wholesome food; where and how to bathe and wash clothing; how to protect the skin from insects; how to build shelter on the move or in winter quarters; and even how to straggle to avoid exhaustion. While some forms of soldier self-care were original, many were carryovers from an antebellum era when changes to personal hygiene paralleled a broader sanitary reform movement. Bathing, for example, had become more common by the mid-nineteenth century, especially among middle- and upper-class white Americans, who connected cleanliness to health, civility, and morality. As travel became easier, those with sufficient means traveled to mineral springs and seaside resorts for health and social reasons. Some reformers believed in "water cure" or "hydropathy," a treatment of total immersion that, along with exercise and dietary reforms, would preserve health and make sickly bodies well again.[9]

Amid these reforms there was broad agreement among powerful members of society that lice marked inferiority. Evicting lice from hair and clothes was a prerequisite for polite society. There were social prohibitions on scratching and picking at vermin in public, followed by a broader effort to scrutinize those in society still afflicted by vermin.[10] Eighteenth-century household manuals, almanacs, cookbooks, child-rearing books, and preachers professed the necessity of keeping free of lice or how to get rid of them.

In 1769, theologian John Wesley declared that "cleanliness is next to godliness" and issued specific instructions for taking care of the body, including the maxim: "Clean yourselves of lice. These are a proof both of uncleanliness and laziness: Take pains in this."[11] In the nineteenth century, one children's book on insects warned that the "loathsome" louse only tormented "the unfortunate and lazy" and could be "routed by the hands of industry and cleanliness." Antebellum gynecologist and surgeon J. Marion Sims learned from his mother that lice "belong always to the black race." By the Civil War, the louse was a known marker of social and racial inferiority.[12]

People who became free during the Civil War recalled lice as part of the reality of slavery and war, but those memories had little in common with Sims or the reformers. Instead, these memories placed lice within an environmental context and prefigured both the humor and strategies for managing lice in armies and prisons. Clara Walker recalled weaving "nits and lice," a coarse, spotted cloth used for overalls. The cloth "was sort of speckeldy all over," which gave the exaggerated impression of lice-infested clothing. Charlie Hudson remembered delousing as a communal activity for the "old folks," who looked over each other's heads for lice. "Whenever dey found anything," the interviewer recorded in racialized dialect, "dey mashed it twixt dey finger and thumb and went ahead searchin'." Other memories placed the blame for postwar infestations by linking the arrival of lice to Union and Confederate armies. Della Briscoe, of Macon, Georgia, attributed the "new plague" of "body lice" to Union soldiers. Lindsey Faucette, in contrast, remembered lice as a product of Confederate soldiers camped around the plantation. "I ain't never seed de like," she remembered. "It took fifteen years for us to get shed of de lice dat the sojers lef' behind. You jus' couldn' get dem out of your clothes les' you burned dem up. Dey wuz hard to get shed of." While the presence of lice decreased for some Americans throughout the sanitation movement, it continued to haunt the most vulnerable in America before and after the Civil War.[13]

Like Civil War nurse Hannah Ropes, men who encountered lice in the Civil War first reacted with shame and embarrassment. They hid the fact that lice afflicted them. A Confederate soldier told his mother that men "prefer to stand the *biting* than acknowledge they were lousy like the 'Yahoos,'" a term that referred to the brutish Yahoos of Jonathan Swift's *Gulliver's Travels*. Before falling into Union hands, John Dooley believed lice were most problematic on active campaign in the trenches, and he saw men sitting on logs searching for the vermin. Oliver Wendell Holmes Jr. confessed the "frightful fact" that "many of the officers including your beloved son have discovered themselves to have been attacked by body lice." Needing a source for the contamination, the officer thought perhaps the lice came from the enlisted men. Cleanliness mattered in the public reputation—or honor—of men in Union and Confederate armies.[14]

While Union and Confederate soldiers found lice repulsive, vermin were more manageable in armies than in prisons. U.S. Army regulations in 1861 identified Saturdays as a day devoted to cleaning and stipulated short hair, neat beards, and "where conveniences for bathing are to be had, the men should bathe once or twice a week."[15] Lice affected campaigning armies to be sure, but disciplined men were confident they could get the upper hand over lice as soon as it became possible to rest, bathe, and boil clothing. Hygiene and manhood, discipline and health were integrated components of the gentleman soldier. While tension existed between a washed and an unwashed class of soldiers, many men worked hard to maintain antebellum standards of genteel cleanliness.[16]

Men of the washed class resented the implication that soldiering amounted to contracting lice. Herbert Carpenter told Martin Roberts, an inquisitive teenager from the same Connecticut town, that the man who "went home and reported that we were all lousy" was misinformed. Carpenter hoped to dispel the misleading rumor that besmirched his public image. "Of course we cant keep ourselves as clean as we did at home," he told the fourteen-year-old, "but we keep ourselves as clean as we can under the circumstances." However, Carpenter admitted there were "dead heads" in the company who were "nasty, and lousy, [and] they never wash their persons &c or clothes." These men included Fred Nichols, a teenager barely older than Martin Roberts but from a poorer family. Carpenter wrote, "I have known one or two instances since he [Nichols] has been out here when the Captain ordered a Corporal to go with him to the brook and see that he washed himself." The other "dead heads" from East Hampton included Newell Root, Gilbert West, and Leander Rich. All shared two things in common: they were younger than Carpenter and came from poorer families. Newell Root was "as lousy as the old cat," and Leander Rich "seems to have lost all ambition if he ever had any." While clean men could "not avoid catching" the lice from the dead heads, strict discipline prevented lice from taking hold. The clean men of the company washed their clothing and used a delousing agent to make sure of it.[17]

While Henry Carpenter felt little guilt reporting the unclean habits of his neighbors, Henry Sellow was more cautious when the self-appointed louse detective wrote him. Sellow admitted that four men from the company, including West and Nichols, had been escorted by a whole squad of men down to the river and forced to wash their hair, skin, and clothing. Nichols had dirt on him from Maryland and Washington, and the others "had got so lousey and dirty you could see the lice crawling on the out side of their clothes," joking that "the lice had the letters *US* branded on their backs." Sellow worried about the social implications at home of his lice gossip. "I would not say any thing about this," he instructed the teenager, "for it may get to his folks and make them feel hard." Whereas Carpenter used the unwashed soldiers to highlight the cleanliness of the washed class, Sellow worried that this social dirt would cause public humiliation at home.[18] The conversations reflected the reality that having lice in the army was not always normal. Disciplined men kept themselves clean and expected the same from others. Despite the presence of lice, prewar standards of cleanliness were also alive and well in Civil War armies.

The Power of Prison Lice

Standards of cleanliness and self-care came under greater scrutiny in Civil War prisons. When men wrote about prison lice, they characterized it as both a new experience and a revolting one. In June 1861, Captain Thomas Baker of the Confederate privateer *Savannah* spent his first five days at "The Tombs" in New York City, "annoyed by bugs, lice, and roaches," before receiving permission to bring in bedding, scrub the floors, and whitewash the room. Early action prevented the lice from getting the upper hand, and only after removing the vermin could Baker "turn in" for the night without "feeling that the bugs and vermin" would "turn me out."[19] Confederate naval officer Thomas T. Tunstall accused the U.S. government of using lice as an instrument of torture. Before embarking on a six-week passage on the high seas, Union officers told Tunstall that he was going below deck, "where 'the vermin would take hold of me.'"[20] From the earliest months of the war, lice could act alongside the walls and guards as part of the carceral landscape.

As with Tunstall's high seas experience with vermin, many first encounters came on the way to long-term prisons. Wash Nelson and James Anderson both fell into Union hands while visiting their families behind the lines. Nelson recalled three aspects of the "John Brown Engine House" at Harper's Ferry in the fall of 1863. The cramped "hole" contained "no beds, no seats, and the walls and floor were alive with lice." At Wheeling, West Virginia, the next temporary hole on Nelson's way to Camp Chase, he found that the room was "neither so small nor so lousy as the one we had left, but the company was even less to our taste than lice, viz Yankee convicts."[21] James Anderson had a similar transition to prison, with both lice and Union men introducing him to prison life. He kept two written records of his captivity, including a diary and a series of unsent letters to an infant son. He first saw vermin onboard a steamboat heading to Nashville where a number of "Copper Heads, Deserters, Bounty Jumpers," and other Union men "abounded in filth and dirt and the vermin it seemed to me would be enough to devour some of them." At the Nashville Penitentiary, where Anderson spent two days on his way to Camp Chase, he discovered that the thin layer of sawdust covering the floor "was almost alive with lice."[22] The connection between the feeling of lice and captivity often began before reaching long-term prison camps.

First encounters sometimes did not occur until men arrived at prison. William Barrow discovered his first louse at Camp Douglas about six weeks after arriving and punctuated his admission with the sound of disgust, "Ugh!" Before capture, Barrow's self-care included taking clothes to a washerwoman and bathing in a creek, and he continued washing at least his face in prison. He had been restless the night before he met the lice, "scratching away at what I supposed to be the *rash*." The doctor's ointment had not helped, and Barrow decided to wash his neck and change shirts. "Lo! & behold! " He wrote. "It was filled with lice, horrid!" The whole barracks soon found themselves infested, too.[23] Tennessee planter Randal McGavock had encountered fleas and other vermin while traveling through Italy in 1851, but he recorded no wartime interactions with them before arriving at Camp Chase in 1862. The barracks, or as McGavock called them, "shantys," were "filthy" places "where vermin and all manner of creeping things infested."[24] Established prisoners helped explain prison realties to new arrivals. James Cooper's "lazy" messmates at Camp Chase warned him about "the number and size of the lice and vermin of all kinds abounding in the prisons." For the new arrivals the news "was sickening to us, as we were just being initiated, but to them it seemed to afford infinite amusement."[25] The amusement would make sense to new arrivals, too, but that would take more time.

Union prisoners had similar reactions when first encountering prison lice. Elisha Reed had the rare privilege of receiving new clothes at a prison in Tuscaloosa, Alabama, and he hoped for an exchange before the lice found their way into them. Although Reed thought himself better adjusted to captivity than other prisoners, he became homesick when he felt a louse. It reminded him of his condition as a prisoner and his anger toward a government he believed had left him to die in the Confederacy.[26] An officer at Macon, Georgia, wrote that his fellow prisoners "are now seated around on their bunks searching eagerly in the seams of their unmentionables for something they dont want to find."[27] Jacob Heffelfinger, wounded and captured outside Richmond in 1862, described his first encounter with lice in a hospital for captured Union soldiers. "The house is becoming infested with lice. How repulsive! To be compelled to lie here, lousy, and no means of avoiding it."[28] One prisoner in Texas found the sight of afflicted prisoners amusing until realizing it would soon become an intimate part of his own experience.[29]

Learning about lice was part of acculturation to the daily rhythms of prison life. At Libby Prison, George Parker called it a "novel sight" to see men in various stages of undress. Some washed their clothing while others sat "in the windows picking lice off their only shirt."[30] Recalling his arrival at Libby Prison shortly after being released, government clerk James Bell wrote, "The climax of all horrors to a decent man was the lice." Bell's word choice— decent—was intentional. As historian Kathleen Brown has observed, decent Northern men and women in the Civil War era considered uncivilized Southerners awash in everything except for morals, bathing routines, and clean clothing. Bell had previously considered lice a problem for uncivilized brutes, such as the Southern white men holding him prisoner. Along the road to prison, Bell had witnessed campaigning Confederate soldiers performing self-care on their clothes, "sitting naked oblivious to our presence, while they pursued their ragged garments in search of vermin." Along that route, Bell had maintained his station above unwashed Southerners, but once in prison "escape was impossible" from the lice.[31]

Prisoners believed these tormenters epitomized captivity. Lice became the mascot of the "Richmond Prison Association," a group dedicated to "fun and mutual improvement" early in the war. Their motto, "Bite and be damned," doubled as the last line in a song written for the organization, and the words also adorned the organization's seal. Lest anyone miss the inference, two concentric circles of lice—a total of forty-eight in all—encircled the motto. The editors of the *Richmond Enquirer* and the *New York Times* were too squeamish to identify the lice on the coat of arms, opting instead to call them "certain small creeping insects" and "well known bugs." The prisoners were less modest about things unfit for the eyes of the newspaper's civilian readership. After the war, a former prisoner explained that there was nothing "more natural" than to include "our constant companion, the 'body louse.'" The writer even recalled that scratching under the arm had become the organization's sign.[32]

Beginning in 1861 and continuing throughout the war, Union prisoners considered Libby Prison an unrivaled metropolis of vermin. Two years after the Richmond Prison Association drew its seal, Harlan Smith remarked on his second full day there that the "boys are busily engaged in destroying body lice." As Barrow had in 1862, Smith punctuated his written reaction in three letters and one syllable, "Ugh." Smith then took a comprehensive census of the room. Estimating that lice outnumbered men one hundred to one, he counted 278 men and projected the body lice population in one room to be 27,800.[33] Writing from memory, John Harrold's words rang of truth when he recalled that the prison seemed to be "'alive' with them — every crack and crevice filled — *working* with these disgusting insects." They respected no personal boundaries as they colonized prisoners' clothing, hair, and beards. The lice made "continual war upon us," Harrold wrote, "and, in spite of our best efforts, they maintained the mastery." With such numbers, lice overwhelmed spaces of captivity and called into question the assumed power relationship between men and insects inside Libby. The prison could not be separated from the experience or memory of lice power.[34]

Although Confederate prisoners did not turn the louse into a mascot, they were as interested in understanding the insects that tormented them. A Fort Delaware prisoner lamented that the "place completely swarms with them," and he remarked, "they appear to be a larger and more ferocious breed than any I have seen in Dixie (this for the benefit of the naturalists)."[35] At Johnson's Island, Robert Bingham took a different type of survey when he began studying the habits of insects and rats at the prison. There were many crickets, grasshoppers, and large spiders, but these creatures were "lazy" and "sluggish." In contrast, the rats were "not sluggish in the least" as their large size indicated, but they "disturb no one." The lice were unique. Not only were lice not "sluggish" at all, but they multiplied and took up their own space. Bingham could not sit on the ground or dry his clothes without being attacked by them.[36]

Studying lice also helped prisoners understand their human opponents. Referring to lice as a biblical plague served the useful purpose of comparing their place to Egypt and their condition to the Hebrews. Describing the "remorseless war" and a "perfect plague," a Point Lookout prisoner described a dismal scene. "Around the yards, by the sides of the barracks, inside the barracks, in the bunks, everywhere," he wrote, "are to be seen groups of men busily engaged, searching the hems and seams of their garments for that loathsome little persecutor which annoyed the Egyptians so much."[37] Mary Terry, a prisoner herself at Fitchburg, Massachusetts, and a suspected Confederate smuggler, received a letter from a male friend released from Fort McHenry. The friend had been in captivity only fourteen days but was "troubled by chinches and one of Pharaoh's plagues."[38] The principal trouble for

Frederic James was "a plague with which one of the Pharaohs of old, together with his Egyptian subjects, were obliged to form an intimate acquaintance."[39] Whether in New England, the Chesapeake, or the Deep South, no one needed to clarify who were the Pharaohs and who were God's chosen people. It just depended on who was the prisoner.

As a versatile symbol, the louse also helped to dehumanize enemies. During the Black Hawk War of 1832, a member of the same militia unit as Abraham Lincoln advocated killing Native American children with a genocidal maxim: "kill the nits and you'll have no lice."[40] Perhaps similarly, the term "graybacks" originated as a way to dehumanize Confederate soldiers in the first year of the Civil War. Future president James Garfield certainly thought the Confederate prisoners arriving at Camp Chase were a "species of the 'great unwashed.'"[41] Regardless of origin, though, the association between graybacks and Confederate soldiers surely popularized the term among Union soldiers. After a lucky wound mangled only his pocket knife and inflected a severe bruise, George Pennington could not run as fast as other soldiers. For that reason, he wrote his sister, "I fell into the hands of the graybacks."[42] As early as spring 1862, graybacks had taken hold and it became the preferred nickname for lice and not an uncommon one for rebel soldiers.[43] The transformation became complete in prison, where the two were interchangeable. In the "Song of Belle Island," a Union prisoner humanized the lice as miniature guards or animalized the guards as big lice:

Bell Island is a splendid camp
We sleep so nice we get the cramp
The tents are open behind and before
And graybacks keep guard around the floor[44]

There is no way of knowing whether the name originated in a Confederate prison, but, like the insect, the term thrived in captivity.

Keeping Clean in Prison

Fighting the graybacks was an important part of prisoner self-care. As with the drainage, ventilation, and deodorization campaigns, both U.S. and Confederate prison officials recognized the general value of washing and bathing, even though self-care was more encouraged in the North. Almost as soon as Confederate prisoners arrived at Camp Chase in 1862, officials hired laundresses from Columbus to attend to prisoners' clothing, and rations in Union prisons included soap throughout the war. Prisoners could also purchase soap from the camp sutler, a vendor with government permission to operate inside the prison, for all but a few months of the war. Rations of soap were almost nonexistent in Confederate prisons, but it was sometimes for sale in the prison markets.[45]

Despite the prevalence of a soap ration in the North, neither Union nor Confederate officials made sufficient accommodations to support washing and bathing. Proposed infrastructure improvements at Northern prisons would have been a great benefit to prisoners who valued washing and bathing, though it may not have helped those who William Haigh identified as the "unwashed" class.[46] In the warmer months, it was possible to bathe under guard in the Chemung River at Elmira, the Chesapeake Bay at Point Lookout, the Delaware River at Fort Delaware, or Lake Erie at Johnson's Island. Robert Bingham considered it a challenge and an accomplishment to strip, wash, and dry his shirt and drawers between breakfast and dinner. Not only did washing take time, but the water pumps on the island were always a popular place for prisoners to wash.[47] Bathing in Northern prisons was much more difficult in the winter. At Johnson's Island, prisoners could find water to bathe only at the pump or, if that froze, carried by hand from holes cut into the ice.[48]

A warmer climate in the South meant Union prisoners had longer access to natural bodies of water, but weather, pollution, and access to soap limited their ability to make the best use of it. At Danville, Virginia, in late spring 1864, soap cost seven dollars per pound, a dollar more per pound than bacon. At Andersonville, prison inspectors encouraged the creation of pools for bathing. There was no guarantee soap could be purchased at the sutler's stand, though Henry Sparks traded his bread for a supply of it to remove the black "pine smoke" from his skin, which would not come off without a vigorous scrubbing. In Richmond prisons, Frank Jennings recalled substituting wood ashes for soap when performing morning ablutions before breakfast.[49]

Even when prisons had only a water pump, a sluggish stream, and little soap, the bathing men continued to wash themselves and their clothing. In 1861, Jonathan Stowe feared vermin would overrun his filthy room in a Richmond warehouse, but he took comfort that he had been "able to wash and keep clean."[50] Six days after being wounded and captured at Fredericksburg, Jacob Heffelfinger considered it a "luxury" to be able to wash his face at the Libby Prison hospital. When Heffelfinger fell into Confederate hands a third time in 1864, he knew to divide cooking and clothes washing with another prisoner and judged the environment on the ability to wash up. While the experience of cooking and washing clothes might have seemed novel at the beginning of the conflict, the disruption of gender norms lingered on in humor. "My wash-woman, Lt. Hurst, being sick," Heffelfinger quipped at Charleston, "I was compelled to take to the tub today" in addition to his duties as cook.[51] Prisoners turned to what they knew about self-care to protect themselves in filthy environments.

The practice of bathing and washing continued even with water men's noses told them to avoid. A prisoner at Fort Delaware described a scene along the river in which "washing men" would charge fifty cents per garment and another three hundred men were engaged in swimming or fishing. However, the proximity to the sinks meant that the water "cannot be rivalled for its filthiness, the smell alone being really offensive."[52] John Baer's morning ritual at Andersonville began by shaking off the accumulations of dirt, followed by "the necessary ablutions for cleansing the hands and face." Baer distrusted the water that passed through Andersonville as "uncomfortably greasy" and admitted that part of the routine was "force of habit."[53] After nearly a hundred days at Andersonville, Franklin Krause asserted, "I go down to the run every morning and wash." If Krause exaggerated, it was not by much. He recorded washing his hands, face, shirt, pants, or drawers on average of every third day after arriving.[54] Frederic James used lye "made of wood ashes" in place of soap, maintaining a washing routine until he became too weak from chronic diarrhea and scurvy.[55]

The realities of prison life left little or no space for modesty. Stripping naked to bathe or wash one's lone set of clothing did not seem to bother prisoners. Embarrassment and resentment did arise when nakedness came under the abusive gaze of prison visitors, especially women. This was most likely to occur at Northern prisons where excursion boats and observation towers allowed paying civilians of all ages to see Confederate prisoners. The *Rochester Daily Union and Advertiser* claimed that with a telescopic lens onlookers could see the lice crawling on the Southerners' skin and clothing.[56] Almost as soon as Robert Bingham arrived at Fort Delaware, he noted that "a good many she Yankee brutes" watched the prisoners swim naked in the Delaware River. In the coming days, as the women's gaze came—or at least felt—closer, Bingham claimed the women used "their opera glasses at a distance of 30 yards" to watch dozens of naked men swimming and washing in the river. Imprisoned men's vulnerability to female gaze followed Bingham to Johnson's Island, where onlookers along the stockade wall came within a dozen steps of the men. "Yankee girls & women," he wrote, "certainly like to look at naked rebels." One girl about fifteen years old became so "anxious" at the sight of Confederate prisoners that she supposedly lost her balance and fell. Disturbed by the inverted gaze, Bingham emphasized the unnatural-ness, unfemininity, and even the clumsiness of it all. Here were brutish Northern women studying a civilized Southern man's body.[57]

Disciplined self-care like washing and bathing may have been sufficient for delousing in Union and Confederate armies, but it was not enough in cap-tivity. Asa Mathews learned this when he arrived at Camp Oglethorpe near Macon, Georgia. Lice had been plentiful inside Libby Prison and in the box-cars that carried Union officers to Georgia, but Mathews believed that "with our privileges for washing we will soon be rid of them, I think." The lice prevailed.[58] Frederic James had similar hopes when he arrived at Salis-bury, North Carolina, from Richmond in early 1864. However, taking no chances, he asked his wife to send a pair of pants that "are *not* lined & will wash," the purpose of both being to make killing lice easier. For "shirts & drawers," he asked for clothing "of close woven flannel with the seams hemed or felled down so that *the lice cannot hide in them*." James received a box of clothing that spring, but it is unclear whether the articles met his specifications. Lice had afflicted James and his mess from September 1863 until February 1864, when James hoped they were getting the upper hand. By the time he reached Andersonville, where he died in September, he had stopped writing about lice, perhaps out of exhaustion. Self-care offered treatment—not a cure—for lice.[59]

How Lice Became Funny

In addition to washing skin and clothing, prisoners perfected an elaborate ritual for delousing that combined self-care discipline and humor to defang the smallest tormenters of prison life. The routine came from necessity. War-time remedies for killing lice included immersing infested clothing in boil-ing water, but prison infrastructure and economics worked against that as an option. Boiling was a luxury few prisoners could afford. Even with a suf-ficient container, the scarcity of fuel meant the choice between washing and cooking. Instead, prisoners turned to frequent cycles of delousing by hand. This method involved stripping down once or twice each day to examine the seams of clothing for lice. Describing a typical morning, George Parker wrote his parents that one by one about half the men in his room of the tobacco warehouse would rise and take a seat near the window, turn their shirts in-side out and begin policing the shirt with fingers. Some prisoners did use their cooking fuel as a way of killing lice. James Eberhart held his clothes over a fire and took pleasure in listening to the lice "crack."[60] Although not an unknown form of self-care in Civil War armies, this delousing became part of daily life for prisoners seeking to avoid the feeling of lice.

Acquiescing to the reality that lice thrived in places men suffered meant rethinking what the louse had symbolized before the war. This started with the name. While having the benefit of dehumanizing Confederates, the term "grayback" worked even better as euphemism. It softened the hard prison reality by replacing a word that marked uncleanliness and dishonor. Picking—and then killing—graybacks gave men something to look forward to when they deloused. Yet "grayback" was just one of many terms Union prisoners invented for lice. As paroled prisoners came to Camp Parole in the fall of 1862, William Flowers noted that a "good stock of Confederate creepers" came with them.[61] Charles B. Stone found not only "grey backs" but also "live stock" and "the natives" who had armor and fought him from ironclads and monitors. Frederic James referred to them obliquely as "genus creepus." William Peabody called them "old settlers."[62] Emphasizing the size, stealth, the nativity, and partisan leaning, these terms all had one thing in common: they made prisoners laugh. Lice euphemisms, from graybacks to genus creepus and Confederate creepers, had to be funny if they hoped to lighten the burden of feeling lousy. The humor was perhaps why even some Confederate prisoners like William Haigh accepted the word and overlooked the dehumanizing double entendre.[63]

Extended military and fighting metaphors helped reshape the image of the prison louse and make delousing an honorable routine. As George Parker explained to his family, the men in Libby called it "skirmishing," and one person might ask another how many "prisoners" they had taken that morning.[64] Implicitly or explicitly gendered male, lice put up quite a fight that elevated the contest between insects and men. The lice Charles Stone imagined fought in chain-mail armor and from ironclads and were "invulnerable to any instrument yet known except the hammer or ax," which he lamented were not for sale in the prison market.[65] William Wilson watched another man "pick a creeper from his pants and proceed to slaughter it. Agreeable sensation!" Soon Wilson was "engaged in [a] wild hunt" for "greybacks" of his own.[66] When Eugene Forbes "commenced a regular 'skirmish drill'" at Andersonville, he "took no prisoners but counted about a dozen dead on the field (my shirt)." Two weeks later, he encountered more "lively skirmishing" that resulted in the deaths of between seventeen and twenty lice.[67] Emphasizing the martial qualities of lice elevated a stalemate between man and insect into a stalemate between male competitors.

The image of skirmishing with graybacks that emerged from prison writing and illustrations was simple and consistent. Henry Van der Weyde's prison sketches from Danville, Virginia, visualized prison touch in two scenes. "Prison Realities" (figure 4) offers a profile view of Weyde's neighbor: a seated, bearded man with unkempt hair, naked from the waist up. This neighbor has just cracked a louse or a nit between his thumbs and has looked up slightly, casting a disengaged gaze downward and in front of the scene of the delousing. In contrast, "Flanking the Enemy" (figure 5) presents a more militarized, masculine—in a word, civilized—view of skirmishing. This frontal view depicts a different man with a healthy beard sitting naked from the waist down, arms resting on his legs and holding his pants between them. Unlike the first sketch, this man's eyes are focused upon the pants, with a kepi shielding his eyes from view. It is easy to imagine that while the former is thinking about lice and the uncivilized conditions of prison, the latter is thinking about capturing and killing grayback prisoners.[68]

Whereas Van der Weyde's sketches reveal the internal struggle of remaining a civilized man in prison, John Jacob Omenhausser depicted the clash of those meanings across the stockade wall. The Point Lookout artist frequently depicted imprisoned men in self-care scenarios, from fishing and selling goods to delousing. In "A Lady Visitor Come to Camp to See the Sights" (figure 6), Omenhausser depicts five people adjacent to the prison door: two prisoners, one Union officer, a Northern woman, and her son. The scene centers on a shirtless, bearded, and muscular man sitting on the ground and holding his gray coat over his blue trousers. The Union officer and the woman have antebellum notions of cleanliness. She has come to gaze on uncivilized men and she thinks she has found them. The officer speaks first, stating, "Heres one of the sights, and you can see a great many more!" The woman replies, "Good Gracious! I come here to see the sights, and I have seen them." Crouched down for a closer view and wearing a gray kepi, the young man projects more curiosity than revulsion. Remarking on their size and gendering the lice male, the boy says, "Mr. its a wonder them big fellows did'nt carry you out of camp." The standing prisoner introduces the idea that this is a continuation of the war. The prisoner responds, "He's fighting under the black flag[.] he shows no quarters," indicating that the skirmisher will execute surrendering lice. The lousing prisoner normalizes the scene as part of the realities of prison life. "Did you all never see a man catching Grey backs before? Say?" In his disbelief, the prisoner not only shows his ability to reclaim the word "grayback"; he also reinforces the gap between the antebellum mores of cleanliness and manhood and those inside the stockade wall.[69]

FIGURE 4 Henry Van der Weyde depicts an unkempt neighbor cracking a louse between his fingers at a prison in Danville, Virginia. "Prison Realities," Henry Van der Weyde Sketchbook, 1864–1865, courtesy of the Library of Virginia, James I. Robertson Jr. Civil War Sesquicentennial Legacy Collection. The original is held by the Danville Museum of Fine Arts and History.

Explaining lice as a continuation of soldiering elevated the conflict between lice and men and allowed the latter to emphasize courage and civility. After Asa Mathews had his "usual skirmish for grey-backs," he compared his up-and-down fortunes with lice to the progress of the Union army. On any given day, rumors might have Union troops "up in the east and down in the west, and vice versa." The vicissitudes of war and prison rumors translated to the battle taking place on prisoners' skin and clothing. "I drive them from my pants and they attack me in force on my shirt," he wrote. "Then I turn and fight them there and they are massed for a break on my other flank."[70] Charles Stone fumed when he learned that some fellow prisoners

FIGURE 5 Henry Van der Weyde portrays a more heroic version of skirmishing with "the enemy" in the same Danville prison. "Flanking the Enemy," Henry Van der Weyde Sketchbook, 1864–1865, courtesy of the Library of Virginia, James I. Robertson Jr. Civil War Sesquicentennial Legacy Collection.

had deserted the Union cause and escaped continued imprisonment by taking the oath of allegiance to the Confederacy. He exclaimed he would rather "rot & be carried from the prison by the vermin that infest it than take the oath to such an unholy alliance."[71] For Stone, there was more honor in fighting the lice than being free from them if that came at the cost of dishonoring himself to his country.

Some Confederate men also reconsidered the reputation of graybacks. As a prisoner at Camp Douglas, George Weston combined all the foregoing elements: the Northern nickname, the idea of a skirmish or hunt, and even a grain of respect. "While looking over my clothes this morning," Weston found five lice, "the regular Grey backs & quite puffed up, by the blood brought from my poor Dilapidated body." Weston's morning delousing

FIGURE 6 Confederate prisoners at Point Lookout embraced the term "grayback" alongside new prison standards of cleanliness. John Jacob Omenhausser, "A Lady Visitor Come to Camp to See the Sights," Civil War Sketchbook, 1864–1865, Maryland Manuscripts Collection, #5213, Special Collections, University of Maryland Libraries, http://hdl.handle.net/1903.1/4939.

ritual mirrored the one practiced by Union prisoners. Even though he thought there were no hiding places in his clothing, Weston took a closer examination after "feeling something nibbling at me last night." In the process he discovered sixteen "large Greybacks" in the seams of his shirt. Although Weston "succeeded in dispatching them," he concluded that "it is no use to kill a louse, a dozen will come to his funeral." Still, the burning sensation interrupted his writing. "I feel a bite now," he wrote, "& have to quit this & go to hunting."[72] Weston, like Omenhausser, showed that Confederate prisoners could use humor to soften prison realities. A civilized, funeral-attending louse was of a more honorable breed than the antebellum lice that had been symbols of inferiority.

By thriving and causing imprisoned men's skin to itch and burn, lice restructured expectations of cleanliness in Civil War prisons. Skirmishing with the lice once or twice a day became a display of self-discipline and honor. That was why William Wilkins disliked Louis Fisher, a German immigrant and a soldier from the regular U.S. Army.[73] Wilkins had learned quickly in prison how, through "scrupulous cleanliness & great care," to keep lice in check. "We search for them in the morning before rising," he wrote, "& it is a comical sight to see a room full of naked men, each sitting up on his blanket & intently examining with the keenest interest, his trousers or shirt." Wilkins implied that the German immigrant might be a source of the vermin; at the very least, the lice overran him. He wrote that Fisher "is actually alive with *lice* & spends nearly all the day, & sometimes, part of the night, picking them off him." In contrast to Wilkins's daily search, Fisher could not keep clean. No longer did just the presence of a louse carry a mark of shame; it was about the inability to keep lice in check with regular—not constant— skirmishes.[74]

Despite prison conditions, men still inferred a vast difference between the washed and the unwashed classes. Washed men reserved the stigma of uncleanliness for men like Fisher who became overrun with lice. James Sawyer recalled feeling "rather ashamed at first" to delouse himself, but in a short time "[we] thought no more of it than to wash your face. Indeed, it became a disgrace not to do it."[75] After all, the lice would catch up with those who lacked self-discipline and industry. While the population of lice made it "impossible to keep them off of you," those men who did not skirmish "would be almost devoured with them."[76] Nehemiah Solon wrote that the men who "neither louse nor wash" became "one mass of filth," and he inferred that they had lost all ambition to live.[77] Prejudice also played a role. Memoirist and artist Robert Sneden held special contempt for European immigrants. He described German and Irish soldiers as "dirty and unkempt" men who created a breeding ground for vermin that affected the whole building.[78]

Sick men also became perpetually lousy, and it added to their own problems and their neighbors'. As Horace Smith's health declined at Belle Isle, he confessed that he could barely "muster strength enough to crack a louse but necessity compels me to muster all the strength I can twice a day for that purpose."[79] At Danville prison, Henry Ladd found it too cold in November to take off his clothes in search of lice. Two days later, he wrote, "Suffering with cold. Nearly naked. Covered with lice. Oh, what a fate! Must we die? Will not God deliver us from this hell?"[80] Some prisoners took it upon themselves to groom the prisoners who were too sick or demoralized to do so themselves. Nehemiah Solon sympathized with the condition of a man who no longer had the strength to skirmish with the lice. "They had eaten holes into his flesh," he wrote, "and the holes were full of loathsome crawling lice eating his very life away." Sick and depressed, "he had given himself up to die but they had taken him to the brook and were trying to get him clean."[81]

LICE HAD STAYING POWER in the memories of prisoners. Memoirists had poor accuracy for events and dates, but their memories reflected wartime prison realities. John Ransom recalled the horror of hunting for "big grey backs" each morning at Belle Isle; he also speculated that lice became unmanageable at Andersonville because prisoners had difficulty skirmishing while aboard crowded trains. Ransom even recalled a dream in which guards hooked up a wagon to a team of lice to carry bread inside the stockade.[82] Charles Sumbardo recalled the transition from disgust to humor. He first encountered what he called a "Southern Grayback" in a Mobile cotton warehouse, which he described as "one of the most touching episodes of army experience." Sumbardo joked that "at first it seemed impossible to regard him with familiarity, but soon he became a constant bosom companion."[83] Jonathan Boynton described the endless task of daily skirmishing. The "graybacks," he wrote, "seemed to thrive on the lean Yankee bodies." Boynton remembered being "fairly alive with them" before even realizing it and "had my hair cut as short as possible to dispose of a fine crop of head lice." Those who neglected to "skirmish," Boynton recalled, were "doomed to endless torture, misery, and death."[84] When survivors thought back to captivity, they remembered the experience of being crawled upon and bitten by unrelenting lice.

At least one man who traveled through prisons in the Confederacy became a well-known entomologist and strong proponent of using chemicals to counteract insects in the early twentieth century. Stephen Forbes, who survived four months as a Union prisoner in 1862, spent much of his later career as a professor of zoology and entomology at the University of Illinois. When imprisoned at Macon, Georgia, he sat among "numerous gallant soldiers diligently engaged in the absorbing sport of hunting—their game not deer and their field a shirt." Five decades later, Forbes continued to speak about insects in ways that echoed how he and other prisoners had written about lice. Lice had been enemies, but the insects were also creatures whose power should not be underestimated. They were honorable competitors. "We commonly think of ourselves as the lords and conquerors of nature," Forbes argued, "but insects had thoroughly mastered the world and taken full possession of it long before man began the attempt." Plants, animals, homes, and even human skin were ever vulnerable to insects. He cautioned, "We can not even protect our very persons from their annoying and pestiferous attacks, and since the world began we have never yet exterminated—we probably never shall exterminate—so much as a single insect species." This was the sort of lesson in the dynamics of power between insects and men that came from the haptic experience of a Civil War prison.[85]

CHAPTER FOUR

Listening through the Cacophony

David Kennedy found as much meaning in silence as noise.

Some sounds, such as those of trauma, were unavoidable in the Civil War or in prison. Men went insane and their "ravings, prayers, and curses" compounded other terrors of captivity. Some men begged for food or "imagined themselves animals" in the hunt for something to eat. Union prisoners encountered the cries of slavery that had animated abolitionist literature and political debates before the Civil War. Describing the whipping of slaves, one ex-prisoner testified to the U.S. Sanitary Commission that prisoners "could hear, —even if they shut their eyes to the horrid exhibition." The "crack" of the gun and the "squeal" of the victim rang out at every location where prisoners accused the guards of murder. The curses and prayers of frustrated, desperate men surrounded Kennedy as much as the prison stockade or the foul air. The noise was inescapable for the simple reason that prisoners had no "earlids" to detach themselves from their auditory landscape—or soundscape. This was the cacophony.[1]

That did not mean that Kennedy was powerless at Andersonville. Discerning ears helped prisoners understand their situation in environments characterized by great demand for hope but little reliable information. While Kennedy unintentionally revealed an Irish accent when sounding out his words, he made deliberate choices about content. His listening, in contrast to his hearing, was a selective process that winnowed noise, and he picked out sounds that mattered most to him. Some of these were animate—that is, living—sounds, including the vocal expressions of suffering and anger. Paroled from the prison interior to work at the hospital, Kennedy found the groans of sick men unbearable and quickly wished to return to the inner stockade. But the curses, sighs, and prayers of discouraged men followed him. "Thay curse their government & the day thay were born," he wrote. "Thay sigh in vaine for their pleasant homes. Take many a sigh for their family the onley object they live for. Maney is the anctious prair sent to heaven from this helish place." All along the inanimate—nonliving—sounds intermingled with the animate ones. The gunshots at night reinforced Kennedy's belief in a persistent rumor that Confederate guards received furloughs for killing prisoners. He heard each shot in the night as the sound of cruelty.[2]

Kennedy's listening also pointed to his religious expectations. As one of millions of Irish immigrants in the 1840s and 1850s, Kennedy was at least familiar with the material and sensory experience of a Catholic mass. As a soldier and as a prisoner, Kennedy heard silences within the din that contrasted with Catholic expectations. His careful listening began before capture and was most focused on Sunday, the day of the week he thought most about his friends and adopted household in Ohio. What had been implicit for him as a soldier became explicit after his capture near Florence, Alabama. When he reached Selma, Kennedy noted, "It is Sunday but it does not apear so to us" and "time drages wearley by." He prayed that his first Sunday in Andersonville would be his last. He wished, "O, if I had the wings of a bird how soon would I sore away." When the second Sunday came, Kennedy revealed the silence that so bothered him. "Sunday comes againe but o what a plaice to spend the Sabath," he wrote. "No chiming of bells. Nothing two put us in mind of its being the lords day. O how I long to be at home to once more go to church." For Kennedy, even the name Sunday sounded "sweet," and he wished to hear "the plaintive straine of the church bells Amidst those ones that I love so well."[3] This silence—the lack of the sounds of church— reminded Kennedy of his condition as a prisoner away from family and friends. Like Kennedy, other men from across denominational lines listened for comforting sounds both in the material world and beyond.

While Kennedy listened to the present for spiritual meaning and thought about the past, he also listened for the future as he made his way from one prison to the next. Only weeks into captivity, the imprisoned men had shouted for joy at Cahaba, Alabama, when guards told them to board trains for exchange. This hope ended in "grait dispointment" seven days later when they arrived at Andersonville. Over the next nineteen weeks, thirteen out of thirty-nine men in Kennedy's company died at Andersonville, equal to the average death rate for the prison over its fourteen-month existence. Amid the daily suffering, Kennedy waited and listened for rumors that they would leave Georgia for the North.[4]

The good news came in early September when Kennedy learned that General William T. Sherman had captured Atlanta. This rumor gained credibility when Confederates scrambled to relocate prisoners farther within their lines. Rumors of an exchange caused "grait cheering & excitement in camp" and Kennedy's hope "to smell the fraigrant aire within our lines" rose again. On September 10, 1864, came even more "joyfull Newes" that his detachment of prisoners should "be redy to start at aney moment." When Kennedy departed by train two days later, he became one of 17,000 prisoners to leave

Andersonville in a single week. Once on the train, packed sixty men to a car, news dashed earlier rumors of exchange: as had happened upon leaving Cahaba, they were again going to another prison. The rail journey took them northeast through Macon and Augusta, then to Charleston. For two days at Charleston, Kennedy came within earshot of his own men, evidenced by the sounds of shells falling into the city. Then orders came to leave again. Kennedy survived captivity, but his diary fell silent six days after reaching Florence, South Carolina. Kennedy had listened to infer the future from the sounds of the present, but he was disappointed time and time again.[5]

The imprisoned listened through a cacophony that included but was not limited to the echoes of battle, guard and civilian voices, military calls, rumors, communal reading, patriotic music, animals, bells, trains, industry, the sounds and silences of suffering, and many others. Reverberations came through the record explicitly, such as Kennedy's use of the inanimate Sunday bells, or implicitly, such as the recording of vocal prison rumors. Depending on time and place, the choices of guards and civilians imposed vocal and instrumental sounds on prisoners. However, the vulnerability of having no earlids went both ways. Prisoners inferred their own interpretations of outside celebration and made tactical use of sound and silence to resist captivity.

Recovering how prisoners listened requires more than inventorying the soundscape. It means listening through the noise for those sounds that meant the most to prisoners like Kennedy. Rather than offering an exhaustive list of sounds, then, there are several categories of listening that helped prisoners cut through the din. These included the vocal sounds of travel and rumors, the instrumental crashes of bells and destruction, the sounds and silences of celebration, the resonances of nature, and the sounds of suffering and perseverance. When prisoners listened, they sought to understand their present, reconcile it with their past, and predict their future.

Listening for Hope

Listening to understand the present and the future began at the moment of capture. Interpreting the sounds of "heavy firing" on May 12, 1864, Confederate prisoner Francis Boyle took solace in the belief—heard through the sound of guns or brought verbally with 3,000 incoming prisoners—that General Ulysses S. Grant's assault had been "desperate but unsuccessful."[6] That same year, the idea that careful listeners inferred meaning from the battlefield also took hold in George Frederick Root's popular song, "Tramp! Tramp! Tramp! (The Prisoner's Hope)." First published in 1864 as a sequel to the popular song, "Just before the Battle, Mother," the title and the second verse imagined listening from the perspective of a Union prisoner:

> In the battle front we stood,
> When their fiercest charge they made,
> And they swept us off, a hundred men or more.
> But before we reached their lines,
> They were beaten back, dismayed.
> And we heard the cry of victory o'er and o'er.[7]

The prisoner's hope came from listening and interpreting the tramping of footsteps, those of a liberating army or a retreating enemy, and the "cry of victory" that spread news beyond the limited view of individuals in thickets and hollows. Confederates sang this tune as well, changing the last line to "and the 'Rebel yell' went upward to the sky." In both versions, sounds traversed the divide between armies and gave men insight into their future as the rifles and cannons fell silent.[8]

Early listening experiences also included contentious exchanges between prisoners and captors, including civilian men and women. Aboard the *Neptune* near Paducah, Kentucky, in February 1862, Confederate prisoner Andrew Campbell could hear the Union troops celebrating the sight of the captured men, who in response cheered "lustily for Jefferson Davis."[9] James Mayo encountered similar taunts from citizens who came to see Confederate prisoners "as if we were so many wild animals," as well as the "sharp rejoinders" from prisoners, which made the trip from the Old Capitol Prison in Washington to Johnson's Island more exciting than he expected.[10] Union soldier George Hitchcock listened to a German regiment forcefully serenade Confederate prisoners with the songs "'We'll Hang Jeff Davis to a Sour Apple Tree,' 'Down with the Traitors,' and 'The Red, White, and Blue,'" to which came "howls and groans from the seething cauldron of grey-backs."[11] Likewise, on a hospital boat within hearing range of Vicksburg, Union soldier Anson Butler watched a passing boat carrying Confederate prisoners on the Mississippi River. Union wounded aboard the *Nashville* could not pass up the opportunity to taunt them. They asked what Confederates thought of their country now and if they wanted "Jackson tobacco" and "wheat bread." They asked what happened to their hats and yelled "O, what breeches, how many lice you got aboard?" Confederate curses responded to Union taunts.[12] As the "howls and groans" from the so-called graybacks indicated, these interactions were more enjoyable for captor than for captive, but the exchange went both ways.

Union prisoners also faced taunts along railroads and in Southern towns and cities. A few days after being captured at the Battle of the Wilderness, Marcus Collis and other men grew tired of listening to Southern women and Confederate officers sing "patriotic airs of the South, and slurs against the Yankees." In response, the prisoners sang their own patriotic songs, including the "Star Spangled Banner" and the "Red, White, and Blue" until threatened by the guards. "Then they had it all their own way," he wrote.[13] Other prisoners on their way to Andersonville encountered heated exchanges in North Carolina. At Tarboro, Robert Kellogg listened to "scores of men, women, & children" who had come to "criticize the Yankee prisoners," and days later more "spicy debates" with guards broke the "usual monotonous manner."[14] Another group of Union prisoners encountered a group of women at Salisbury who came out to spit on them. One of the most heated exchanges came at Petersburg in the aftermath of the Battle of the Crater, when black and white Union prisoners were marched through the streets to racial taunts, including "See the white and nigger equality soldiers" and "Yanks and niggers sleep in the same bed!"[15]

Listening helped prisoners infer the mood of a town as well as the local partisan divisions and loyalties. Confederate James Franklin, passing through Westminster, Maryland, after being captured at Gettysburg, remarked that the prisoners created a stir among the citizens. "The young ladies," he wrote, were "very witty on the subject of our personal appearance." After spending the night in Westminster, Franklin noted the strange silence on the Fourth of July. There was "no ringing of bells, no little boys exploding their fire crackers and squibs in the streets, but everything wore a serious aspect." From this he interpreted that the citizens placed little faith in the rumors of a Union victory. Passing through Baltimore, the prisoners read silence on the Fourth of July as unspoken support for the Confederacy, which emboldened them to sing. "The stirring notes of 'Dixie,'" Franklin wrote, "must have made their hearts warm to the 'Sunny Land.'"[16] One year later, when E. L. Cox stayed in the Norfolk guard house on his way to a Northern prison, the usual sounds of cannons and bells were present, but with an important addition. The night before the holiday African American women had passed by his guard house to "scoff and sneer" at the Confederate prisoners.[17]

For Union prisoners, in contrast, slaves displayed subtle words, sounds, or silent glances of encouragement. Enslaved African Americans had long used sound and silence as a means of existence and resistance, and for good reason. During the Civil War, even small acts of resistance, such as exultation at Union victories, could inspire violent reprisals.[18] Union prisoners recalled subversive silence and sympathetic looks from the enslaved and free people of color. Ezra Ripple remembered that white Southerners treated prisoners "as they would cattle" by talking about them "in our presence as if we were devoid of the sense of hearing." In contrast, Ripple inferred support from the enslaved. "In the eyes of one class there was always that look which said to us plainly as *words* could say it, 'we pity you,' 'we are your friends.'"[19] Daniel Kelley remembered a similar occurrence on the railroad between Columbia and Orangeburg, South Carolina. While passing a "negro hut," Kelley recalled seeing a black woman standing silently in a doorway revealing a small American flag.[20] In hushed and ambiguous displays, Union prisoners found reassurance that they had friends in the Confederate South.[21]

Careful listening took on new importance at long-term prisons. Prisoners reacted differently to the noise. Captured at the Battle of Chickamauga, Michigander Alonzo Keeler became accustomed to the hubbub of Libby Prison after one week. "Whistling, singing, dancing, crowing, barking, braying," he wrote, "& everything as usual." Keeler seemed to thrive on the rumors, the reading of a satirical newspaper, and he tolerated the "tramp, tramp" of men keeping themselves warm at night.[22] In contrast, Robert Bingham's sensitive ears caused him much suffering day and night. He described Fort Delaware as "a perfect babel—noise, noise, noise. I never thought the human voice so discordant before."[23] Most prisoners remarked on noise as an inescapable matter of fact. At Andersonville, John Baer described the "sound of many voices" that met "our ears," ranging from conversations about home and loved ones to heated disputes and inarticulate cursing.[24]

When men arrived at prison they continued to listen for information about their present and future. At Andersonville, Robert Kellogg read or listened to smuggled newspaper accounts of fighting in Virginia read aloud to him. Silence about the outcome in the papers and from the guards sounded promising because Kellogg reasoned that "if Grant is whipped, the Rebs will not be long in letting us know it."[25] The lack of normal channels of communication increased reliance on oral networks, which culminated in an omnipresent buzz of prison rumors. James Burton described prisoners grabbing for rumors of a prisoner exchange "as a drowning man does at straws. Result about the same so far but hope on hope is the motto."[26] Prisons became constant rumor mills because it fed what men wanted to hear.

Prisoners spent much of their time listening for news and debating its authenticity in a continuous cycle of hope and despair. Those detained in cities often had access to newspapers, and even captives at remote prisons had some access to smuggled newspapers. However, the scarcity of papers meant that prisoners regularly consumed news in the form of a public recitation. When a paper appeared inside the prison at Millen, Georgia, one man recalled that "a crowd would gather around that they might hear if it gave any information concerning the exchange, catching at the least word which held out a possibility of hope."[27] John Baer started an exchange rumor at Andersonville for the academic exercise of testing how quickly it became common knowledge. "By evening it had gained enough that some man had heard the rebel Commissary say so," he wrote, and by "the 3rd day some one had heard it read in the Macon papers." Soon even members of his own mess believed the rumor and he had trouble dissuading them of the belief that they would all be exchanged in early August. He attributed the strength of the rumor to "an ardent desire that it might be so," and the men who surrounded him "could scarcely let it pass as mere rumor."[28] Frustrated with the lack of reliable news and to pass the time, some men turned to satirical newspapers, including the *Libby Chronicle* and the *Fort Delaware Prison Times*, that the imprisoned editors compiled and read aloud.[29] From the front line to the prison pen, men listened for hope that their luck would improve even if they had to imagine it.

Alarm Bells and Homesick Peals

While the buzz of rumors, news, and debate animated cycles of hope and despair, the imprisoned listened carefully to inanimate sounds as well. These frequently had to do with time and the perception of the monotony of captivity. The relationship between bells and clocks had a long genealogy, and there were practical reasons sound became a key conveyer of time. Prisoners, especially Northern men, were often robbed of watches.[30] Moreover, prisons used sound—the voices of guards, bells, and musical notes— to mark hourly and daily rhythms. At Fort Delaware, the Union garrison observed sundown and the lowering of the U.S. flag with the firing of cannon. Confederate officials at Andersonville used seventeen calls during the day from reveille at daybreak to taps at 8:30 P.M. These calls mixed the natural time of sunrise and sunset with clock time in ways that factory and plantation bells rang for decades and church bells for centuries. On paper if not always in reality, a stable call rang out half an hour after daybreak and the breakfast call sounded at 7:00 A.M. In the evening, the supper call came sometime after parade at 5:00 P.M. and taps. Some calls affected prisoners more than others, but these sounds were imposed upon their ears around the clock.[31]

Listening to the present, prisoners kept track of time through sound, whether or not they had personal watches. As a wounded Union prisoner on two occasions, Jacob Heffelfinger routinely substituted Confederate bugle calls, especially retreat, for numerical time.[32] At Belle Isle, Union prisoner Thomas Springer listened carefully for the ration calls and complained about their unpredictable rhythm: in three days, the breakfast drum or "grub call" sounded at 10:00, 11:00, and 11:30 A.M. The supper call was just as unreliable, sounding at 3:00, 4:00, and 4:30 P.M.[33] The inconsistency of aural time did not make it less important; if anything, intermittent calls reinforced careful listening because it meant the difference between receiving rations and medicine or going without. These instrumental notes mingled with sentries' hourly cries, announcing time aurally whether prisoners wanted to hear it or not.

The sounds of the present clashed with cultural and religious ideas about the cadence of days, weeks, months, and years. Important national anniversaries were celebrated with toasts, speeches, bells, fireworks, cannons, and loud celebrations. On Sundays, however, Christian listeners across denominational lines expected to hear church bells, the sober tones of religious leaders and hymns, and Sabbath quietude.[34] They had little tolerance for anything else. While traveling through Mississippi in the 1830s, for example, Joseph Ingraham wrote that on Sunday, "a more hallowed silence then reigns in the air and over nature." This Sunday quietude was not silence per se, but rather serious, structured sound "like a 'still small voice'" in which the "light notes of merry music, or the sounds of gay discourse, would seem like profanation." For this reason, disturbances at Natchez appalled Ingraham. "Sounds of rude merriment," he wrote, "mingled with the tones of loud dispute and blasphemy, rose with appalling distinctness upon the still air, breaking the Sabbath silence of the hour, in harsh discord with its sacredness."[35] For listeners across denominational lines, Sunday had a sacred but fragile soundscape, easily disturbed by the noise of drunks, gamblers, and peddlers.

The Civil War had already disturbed the sounds and silences of Sunday. Some congregations voted to donate their loud, brass bells to the Confederacy to be melted down and cast into the loudest instruments of war—cannons. The *Montgomery Daily Advertiser* highlighted the case of the Methodist Protestant church of Autaugaville, Alabama, and wished that the bell, once used to "call in sinners to attend divine service," might soon "be in a condition to ring out the death knell of the dastard invaders of our soil."[36] The calls of church enlisted for the war.

From 1861 to 1865, martial sounds broke the Sabbath's calmness in spite of limited efforts to accommodate Sunday observers. This was especially the case in prisons, where Sunday sounded no different from other days, and this contributed to a sense of painful monotony. Before his capture, Vermont Congregationalist Daniel Cooledge had complained about Sunday dissonance in the Union army. His sentiment represented what historian Lorien Foote describes as the gentleman class of evangelical soldiers who had hoped to preserve the Sabbath in wartime. "Moving our camp and chopping [wood]," Cooledge wrote, "makes it seem as far from the Sabbath as possible."[37] He worried about the habits of the men around him, and like many soldiers believed he would better appreciate religious services when he returned to civilian life. Fighting did not pause for Sunday rest either. Listening to martial sounds on a Sunday, Cooledge reflected that "the booming cannon and the excitement of the roar of distant strife" diminished the sense of the Sabbath's sacredness. He longed for the church bells of Vermont, and the whole affair felt like a dream.[38]

Captivity only intensified Cooledge's discomfort. He fell wounded—on a Sunday, no less—at Savage Station, Virginia, and was captured the next day. Exchanged after three weeks of hearing no church bells at all, he took comfort in the sounds of the U.S. General Hospital in West Philadelphia. "The bells," he wrote, "sound quietly on the ears and show that I am in a land where churches and church goers are once more found."[39] One year later, Robert Bingham fell into Union hands, and recorded his transition to prison through the similar complaints. As Ingraham had written in the 1830s, Bingham bemoaned irreverent prison noise in 1863. He ended his first week in captivity at Fort Norfolk, Virginia, and believed it "the worst Sunday" because it was "the least like Sunday—no quiet—no holy calm." Instead of comfort, Bingham found anxiety. "I feel so restless," he wrote, "and there is so much fuss I can't abstract myself from it all." That week the prisoners left for Fort Delaware, a place that also lacked the sober quietude Bingham sought. On his second Sunday, he exclaimed, "There is little Sunday in a prison—no quiet—no calm." By early August, Bingham had moved to Johnson's Island, but the noise followed alongside the deadly sin of reading novels. Regardless of region, young men had been warned to avoid novels if they hoped to achieve manhood. Regardless of the warnings, novels proliferated, and few educated men resisted the temptation of reading in prison, including Bingham, who consumed Charles Dickens among other authors. Still, the scene troubled him. "Sunday here does not differ from the other days," he wrote. "There is no quiet—no holy calm. The same card playing, the same novel reading, the same profanity goes on as other days." It all contrasted to his memory of the "holy, quiet Sundays" he had spent with his wife, Della, in North Carolina.[40]

Both the noise and the monotony of day-to-day life jarred with peacetime sounds. Those less specific than Bingham and Cooledge hinted at Sunday noise and monotony indirectly by complaining about the passage of time. On Sunday, more than on other days, prisoners complained about the sameness of each day.[41] When William Peabody wrote "This is Sunday, not much like N. England Sunday, more like Hell I think and a tough one too," he hinted at the Andersonville soundscape and the pace of time described by other listeners.[42] Many would have agreed with William Wilkins that the "clamor, shouts, oaths & wrangling" of prison clashed in sharp discord with "a sweet, quiet Sabbath at home."[43] Sunday offered no pause that set the day apart from the rest of the week as it had in the past. Sunday sounded like all other days of war and prison.

While these religious listeners cared about quietude, they also listened for particular sounds of reverence, familiarity, and the comfort of loved ones. When Jacob Heffelfinger lay in his first Confederate field hospital, he remembered his family entering the "house of God, where they now have the privilege of mingling their voices in prayer and praise."[44] In a similar way, Confederate prisoners like Randal McGavock noted the absence of church bells. "Another Sabbath day has come but we hear no church going bells and we see none of those loved ones that we are accustomed to go to church with."[45] David Kennedy emphasized the soundscape of Andersonville on Sundays perhaps more clearly than anyone else, emphasizing the disconnect between the present and the past and the uncertainty of the future. "I almost give up in dispaire," he lamented, "that I shall ever heire the word of god preached in yankey land againe." Like clockwork, the absence of the "sweet chiming of the bells" broke the Sunday soundscape. "It is Sunday," the Irish-born Ohioan wrote, "but we can hardley relise it."[46]

Although men like McGavock and Kennedy loathed the absence of church bells, those who heard bells found that context changed the meaning of familiar sounds. Church bells sounded strange and foreign to prisoners far away from home and family. At home church bells had a summoning effect, but these bells did not call to prisoners of war. In this way, the sounds had the same effect as the silences—both could intensify the feeling of separation from loved ones. At Macon, Georgia, Asa Mathews wrote that "at the usual hour the church bells rang but they're to us homesick peals. The day passed with heat and the usual monotony." Mathews admitted that the prison was "more quiet," but he could still hear cards and checkers.[47] Mary Terry, a Southern sympathizer and suspected spy imprisoned in Baltimore, initially considered it "a blessing to live within the sound of the church going bells."

As if on second thought, however, she reconsidered: "what a sad thought, I cannot sit under the drippings of the sanctuary." The next Sunday was gloomier because Terry "heard nothing, no preaching to, or praying for prisoners," and it was a remarkably "long sad day."[48] Whether depressed by the absence or presence of bells, many prisoners listened for the antebellum sounds of Sunday but could not hear them. Listening separated the present from the past.

Some prisoners recovered the missing element by carving out religious space within prisons. "The church bells ringing the calls for services seem like sweet music," Lewis Bisbee wrote in Savannah, Georgia, and "the sacred influence of the day seemed to pervade the camp more than usual." For once at least, Bisbee thought, it "seemed very much like Sabbath today."[49] To someone who had spent nearly three hundred days in captivity and thought exchange near, this particular Sunday may have indeed sounded sweeter than other days in prison. Bisbee and others attempted to revive a sacred soundscape inside prisons, an accomplishment that postwar narratives stressed more than wartime diaries. John Baer at Andersonville noted that on Sundays at 11 A.M. and at sunset "the voice of deep and earnest prayer" from hundreds of voices momentarily rose above "the din and confusion of camp."[50] At Johnson's Island, one prisoner told his mother that men could "scarcely get a seat, within hearing, unless he goes [to religious services] very early."[51] Still, listeners disagreed whether the holy sounds of Sunday could be heard above unholy noise. "There is perhaps a little less gambling," Bingham conceded after weeks at Johnson's Island, "but the same novel reading & perpetual noise."[52] Whatever prisoners interpreted from Sunday sounds and silences, their concerns were about their past experience, their present condition away from loved ones, and their discomfort at not knowing their future.

While church bells, whether present or absent, caused restlessness, Union prisoners in Richmond took pleasure in listening to alarm bells. The *Richmond Enquirer* angrily noted that Union prisoners on Belle Isle "could not restrain the exhibition of their diabolical joy on hearing the alarm bell."[53] They could have included the other Richmond prisons as well. At Libby Prison in May 1864, John Gallison and others sat up at night trying to interpret the ringing of bells, the tramping soldiers moving through the streets, and the brass bands.[54] That summer, George Albee, a firefighter from Madison, Wisconsin, woke up to alarm bells several nights in a row and on one day the bells "rung vigorously for half an hour or more but we saw nothing." At first he struggled to separate the meaning of bells from their antebellum context.

He wrote, "My first impulse is to jump & run to the fire as I used to do." Over-lapping with instinct, Albee felt distinct pleasure listening to the ruination of Richmond. He concluded that "if incendiaries are at work[,] they work faithfully" and joked that "as this is the 'heart of the rebellion[,]' the rebellion is warm hearted at present."[55] Listening to alarm bells could be more pleasant than church bells because what meant an emergency to Confederate soldiers and Richmond citizens gave hope to Union prisoners.

Nowhere were the sounds of destruction heard more plainly as the sounds of hope than in Charleston, South Carolina. From summer 1863 until the surrender of the city in February 1865, white Charlestonians heard themselves under constant attack by Union troops gaining a foothold along the coast. As the sounds of bombardment became inescapable, soldiers and civilians had no choice but to listen to the noise of destruction that blasted away at their tenuous independence. In effect, the city became a captive audience as well.[56] For Union prisoners, the same sounds of destruction were pleasurable. James Burton found them amusing and took satisfaction in knowing someone was paying for the rebellion. "It must disturb the dreams somewhat," he mused at the Washington Race Course, "to have one of those large shells come down through the top of the house and explode."[57] One man recalled that the sound of shells "made music for me, and I loved to listen to them in their flight, and to catch the downward rush and deafening crash of their explosion, for they seemed, not like missiles of destruction, but messages from near-by friends."[58] For Jacob Heffelfinger, the sounds were a reassuring reminder "that Uncle Sam is still full of life and vigor."[59] As Confederates marched him up King Street to take the train to Columbia, South Carolina, he found great pleasure in the "broken city" that surrounded him. "Devastation reigns supreme," he wrote, and the once-boastful city sounded quieter on a Wednesday than Sunday in the North. Pleasant sounds of destruction broke the monotony of prison life. The resulting silence carried his mind back to Sunday and to his Northern home.[60]

Weaponized Listening

In concert with bells, the sounds of music, whether somber or lighthearted, mattered to prisoners. Both Union and Confederate prisons had glee clubs and acting troupes, which performed for fellow prisoners, guards, and civilians. There were the "Libby Prison Minstrels," the "Rock Island Minstrels," and, at Johnson's Island, the "Island Minstrels," the "Rebel Thespians," and the "Rebelonians." One performance at Libby Prison in 1863 contained three parts. The first consisted of an instrumental overture and songs from "Who Will Care for Mother, Now" and "Do They Think of Me at Home." The second part included a violin and flute duet, songs, and a dialogue called "Rival Lovers." The third part consisted of two one-act plays, "Countryman in a Photograph Gallery" and "Masquerade Ball."[61]

Prison performances combined familiar and original material that could be deeply partisan. At Johnson's Island, Confederate prisoner William Peel noted that "a couple of Yankees who were present" were not as pleased with the humor as he and his fellow prisoners. At Camp Asylum in January 1865, white women of Columbia, South Carolina, came to listen to prisoners' music. In addition to an instrumental band, the glee club sang "When Sherman Marched Down to the Sea." This original song, written by Samuel Hawkins Marshall Byers at Camp Asylum, had been inspired by reports in a newspaper an enslaved man had smuggled to the officers.[62] The title of Byers's song became the popular name for Sherman's campaign between Atlanta and Savannah, but not all the listeners at the Confederate prison were pleased with it. "One of the ladies seemed quite indignant," Sylvester Crossley wrote, "and says she can sing a better song than that herself on General Lee." He inferred quiet support from many of the other women, who "seem inclined to pity our condition rather than annoy us." The prisoners danced, and the imprisoned band played to both the silent sympathizers and the outwardly indignant.[63]

As with Sundays, prisoners listened for familiar sounds on national holidays. The sounds of the Fourth of July were important to Union and Confederate prisoners just as they had been before the Civil War. After secession, Confederate soldiers and civilians debated whether to celebrate or mourn the national holiday of their old county.[64] In Northern prisons they had no choice but to hear sounds of celebration that rejected the legal existence of their Confederacy. A political prisoner from Baltimore at Fort Warren in Boston Harbor disliked the noisy celebration on July 4, 1862. The most disturbing part of the day was neither the band nor the "Star Spangled Banner" but a national salute of thirty-four guns. The firing of cannons reached Confederate prisoners' ears as an assertion that they had forsaken their national identity.[65] Likewise, two years later at Camp Chase, Tennessean James Mackey noted that the garrison had fired "thirty-five guns," which he believed was "at least eleven more than was necessary."[66]

These sounds of celebration could also reinforce Confederates' belief that they—not their Union captors—were the true inheritors of the American Revolution. In 1863, Bingham awoke to the sound of salutes. "What a mockery," he wrote. "Salutes to celebrate a declaration of independence fired by the most infamous tyrants that disgrace the earth."[67] From the Baltimore jail, Mary Terry had had similar thoughts. Listening to the commemorative cannon salute, she remarked that "blindness to the future is kindly given," because if her father could have seen the future, "it would have turned his heart to stone."[68] Confederate prisoners like Terry, Bingham, and Mackey wished for silence on the Fourth of July. The celebration just reminded them of the death of the Union and their embattled quasi-nationhood.

In contrast, many Union prisoners in the South heard only silence on the Fourth of July and wished for a much louder celebration. Frank Hughes noted that the flags in Macon, Georgia, were at half-staff on the Fourth of July. "Not a word is heard to day," he wrote in 1864. "The only way of celebrating the glorious old 4th is profound & silent meditation."[69] At Andersonville, Eugene Sly hoped never to hear another one like it. "The men make less noise than before in several days," he wrote, "& it seems more like a day of mourning than like a *Fourth of July*."[70] Although some Union prisoners tried to stir up a celebration, many found it too quiet.[71]

Union prisoners used the Fourth of July as an opportunity to make Confederates hear the songs of a country they had betrayed. Newly captured prisoners at Gettysburg sang patriotic songs on the Fourth of July in protest of their captivity. Confederates on this occasion did not silence them, which prisoners inferred as another positive sign about the outcome of the fighting.[72] Prisoners gathered around a small American flag early in the morning at Macon, Georgia, singing "Rally Round the Flag," and "The Star Spangled Banner," while "cheers, full of heart and soul, rent the air." Later in the morning there was a prayer followed by speeches that were "heavily responded to by the crowd." The guards listened to this celebration with alarm and sent orders "that there should be no more speaking." Prisoners eventually complied, but not before giving cheers "for the flag, for Abraham Lincoln, Gen. Grant, & the Emancipation Proclamation." That night the prisoners rekindled the commotion, improvising fireworks "out of boards, and pitch pine pegs."[73]

Making the prison resonate with Union sounds broke the silence imposed by Confederates. As far west as Camp Ford, Texas, Union prisoners gave toasts and listened to the glee club before guards broke up the celebration.[74] Although many Andersonville prisoners heard little celebration on the Fourth of July, there were small demonstrations. One small group gave "three cheers for the [Union] army before [in front of] Richmond and three groans for the Confederacy." A few men who had smuggled percussion caps into the prison used them as fireworks.[75]

The Fourth of July was an aural holiday par excellence, but Union and Confederate prisoners picked up on other periodic sounds of celebration coming from the guards. The popular song "John Brown's Body" originated at Fort Warren in Boston Harbor and became popular among Union soldiers before emancipation was an official goal of the Union army.[76] That the song had roots at a coastal fortification meant that prisoners of war may have been among the first Southerners to hear it. George Brown, the imprisoned mayor of Baltimore, listened to the sounds of Union celebration after their victories at Forts Henry and Donelson, remarking that it was "all very proper except that they had the bad taste to sing the northern battle song of Old John Brown, marching on to glory, Hallelujah."[77] Confederate prisoners preferred to listen to the sounds of brass bands when they did not play national airs. Brown found it unpleasant to "listen to hail Columbia" while a prisoner of war.[78] In contrast, Bingham awoke one July night to "some very good music—no Yankee about it—no national airs—but it was very sweet music—a brass band."[79]

Union prisoners in the South singled out slave songs as thought-provoking and more uplifting than Confederate tunes. Antebellum travelers in the South had listened carefully to the singing and music of enslaved African Americans in the context of slavery debates, and Union prisoners picked up on these sounds as well.[80] At Andersonville, Eugene Forbes knew that the enslaved were working all night, "as we could hear their singing, which always sounds inexpressibly mournful to me, as if the wail of the oppressed was rising to Heaven."[81] Listening to slave music reminded prisoners of the enslaved people's humanity as well as the ideological goals of emancipation. Willard Glazier listened to singing attributed to captured soldiers in the 54th Massachusetts and remarked that "no race so delicately sensitive to the emotional can be essentially coarse and barbarous."[82] African American music reinforced individual commitments to emancipation at the same time as alliances strengthened between whites and blacks in the Union army.[83] The power of sound and the importance of listening facilitated this transition among Union prisoners.

Whenever possible, Union and Confederate prisoners had rambunctious celebrations on Christmas. A political prisoner at Fort Warren, Massachusetts, described Christmas in coded language to his mother. The prisoners sang songs, cracked jokes, and held a mock trial for an "obnoxious individual whose effigy we sentenced to an ignominious fate, after a solemn trial." The unnamed "obnoxious individual" must have been a Northern political or military figure, as the letter was designed to pass through the prison censor's watchful eye. "These are secrets," he wrote, "not to be communicated now or here."[84] A Union prisoner in Richmond described howling so loud around Christmas that it "made the guards tremble. They no doubt thought we were about to make a break for liberty."[85] Another man recalled singing "Rally Round the Flag," and emphasizing the words, "'Down with the traitor, up with the stars,'" to make sure "the traitor guard on the front sidewalk" heard their voices. They sang until guards threatened them.[86]

The Sounds of Prison Nature

Sensitive to the peal of bells and celebration on particular days of the week and year, prisoners also listened to the natural environment to understand their place and express their condition. This ranged from the solemn howl of waves and wind at Johnson's Island to the cloud of insects at Andersonville and the "hum of their innumerable wings," which reminded one prisoner "of an approaching wind."[87] Like the biting of lice, prisoners used nature's hums, howls, and music to understand their place and condition, which, like time, had antecedents long before the Civil War. Solomon Northup, kidnapped and sold into slavery, had described a "pleasant morning" in the South through the sound of birds. "The birds were singing in the trees," he wrote. "The happy birds—I envied them. I wished for wings like them, that I might cleave the air to where my birdlings waited vainly for their father's coming, in the cooler region, of the North." David Kennedy and Samuel Gibson had thoughts at Andersonville similar to those of Northup in Virginia. Listening through the human and natural cacophony for place and condition, prisoners found a versatile symbol in songbirds.[88]

Prisoners used the sounds of birds to define place. Hiram Eddy, a lover of bird songs before his capture, compared the Southern songbirds to those in Connecticut on his way from Virginia to North Carolina. He heard his first while leaving Richmond and crossing the James River. "It was only one surge of Nature's music," he wrote, "but it reverberated around all the galleries of my soul, thrilling my very heart." Still, he was disappointed and discerned sectional differences between the North and South through the sounds. Virginia and North Carolina, Eddy declared, were not good places to listen to birds. "They cannot sing so joyously where such a blight & darkness [reigns] & throws its chill over everything as slavery does here. It seems to affect everything." The sounds of Southern songbirds were inferior to those in Connecticut. Eddy had not heard "the robin sing his melting song" at daybreak or "withdrawing them in deepening splendor" at dusk. The "laughing bob-o-link" did "not become delirious in song," and the "brown thrasher does not make the bushes vocal while she discourses sweet music." The only songbird Eddy heard was a "cat-bird," which he thought must be a species of mockingbird.

While Eddy considered the song of the catbird unremarkable, the sounds tethered the present to the past by evoking memories of home. It reminded him of watching birds from his study. He wrote, "How delighted was I with their songs, little thinking that the next time I should hear them would be far away from their evergreen perches, 'midst strangers & enemies!" Eddy imagined that those birds had flown down from Connecticut to "a strange land" where he could not sing himself. "This little bird says kindly," he wrote, "I will sing for you. This is the only real singing-bird which I heard. And I saw but few." Aside from songbirds, Eddy found a red-headed woodpecker, which "thrust the scenery of my boy-hood into my face." Bringing his bird-watching back to place, he admitted to seeing the "nastiest of all the bird tribe," the turkey buzzard.[89]

Prisoners like Eddy connected the sounds of songbirds to the place and condition. Comparing himself to a bird, James Burton wrote at Anderson-ville that it was "a beautiful morning to pine for caged birds." Vermonter Charles Chapin listened to the tune of a mockingbird outside the stockade at Andersonville on the Fourth of July. In contrast to Eddy, Chapin wrote that the mockingbird "is the nicest bird I ever heard." The next day, however, Chapin discovered that Confederate guards or, more likely, enslaved people, had "cut down the tree & drove off our mocking bird." The resulting still-ness "makes it seem lonesome."[90] Others remarked on the contrast between pleasant sounds of nature and the context of war and imprisonment. Frank Bennett found it difficult to reconcile "birds singing merrily" with the real-ity that "this can be a time of war."[91] Likewise, when Charles Blinn discov-ered that "sweet birds are singing in the oak grove" outside a stockade in Lynchburg, Virginia, he demurred: "They make not happy a prisoners life."[92] What these men interpreted as the happy and free sounds of birds contrasted sharply with what they felt as prisoners.

Confederate prisoners, like Eddy, also used birds and nature to depict sec-tional differences. Southern ears heard the North as a wilderness or frozen desert, in contrast to the opulence and warmth of the South. Randal McGa-vock contrasted the "cold, dark, and disagreeable day" at Fort Warren, Mas-sachusetts, in May 1862, with how he imagined his Tennessee home where "the flowers are blooming and the birds singing."[93] Others described Northern prisons as eerily void of animal life. Samuel Boyd wrote home to

Tennessee from Camp Chase, Ohio, in March 1865 that he had neither seen a bird nor "heard a chicken crow or a cow low or a horse neigh & have heard a dog bark but once."[94] Captured at Gettysburg and lying in the hospital at Johnson's Island, William Peel listened to blackbirds in the prison yard, a woodpecker hammering a dead buckeye tree, and ducks returning north. These sounds stood out to Peel because "the almost entire absence on this forlorn island of animal life except the prisoners & the necessary guard, to which I may add an innumerable host of rats, & a few pet cats, renders them circumstances to be noticed."[95]

Prisoners also used the sounds of nature to express contentedness and re-assure loved ones in shared difficult times. By May 1864, Frederic James had been a prisoner for eight months. Captured in an ill-fated amphibious assault on Fort Sumter in Charleston Harbor, he had already experienced a circuitous trek to Columbia, Richmond, and Salisbury. Soon he would be on a train bound for Andersonville. Ellen James, Frederic's wife, had written to him that spring with terrible news and a request. His eight-year-old daughter, Mary, had died, and Ellen James wanted her husband to write his surviving daughter, Ellen "Nellie" James, a letter about the meaning of her older sister's death. In his private diary, James described the enervating effects of the prison envi-ronment, but none of this appeared in the letter to six-year-old Nellie.

In his letter to young Nellie, James depicted a tranquil, heavenly envi-ronment that reinforced a spiritual message about God, Jesus, and an after-life where the whole family would reunite. From the windows he could see forests and wheat fields and hear the songs of colorful birds. "We have a plenty of music too," James wrote, "for there are a great many birds here & you know that they are great musicians & don't send a monkey around to ask us to pay them for singing, as the organ grinders do." In contrast to the street musicians, James wrote that nature's musicians "sing as merily as can be, just for the fun of it, because they are so happy." The sound of the birds drew back to his larger themes about faith and happiness. God had made birds col-orful and sonorous, the father explained, "to be happy & make others so." While the bird-song letter was not the first Nellie had received from her father while he was at war, it was the first she had received as an only child. It was also probably the last letter. Three weeks after writing, Frederic James arrived at Andersonville, and in a few months' time became burial number 8,885 in the prison graveyard.[96]

The sounds of birds became a part of the way prisoners described their experiences. While the metaphor of the "grapevine telegraph" remained a more common way to describe rumors, a Confederate prisoner at Fort

Warren noted that even though "there is neither free press, nor free speech, outside of this Prison, yet little birds will in the Springtime warble sweet music & we hear it, and the rapid progress of events cheers me with the hope that all will soon be over." The comparison of people to birds occurred on occasion as well. A racist Union officer on his way to Camp Oglethorpe in Macon, Georgia, compared the voices of enslaved African Americans to blackbirds, and a Macon newspaper found "caged birds" a useful description for the homesick "little fellows" at Andersonville. Birds proved to be a malleable symbol for conveying ideas about time, place, and condition.[97]

ALONGSIDE RUMORS, BELLS, AND BIRDS, Union and Confederate prisoners were exposed to sounds of suffering that echoed in wartime and postwar writings. These sounds were used in debates about imprisonment, but they were also part of an internal struggle about perseverance and manhood. As Drew Gilpin Faust has shown, the manly Christian death in the Civil War era required visible and audible signs of contentedness — not contempt or fear of eternal fate.[98] The *Richmond Examiner* emphasized this idea through the juxtaposition of wounded Union prisoners and Confederate soldiers. From wounded Union prisoners, the "cries and groans of distress can be heard" and "the whine and groan and fearful contortion of countenance to be met with on every hand is fearful to behold." In contrast, at a hospital for Confederate wounded, "Pleasant faces are to be met with, groans and sighs are repressed, and the wounded joke and laugh about their wounds as something to be proud of." The difference, according to the Southern writer, lay in the chasm between the manly pursuit of a "just and holy cause" and the unmanly "wicked and unjust crusade." George Stevens, a Union physician, heard the opposite in the aftermath of Gettysburg. While the Union wounded soldier would "say nothing," a wounded Confederate prisoner "would whine and cry like a sick child." In the sounds of suffering, listeners inferred manly quietude or cowardly agitation.[99]

When relatives could not judge the last moments of a loved one's life for themselves, they sought comfort from witnesses. William Bonsell had not known John Pond before Andersonville, but as he told Pond's sister in 1867, "I was attracted to him by his manly, noble, and high toned character, his unswerving patriotism and his genial social disposition. In such places, men become clannish, a few congenial spirits get to gather and try to drive away the horrors of the place by cheerful conversation." The men kept up a cheerful spirit by talking about the past, home, favorite books, or "building air castles for the future." The two men became temporarily separated in the fall of 1864 during the movement of prisoners from Andersonville to Charleston and Florence, and then permanently separated when Bonsell left for a prisoner exchange. Pond stayed behind and died in Wilmington, North Carolina, on his way back to Union lines in the final months of the war. Unable to provide specifics about Pond's death, Bonsell reiterated his quiet perseverance at Andersonville. "As a friend he was always genial, cheerful, and social, and I have to cherish his memory as one of the few true men, it has been my fortune to meet."[100] In providing comfort to the dead man's family, Bonsell signaled confidence that Pond had died in a state of contentedness and quietude. He died as close to a good death as possible for a prisoner of war.

While prisoners also inferred perseverance in quiet suffering, they seemed more open to dismiss sounds of discomfort—sighs—as unmanly noise. At Johnson's Island, the prisoner poem "Half Past Ten O'Clock" described the "Silence over [Lake] Erie's Waters" and the "melancholy silence" of prison quarters that was broken by the sentry's cry, "All is well," at each half-hour mark in the nighttime hours:

"Half past 10 o'clock" is calling
"All is well"! Ah! Whence that sigh?
'Twas like grief in cadence falling
From some o'er charged heart close by
Like a weary zephyr dying
Where October's leaves are lying
Yet the Sentry is replying,
"All is well."[101]

For that writer, at least, the prisoner's sigh was a more natural sound than the sentry's discordant words that clashed with prisoners' emotions. All was not well for the listening prisoners. In May 1865, William Haigh recorded, "The Prisoner's Sigh for Home!" that contrasted prison with home and family "where the birds are singing."[102] For prisoners, manly persistence meant quietude, but that did not preclude all sounds of heartfelt anguish.

Confederate prisoners processed the spring of 1865 with melancholy silence or strategic quietude. As rumors had turned out false so many times before, Confederate prisoners could hardly believe their ears when the death knells of the Confederacy came that spring. Although demoralized throughout the winter of 1864–65, the news of Lee's surrender came as a surprise in the form of rumors and cannon salutes. For Francis Boyle, the news came "like a clap of thunder upon us—even those who feared and expected this thing are astonished, even stupefied, at the terrible news." Confederate prisoners also responded to the reports of Abraham Lincoln's assassination with cautious silence amid uncertainty about what the president's death meant for their fate. Fear of reprisal led prisoners to avoid exhibiting even a whisper that might be interpreted as rebellious exultation.[103] Perhaps, for once, there was quietude in prison. What that meant, of course, was up to individual prisoners and the listening guards.

CHAPTER FIVE

The Thoughts and Acts of Hungry Men

Privation was not unique to Civil War prisons, but rarely in nineteenth-century America did hungry people write so much about food.

As with other aspects of prison experience, time and place mattered. An 1862 Christmas prison scene depicted in a Chester, South Carolina, newspaper was far from representative. That December came at the height of prisoner exchange and Fort Delaware contained only 106 prisoners; after a few deaths and many more exchanges, only five men remained when the Emancipation Proclamation took effect on New Year's Day. As a result of emancipation and the Confederate response to black Union soldiers, the prison population mushroomed to 2,800 one year later and 7,700 after two years.[1] The small population in 1862 made little difference, though, to Southern-sympathizing women in Philadelphia who witnessed the approach of Christmas through the lens of sectional war. The writer described a street-side spectacle of shivering African Americans selling "green wreaths and boughs for Christmas trees." All the while, she claimed, abolitionists "swept aside these hungry sons and daughters of Africa with their fine Christmas turkey in their baskets." The season that kindled the woman's sharp criticism encouraged her to make sure that nearby Confederate prisoners had enough to eat.[2]

Although published anonymously, the woman who described Christmas in Philadelphia was Esther B. "Essie" Cheesborough, a South Carolinian whose antebellum writing appeared in the *Southern Literary Gazette*, the *Southern Literary Messenger*, and *Godey's Lady's Book*. Cheesborough lived in Philadelphia by the late 1850s, but she held secessionist convictions and raised money to feed and clothe Confederate prisoners of war from at least the fall of 1862 through the spring of 1863. She thought the men "should have their Christmas dinner sent [to] them by loving and sympathizing friends."[3] Therefore, Cheesborough collected food donated by Southern-sympathizing women in the city.

These self-styled "rebel" women, masking mince pies and other desirable goods under their cloaks, amassed a smorgasbord. The meats amounted to two turkeys, one ham, one round steak, and four pounds of sausage. There were also two cakes, ten pies, ten biscuits, and five loaves of bread, with pounds of butter and a variety of sauces from mustard to catsup. The fruit consisted of forty-four apples, dozens of oranges and lemons, as well as figs, raisins, and other sweets. A supply of tobacco topped off the boxes. Cheesborough concluded, "Thus gayly passed the Christmas hours in Fort Delaware; darkness had been turned into light, and the shadows of despondency chased away by the cheerful sunshine of pleasure." Despite her belief that "the Lincolnites" considered the work "high treason," Cheesborough's efforts were perfectly legal.[4]

This work by Cheesborough and other "rebel" women was not uncommon. Confederate prisoners with connections in the free states, the Border States, or in parts of the Confederacy controlled by the U.S. military could receive food and supplies through the mail for most of the war. It was more difficult, though not impossible, for food to travel from the Confederacy to Northern prisons, or from Northern states and Union-held areas to Southern prisons. Status, wealth, and prewar connections also mattered. Outside donations divided prisoners into two classes: those with access to money, friends, or family, and those without money or such a support network. Union officers at Libby Prison, Camp Oglethorpe, and elsewhere ate better than Union enlisted men, especially before December 1863, when they could rely on packages from friends and family. Confederate officers at Fort Warren, Fort Delaware, and Johnson's Island included many elite Southern men who were well provisioned by friends, family, and strangers until at least mid-1864. While the U.S. government restricted contraband items, including whiskey and weapons, they allowed prisoners to receive food, tobacco, and clothing. Only in response to hunger among Union prisoners in the South did U.S. officials cut rations and restrict the delivery of food to Confederate prisoners. This had the effect of leveling class divisions across Northern prisons, and hunger became a more widespread reality felt in prisons from north to south and east to west.[5]

Cheesborough was not done after Christmas. She sent a belated Christmas present to officers at Fort Lafayette in New York Harbor, which contained fifty prisoners at the time. The shipment looked similar to the package delivered to Fort Delaware: one ham, three pounds of sausage, two and a half pounds of cheese, six pounds of biscuits, two pies and ginger cakes, apples, two pounds of butter, tea and sugar, pickles, catsup, and mustard. This food supplemented rations that, according to Union officials, equaled those of Union soldiers in the field. By one historian's estimate, the baseline rations for Confederate prisoners and Union soldiers before mid-1864 amounted to an astounding 4,500 calories per day. Afterward, the U.S. government reduced rations for Confederate prisoners, though reduction of caloric intake is unclear.[6]

There was more to prison hunger though than modern calorie estimates can reveal. The types and variety of Cheesborough's foods indicated an emphasis on choice—the key element of exercising taste—and not on mere survival. So too did the other consumer goods: soap, tobacco, and clothing ranging from socks and shoes to shirts, neckties, and a black silk cravat. Donations helped prisoners maintain what they considered the standard of living for gentlemen. Still, Cheesborough's operation was unsustainable. By the time General Robert E. Lee's Army of Northern Virginia invaded Pennsylvania in 1863, Cheesborough had returned to South Carolina. For the rest of the war, she lived a peripatetic life between South Carolina towns as a tutor and an author of articles for the *Chester Standard* and other Southern newspapers.[7]

Despite postwar recriminations about so-called Andersonvilles of the North, malnutrition in Northern prisons never approximated that in the Confederate South. Yet therein lies the peril of making sense of prison food: relative hunger and intentional starvation have been among the most vexing questions surrounding prisoners' experience. Writing on the subject reveals more assumptions than answers, including whether the Confederacy could have fed their prisoners better and whether U.S. retaliation in 1864 was brought on by rational pragmatism or a vindictive "war psychosis." Moreover, focusing only on policy overlooks the autonomy of prisoners to be the judge of their own experiences.

Two patterns emerge when studying prisoners' thoughts and actions surrounding food. First, Union and Confederate prisoners agreed that hunger was a decivilizing force and made choices to improve their condition across various levels of privation. Second, hunger became more widespread and severe over time. Many Union prisoners believed that Confederate officials intended to starve them, and Confederate prisoners also went hungry in the last year of the Civil War. Retaliation against the latter did not cancel out the suffering of the former, and litigating policy distracts from the human story. How prisoners understood captivity through food and made choices to improve their condition restores individuality to their experiences.[8]

Prisoners spent so much time thinking, writing, and talking about food, in such differing material circumstances, that there was no single "common experience" of eating in captivity. Prisoners faced a range of experiences, with the Fort Delaware Christmas dinner on one end of the spectrum and the emaciated Union prisoners who returned in 1864 and 1865 on the other.

Recovering the range of experience also means considering what taste meant in the nineteenth century. The sense of taste has traditionally been grouped with smell and touch as the three "lower senses," in contrast to the "higher senses" of sight and hearing. If sight was precise and rational, taste was vague and laden with biases. The writer for *Harper's New Monthly Magazine* in 1855 racialized the mouth and lips, describing the lips of black people as "thick, fleshy, and protruding," which to the writer signaled "a much duller, more material nature of mind and of senses." According to the same writer, women tended to consume food alone because it was an "unpoetical process" and because the writer sexualized the lips.[9]

The tension over eating cut even deeper because all living things need food to survive. If there was a meaningful difference between civilized tasting and animalistic feeding, eating required stratification. The nineteenth-century French gastronome Jean-Anthelme Brillat-Savarin said as much in two of his self-aggrandizing aphorisms: "Animals feed; man eats; only the man of intellect knows how to eat" and "Tell me what you eat: I will tell you what you are." Western elites used taste to distinguish classes of people and people from animals. The recurring inner question for imprisoned men was just where they fell on this spectrum.[10]

It is useful to resist overemphasizing what Civil War prisoners would not have thought about when eating. Twenty-first-century historians would not be wrong to point out that Cheesborough's inventory hinted at certain macronutrient needs—protein, carbohydrates, and fat. However, that insight would not have resonated with prisoners in the same way. Civil War–era Americans saw no nutritional labels blasting the number of calories, no list of nutrients or ingredients, and no expiration dates. Counting calories tells us more about how twenty-first-century consumers experience food and drink than those of the nineteenth-century world. Modern labels place rational vision over subjective taste, allowing consumers to make choices about what they should consume, when they should say "no" to their appetite, and how to conform to social expectations of bodily appearance. Vision, in an era when dieting and gluttony comingle, is more central to eating than it was in the 1860s. Prisoners judged food on vision as well, but they gave considerable weight to their nonvisual senses when navigating the world of wholesome and unwholesome food in the era before refrigeration.

Prisoners believed that food was one of the keys to civilization, whiteness, and able-bodied manhood. While individual circumstances and experience varied, captivity and hunger changed how imprisoned men related to food. Unwholesome food might disable them inch by inch; therefore, they looked to friends, family, and strangers for support as well as their own ingenuity in suiting taste to circumstance. They did this because hunger threatened to make an animal out of an epicurean.

Hunger and Captivity

In the 1850s, the basic American diet consisted of meat, bread, and, to a much lesser extent, vegetables. Regional and social variations emerged within this dietary framework. Americans ate pork across the United States, but some planters and physicians considered the meat more suitable for slaves and laborers than refined men and women because it was more difficult to digest than beef, and thus unfit for more delicate stomachs. Southern planters ate less pork than slaves and had more diverse diets. Corn, also a national staple, had regional inflections. Southerners often ate cornbread alone or sometimes with wheat bread. New Yorkers and New Englanders preferred wheat bread and beef over corn and pork. Between 1854 and 1860, New England farmers raised more sheep than pigs, and consumers bought two and a half times more beef than pork.[11]

Food supplies in the Civil War connected the home front and the front line. Abandoned fields, the footprints of armies, and destructive battles exemplified not only the ruination of war but also the resilience of nature. One soldier described the resurgence of blackberries, which grew well in damaged ecosystems, on the Resaca battlefield "as if human blood had fertilized the soil."[12] Soldiers scavenged, fished, experimented with local foods, and shared meals and hunger with civilians and prisoners. Southern white women led at least thirteen bread riots in Confederate cities, in part because soldiers took food from civilians, targeting enemy houses and sometimes engaging in nonpartisan plunder. One Confederate soldier compared his army to an aptly named armyworm, slinking through gardens and devouring the contents. Soldiers called "foraging" what civilians called stealing; but either way, it was a solution to the monotonous and often unwholesome staples of army life. By purchasing, foraging, or stealing, soldiers participated in an ever-changing wartime network of food and preserved the liberty of individual taste.[13]

While many experienced hunger during the Civil War, captivity further limited the options of the hungry. William Dolphin knew hunger in the Union cavalry, but two years into his three-year enlistment he also knew how to feed himself in wartime Virginia. In August 1863, Dolphin got into, as he euphemized it, "a fuss with [an] old citizen" who tried to stop him from stealing chickens and potatoes. The encounter ended when Dolphin struck the old man "over the head" with his fist or a weapon. The stew Dolphin stirred that night testified to his triumph over the dotard.[14] The assailant and his messmates regularly stole—he called it stealing—or hunted to supplement rations: a bag of oats, eels from the river, vegetables for succotash. They became less bold within hearing range of the "rebel drums." Dolphin stopped writing about food for seven days leading up to the Battle of Liberty Mills. He was likely captured hungry.[15]

The relative ease of supplementing rations came to an abrupt end. Dolphin either discovered he should not employ the same methods against fellow prisoners or was not in a strong enough position to do so. Although many prisoners stole, and Dolphin did steal from Confederate guards, stealing from one another was a zero-sum game. Within days he felt "half starved," and this became a recurring theme at Libby Prison and Belle Isle over the next several weeks. The "d—d harsh" food, whether it was the "louse soup" or bread, left Dolphin as "hungry as Satan."[16] From Belle Isle, Dolphin heard—or heard rumors of—bread riots taking place a few blocks away in Richmond, and his temper resurfaced into a simmering "fuss" with another prisoner. Conditions improved slightly in November when donations of coffee and tobacco arrived from Baltimore and "uncle Sam's grub" came from the United States Sanitary Commission. Still, "the Best Pork I ever eat" made Dolphin angry because he believed he had been shorted by the Confederates. "They have fed us out of the Pork once," Dolphin wrote, but he asserted that they fed "the guards 5 times. D—d Scoundrels." By the onset of winter, Dolphin had begun selling his clothing for food and tobacco.[17]

Dolphin's experience was not unusual. Hunger changed how men thought and acted in captivity. The wholesomeness of food mattered as much as quantity, and some men went hungry because their senses warned against eating what they were issued. Reflecting the senses of smell and taste, prisoners called suspect rations strong, rancid, foul, sour, or tainted, and writers stretched for effective comparisons during and after the war. Union prisoners at Belle Isle and Danville described soup as having a "bitter nasty taste" or tasting "flat like dishwater."[18] The postwar remembrance of disgust paralleled accounts written in captivity in spirit if not always in detail. One former prisoner at Point Lookout recalled detecting a peculiar taste in the soup before discovering a used tobacco chew.[19] A Union memoirist recalled that in addition to the "strong, rancid, and maggoty" bacon they received, were beans that "were small, red or black, a little larger than a pea, with a tough skin, a strong bitter taste, emitting a flavor much like an old blue dye-tub."[20]

Texture also mattered in judging the wholesomeness of food. For decades before the Civil War, Northern travel writers had criticized the texture of Southern cornbread, and prisoners continued in this tradition. One antebellum traveler compared cornbread to a pioneer because it cleared a path "scratchingly down the throat." Frederick Douglass pointed out the important class distinction, juxtaposing coarse "unbolted meal" that slaves ate with the refined flour baked into the bread eaten by their masters.[21] The better cornbread recipes combined eggs, milk, and wheat flour with cornmeal. Cheaper recipes, from "corn dodgers" to "hoecakes" and "pones," consisted of only the basics: water and cornmeal, with or without salt. The cornbread eaten by Confederate soldiers and Union prisoners resembled something closer to what Douglass remembered than even what travel writers consumed.[22]

Northern men brought this prejudice against cornbread with them into the war. Long before his capture, Union soldier John Hoster had argued with a Southern woman over the fitness of cornmeal and raw beans after finding these rations in the haversacks of Confederate prisoners. The woman was proud that Southern men could fight on such rations. Hoster, echoing the spirit of Brillat-Savarin, told her that Southern men could live and fight on hog meal only because they were "so near like that animal."[23] In a similar way, the *Indiana State Sentinel* reprinted a satirized rebuke of the U.S. policy of feeding "pone-craving prisoners" more expensive wheat bread. The writer mused that perhaps forcing "maize-loving rebels to eat Northern wheat bread" would turn them into civilized, law-abiding citizens. "With every mouthful of wheat bread, the hungry rebel swallows and incorporates into his treasonable system so much loyalty and patriotism."[24]

While Northern newspapers joked that Southern men could become civilized by changing their diet, distaste for Southern food became chronic for Union prisoners of war. From Montgomery, Alabama, Nathaniel Kenyon described prison food as a coarse mixture of corn and cob, "making a very good food for horse[s] and cattle but poor feed for human beings unless in a starving condition."[25] Cornbread became the subject of inside jokes. James Burton commemorated his birthday with a dry joke about the monotony of food at Andersonville. "I must have something in a way of a feast," he proclaimed, "and I think I'll have a little *corn bread & fried bacon* for a change."[26] Others mulled the treasonous implications of being corn-fed in Southern prisons. James Vance believed that "we are going to be Regular Cornfeds from the way we are stuffed with corn in various ways." After two months of nothing but "corn and stinking meat," Franklin Krause was more than ready to put the "Corn-federacy" behind him.[27]

From sober metaphors to humor, cornbread was not just distasteful but decivilizing. David Kennedy loathed the strong-smelling beef at Andersonville, but he saved his ire for the half-cooked cornmeal mush. When this Irish immigrant and farm laborer stated that the cornmeal would "give a hog the colic," it was not necessarily hyperbole because he knew hogs well.[28] Samuel Melvin took the spirit of Brillat-Savarin's aphorism about eating and being to its logical extreme. The beans made his stomach hurt, the cornmeal gave him diarrhea, and he considered unsalted mush degrading. Moreover, the cooking, including preparing wood for a fire, and eating had to be done with the fingers. It was too much for him. "This is the roughest pen that ever civilized man was put in," he wrote. "Here all is bestial, just like a hog pen, & hogs we must be, for like hogs we live, like hogs we act." Prisoners used the hog metaphor to describe the smell of prison as well, but there was nothing more hoggish than feeding like animals instead of eating like civilized men.[29]

Union prisoners like Melvin also loathed cornmeal because they believed it caused the chronic diarrhea that killed so many of them. For prisoners, calling it chronic diarrhea or starvation was a matter of semantic difference at best, or euphemism at worst. When four hundred paroled prisoners, mostly enlisted men, arrived at Annapolis, Maryland, in the spring of 1864, the sight shocked officers and hospital attendants. Rejecting the medical diagnosis of chronic diarrhea, they called it by the prisoner name: starvation. The emaciated prisoners had come from Belle Isle, and the living skeletons expressed strange tastes "for things which they ought not to have," including water from the James River and "anything that a dog can eat."[30] Ex-prisoners had lost control of their appetite, stealing food from each other and the hospital. Dorothea Dix described the prisoners as "reduced to idiocy," begging for the privilege of looking at an apple if they were not allowed to eat solid food. Another attendant said that the prisoners "were in a state of semi-insanity, and all seemed, and acted, and talked like children, in their desires for food, &c."[31] Onlookers feared that the starved men would eat themselves to death if given the opportunity.

While prisoners brought the meaning of hunger to Northern ears, photographers and publishers brought it to public eyes. Since the invention of the daguerreotype in 1839 and the popularization of ambrotypes, tintypes, and cartes de visite in the 1850s and 1860s, many Americans believed that photographic images provided an intimate connection between subject and viewer. In the Civil War era, eyes pried into photographs, searching into the character and soul of men, women, children, and sometimes the deceased.

To U.S. citizens and military officials, emaciated prisoners confirmed the worst rumors about life in Southern prisons.[32]

Illustrated newspapers and faith in the objectivity of sight spread the knowledge of hunger. On June 18, 1864, images taken by a congressional committee were published in *Harper's Weekly* (figure 7) and *Frank Leslie's Illustrated Newspaper* (figure 8). The front-page illustrations carried only titles—they did not need explanation. Inside, descriptions of the size, shape, frequency, and taste of prison rations supplemented what readers already knew from the cover. Jackson Broshers, one of the two prisoners on the cover of *Harper's Weekly*, thought they had been fed mule meat in Southern prisons. "I never saw such looking meat," he said, "and never tasted any of the same queer taste." He had initially weighed 185 pounds, nearly forty-five pounds more than the average soldier, and came to Annapolis weighing only 108½ pounds. The physician examining the condition of returned prisoners described them as looking like apes, and both the images and the descriptions were presented as undeniable evidence of a great crime.[33] Visualization underscored the authenticity of starvation—seeing was believing.

The images also marked a change in U.S. policy toward Confederate prisoners. From 1862 through the spring of 1864, U.S. Commissary-General of Prisons William Hoffman displayed a thrifty but consistent policy of treating Confederate prisoners and paroled Union prisoners on equitable terms.[34] The returned enlisted men changed his mind. "That our soldiers when in hands of the rebels are starved to death cannot be denied," he wrote to Secretary of War Edwin Stanton. While Hoffman considered the effects of weather and clothing, he pointed to insufficient and unwholesome food. The cornmeal "was made of coarsely ground corn, including the husks, and probably at times the cobs, if it did not kill by starvation it was sure to do it by the disease it created."[35] Hoffman asked for measured retaliation against Confederate officers in the North. A year earlier, General Orders No. 100, or "Lieber's Code," stated that "prisoners of war shall be fed upon plain and wholesome food whenever practicable and treated with humanity."[36] The code also utilized the principle of retaliation to make it enforceable: if prisoners in the South did not receive rations similar to those of Confederate soldiers, the U.S. government reserved the right to adjust the rations of Southern men in Northern prisons to comparable levels. In the summer of 1864, these images resulted in the reduction of Confederate rations as well as a prohibition against food through the mail and prison markets.[37]

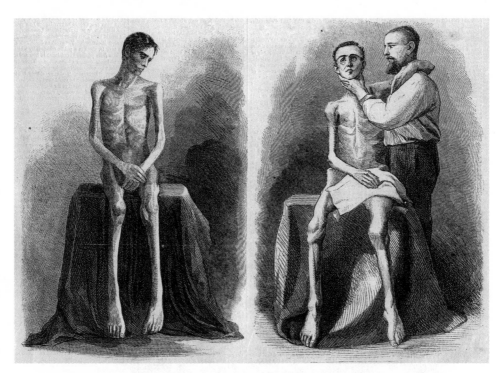

FIGURE 7 For many Northerners, these images confirmed the worst fears about prison food in the Confederacy. These lithographs visualized hunger. "Rebel Cruelty—Our Starved Solders—From Photographs Taken at United States General Hospital, Annapolis, Maryland." *Harper's Weekly*, June 18, 1864. Collection of the author.

Confederate leaders dismissed charges of starvation as Northern propaganda, but some observers echoed Hoffman's assertion that the coarse cornmeal had harmed the prisoners. When Dr. Joseph Jones inspected Andersonville in 1864, he stated that suffering resulted from a change in diet from potatoes and wheat bread to cornmeal. Jones wrote that the cornmeal was "disagreeable and distasteful" to prisoners and it ravaged their intestines. "Those who have not been reared upon corn-meal, or who have not accustomed themselves to its use gradually," he wrote, "become excessively tired of this kind of diet when suddenly confined to it without a due proportion of wheat bread." Prisoners might choose to go hungry because they associated it with the chronic diarrhea killing so many prisoners. Confederates explained away prisoner mortality as being a result of weaker Northern stomachs.[38]

FIGURE 8 Debates about the prison hunger did not wane in 1865. "Relics of Andersonville Prison from the Collection Brought from There by Miss Clara Barton and Dorence Atwater, Aug., 1865, and Photographed by Brady & Co. for the Great National Fair, Washington, June, 1866," Library of Congress, Prints and Photographs Division, https://www.loc.gov/item/2011648399/.

The Behaviors of Hungry Men

While prison officials thought about hunger at the macro level, imprisoned men responded to hunger as individuals. Whereas odor took up a physical space, food preoccupied the inner thoughts of hungry men. Confederate John Allen followed the whims of his stomach as he transitioned from hardened soldier to seasoned prisoner at Fort Delaware in 1864. Food dominated his writing. For weeks at a time, he kept nothing more than a food journal: coffee, bread, and beef for breakfast; soup, potatoes, and bread for dinner; and coffee, bread, and beef for supper.[39] Henry H. Stone kept two accounts of his route from Spotsylvania to Andersonville to Charleston as a prisoner. The first record described acute hunger. Stone thought "only of my belly," compared cornmeal to "horse food," and yearned for wheat flour. His second journal was simpler but equally compelling. Beginning July 1, 1864, Stone recorded what he ate—and only what he ate—in the cash account pages of his pocket diary, skipping only a handful of entries for the next 160 days.[40]

Prisoners like Allen and Stone found themselves compelled to write about food because they were hungry. Stone remained dispassionate in his food journaling. He recorded "meal beef salt" and "Grits Potatoes" without elaboration or vituperation. It was the compulsion to record, instead of the descriptive quality, that revealed the importance of food. It mattered to Stone whether he received salt and it mattered whether he received meat, which he did not during his last twenty days of captivity. The pressure to record every meal lasted only as long as captivity. Stone switched back to keeping only one journal the day he stepped aboard a U.S. ship in Charleston Harbor. Back to one journal, he beamed, "My spirits are as gay as a peach," and he looked forward to being "in the land of plenty." The food journaling had served its purpose and with freedom from prison came freedom from hunger.[41]

The omnipresence of food extended into public conversations and dreams. George Hegeman thought it "laughable to hear some of the young men and boys from the rural districts talk of the goodies, pies and puddings their mothers made at home, and actually smacking their lips over the recollection."[42] Another man recalled that his mess carefully recorded each other's recipes and resolved to "have a big lot of those things cooked, baked, boiled or fried under our own supervision and give them a good soul-satisfying test ourselves."[43] William Peabody had recurring dreams of food. Addressing his wife, Hannah, in his diary, he wrote, "I often dream of you and Ham & Eggs, but [I] don't get a chance to eat with you." One version of Peabody's dream juxtaposed friends and family with food. Peabody could see his friends and family and he could see a set table with ham and eggs. However, Peabody found that he could not eat. Despite dreaming, he still knew that he was "in the bull pen," slang for the prison stockade, and could therefore only see the food.[44] Hegeman survived his prison experiences; Peabody's dream was foretelling. He never ate with his family in this world again. Thinking, writing, and dreaming about food became a key occupation of the hungry whether they lived or died.

Hunger affected what prisoners considered palatable by blunting the smells, tastes, and texture of prison food. In this way, prisoners traced the transition of a new arrival, or "fresh fish" in prisoner slang, to a seasoned prisoner. At Fort Delaware in 1863, James Franklin could eat crackers and meat from the beginning, but he and the new prisoners could not stomach the maggoty soup, which they "abandoned at the first taste of it." However, Franklin noticed that veteran prisoners "appeared to enjoy it amazingly," and within a few days he "devoured it with as great relish as any one of the rebels."[45] Horace Smith complained about the absence of salt in the meat and the presence of bugs in the rice at Belle Isle. Yet he confessed, "it tastes good to us for we are about half starved and we are not allowed to buy anything here at any price."[46] Established prisoners welcomed what new arrivals could not stomach.

In extreme cases, hunger changed taste by unmooring the line between the edible and inedible that separated men from animals. Frederic James described fellow prisoners at Salisbury Prison as having "gone to grass" because they were boiling and eating clover.[47] George Hegeman, at Belle Isle, admitted to caving in to the demands of hunger when it took too long to properly cook cornmeal. He began eating cornmeal raw because he "could not wait to cook it" even though the rough meal and husks "felt like eating tacks." He daydreamed about eating one of the cats milling around the prison and later that year his mess succeeded in catching a loose hog and a stray dog. "This is the first time I ever tasted dog," he admitted. "I consider it wholesome and nourishing without the taint one would naturally suppose dog meat had." He claimed, perhaps to make it sound more palatable, that it was stolen. It was the prison commandant's dog.[48]

As in the rare example of dog eating, hunger led men to seek nourishment in food they would have been ashamed of consuming in freedom. Recalling his experience at Camp Chase, Henry Mettam remembered the prisoners taking note of a fat cat in the prison "filled with food that should have been ours." They skinned and cleaned it like a rabbit, soaked it in water, and made stew with onions and potatoes. Mettam enjoyed the taste of it while in prison, but it affected him so much after the war that he could no longer stomach rabbit.[49] E. John Ellis found a cat cooking at Johnson's Island and wrote, "Oh! Epicurus, a cooked cat. I placed it close enough to my olfactories to get the scent and was tempted to taste it, but my prejudices were too strong."[50] For Mettam, if not for Ellis, hunger overcame the antebellum palate.

While cats and dogs were possible sources of food, rat eating became a symbol of privation during and after the war. This was more common among Confederate prisoners for several reasons. Rat eating had already occurred in parts of the Confederacy, and preparing rat was not substantially different from squirrel. Jefferson Davis made this comparison perhaps to make the rodent sound more appealing to rural Southern tastes. Still, besieged Confederate soldiers and civilians and Confederate prisoners made up their own minds about rats on a case-by-case basis.[51] The raised barracks of Northern prisons also offered better environments for large populations of rats than Southern prisons, and periods of peaceful cohabitation made rat hunting easy. In 1863, when Robert Bingham first noticed the large rat population at Johnson's Island, he only noted that they did not disturb the prisoners. For at least the first two years, prisoners did not disturb the rats much either. John Dooley recalled that rats became "so tame that they hardly think it worth while to get out of our way when we meet them." Rat hunting did not become popular until late in the war, but it was aided by the cohabitation of rats and humans for a much longer period of time.[52]

Stories of rat hunting became common only after the U.S. government cut rations and restricted the delivery of packages. Dooley described the "rat business" as a nighttime activity in which men captured rats to cook themselves or sold the meat. Across Northern prisons that fall and winter men recorded or recalled the practice. Members of Thomas Sharpe's mess cooked a breakfast of "a big *grey rat*" they "caught in a dead fall." Others remembered cleaning rats as they had prepared squirrels at home and brining the meat in saltwater before cooking. According to the *Fort Delaware Prison Times*, rat meat was still popular in April 1865.[53] Not all Confederate prisoners were convinced of its necessity. At Fort Delaware, John Gibson could not determine if the cause of the rat eating was "our short rations" or "an experience of someone who wished to be odd."[54] Marcus Toney was even less charitable to the "noise of the rat hunters" that kept him up at nights at Elmira. For Toney, the behavior was as unnecessary as it was uncivilized. "If men were actually starving," he wrote, "there might be some excuse for this heathen behavior."[55] For some, rat eating was the necessary reality of prison life; for others, it served as a reminder of the hierarchy of eating from civilized taste to animalistic eating.

It was not just what prisoners ate that felt decivilizing but how they thought and acted around food. Hugh Moore recalled an inner struggle at Florence,

South Carolina, when another prisoner wanted a share of his rations of corn-meal mush and red peppers, for which he had just sold his knapsack to a guard. "There was a fight going on within me between the man and the animal, which lasted all the time the mush was cooking," he wrote. "I had divided [rations] with him before, but this was harder, for the cold and hunger was harder to bear now."[56] Luther Billings recalled it was common to see officers fighting "like dogs over a dirty bone or crust of bread," and prisoners ate rations as quickly as possible to prevent others from stealing them.[57]

While hunger compelled prisoners to eat with their hands, it also affected how they used their hands to make meals. The hungriest in nineteenth-century America, especially among the poorest working-class families and westward settlers, made certain that no bones went to waste. Prisoners described processing bones in ways that historical archaeologists have found evidence of at the Donner Party site and in Chinese mining camps.[58] The hungriest Confederate prisoners recalled taking care to extract marrow from bones issued to them in rations. Marcus Toney described the vigor with which men devoured soup, bread, and even bones "as eagerly by some of them as if they had not tasted food for some time."[59] Prisoners considered bone butter a luxury and produced it by splitting bone joints, boiling the fragments, and collecting the residue. Confederate prisoner John King recalled taking discarded bones into his bunk "and after gnawing the soft ends, sucked at the bone for hours at a time. I wasn't the only one. No bones went to waste as long as there was any substance left on them."[60] While some carefully processed bones, others greedily gnawed on them for additional sustenance.

Union prisoners used similar methods to process bones. At Salisbury, William Tiemann recalled that he preferred rations of meat and bone to meat alone. "These were esteemed a great luxury," he wrote, "as they were broken up and boiled in water to make soup, or if the recipient was so fortunate as to possess the wherewithal to purchase rice they were cooked with that, the marrow and grease combined with the rice making a most palatable and savory mess!" At Christmas, Tiemann and his messmates determined to make a dinner suitable for the occasion. Tiemann recalled that he "proceeded to break up our share of the bones, cracking them into small pieces about one half inch in size and very rich and full of marrow they were, and I fairly gloated over them as I thought what a rich and palatable mess they would produce when boiled with the rice!!!"[61] Remembering the anticipation while boiling beans and rice, Tiemann wrote that he and the other hungry cooks "smacked our lips." When the hungry satisfied their appetites, it came by scavenging and extracting every bit of sustenance.

External Supply Lines

The bone processing in Union and Confederate prisons is a reminder that prisoners adapted to survive the hunger of Civil War prisons. They looked inward and outward to improve their conditions, calling on external support networks, internal markets, and ingenuity. Success depended on many factors and resulted in a highly individualized range of experiences from feast to famine.

Degrees of access to money, friends, and family divided the experience of prisoners. Confederate prisoners, especially officers and political prisoners, improved their conditions through purchase until late in the war. Captured at Fort Hatteras, North Carolina, in August 1861, Thomas Sparrow endured what he called a "gilded slavery" on his way to a succession of Northern prisons. As with men who called eating with their hands uncivilized, it relieved Sparrow that at Fort Warren he could put an oil cloth over the table and eat from stoneware rather than tin plates and cups. "We had also light bread and butter," he wrote, "& have begun to live like white people." On Christmas Eve, Sparrow had eggs, brandy, sugar, and oysters delivered to the prison, and on Christmas Day the prisoners drank eggnog in the morning and had turkey with cranberry sauce for dinner.[62]

These well-connected prisoners pooled resources, especially on holidays, and their feasts contrasted sharply to prison conditions later in the war. Contributions provided Thomas Hall, the imprisoned editor of the *Baltimore South*, with a large stock of food for the beginning of 1862, including turkeys, cakes, "mountains of preserves & pickles" as well as "*six* gallons of egg-nogg."[63] Hall had expected a poor Christmas but was "agreeably disappointed to find that the sun did shine, that the turkey & plum pudding retained their natural flavor," and that eggnog and brandy had the same effect on the "humor & hilarity" of the group.[64] Henry Warfield, a Maryland state legislator, agreed with Hall's assessment. "From the Alleghenies to Old Worcester," Warfield wrote, "came avalanches of fish, flesh, & foul." Although imprisoned, the tastes of home still reached Confederate prisoners at Christmas in 1861.[65]

The prisoners continued to eat from these provisions well into 1862. Hall did not consume the last of the turkeys until the end of January, and he promised his mother that complaints of hunger were the "mere figure of effect."[66] That spring, Edward Drummond thought that he "could not have chosen a better place for imprisonment" than Governor's Island in New York Harbor. Drummond not only had a grand view of New York City and Brooklyn, he also had access to meat and bread three times each day and coffee twice a day.[67] At Fort Warren, Baltimore mayor George Brown's mess took meals with Antonio, an Italian man trained in French cooking. By Brown's own estimate, he gained fifteen pounds in the early months of captivity.[68]

Prisoners like Sparrow, Hall, and Drummond indicated how the mail and external markets could supplement rations. While Drummond complained about cold coffee or raw meat and Hall longed for a well-cooked meal out, both were in a special class of prisoners. Not long after Durham arrived at Governor's Island, Baltimore women sent the prisoners clothing and "eatables of most every kind," including jelly, fruit, and cakes.[69] Hall regularly purchased tea, extra coffee, and vegetables, and he requested long lists of food from home. "All contributions in the shape of biscuits, crackers, sandwiches, cold meats, such as tongues, pressed corned beef, spiced beef or beef a la mode, hams, cheese, bologna, sausage, pickles, preserves," he wrote his mother, "[in] short anything and everything which will stand a journey and 'keep' will be thankfully received."[70] After receiving one of his packages at Fort Warren in February 1862, Hall thanked her. "The beef and ham are delicious," he wrote. "I have tasted nothing nicer since I have been in prison, nor often out of it." The taste of the ham at Fort Warren reminded Hall of the one sent to him at Fort Lafayette, which he described as "the first decent morsel I put in my mouth" since arriving there.[71] The U.S. mail gave secessionist men a degree of freedom in choosing what to eat.

Those with money and friends consistently ate better than the rest. Through prison censors, solicitors maintained cheerful dispositions to worried family members while also soliciting money and food. Captured at Fort Donelson, Charles Ray told his parents not to worry about him at Camp Chase because the men received hominy, coffee, tea, sugar, bacon, pork, and beef. He inferred that the guards "intend to treat us well and win us back and all live like brothers again."[72] Joseph McGehee, another Camp Chase prisoner, explained to his mother that the prisoners had plenty of food but also noted that "those who have money can furnish themselves in anything the market affords."[73] Describing abundant food helped pacify concerns from home, but references to money and the market indicated a class division central to captivity. From the beginning, the poorer prisoners suffered. "I have to do without many little necessaries, which others enjoy," W. M. Smith wrote to a friend. He had been spending his small quantity of money on milk, "which, when I can get [it], I mostly live on." In a subtle solicitation to a possible creditor, Smith promised he would prefer to have $50 in the present than $150 in the future.[74] Food and money for these prisoners and their correspondents became tantamount to experience.

While Confederate prisoners could write to friends or family in regions of the Upper South with ease, sending mail from behind Confederate lines was more expensive, took more time, and was less likely to reach its destination. Some Union prisoners at Belle Isle benefited from packages sent by the United States Sanitary Commission. Thomas Kimball Jr. received tea, sugar, butter, and apple butter, and he thought the contributions were "a perfect godsend to us who have no money to add some thing palatable to our rations of bread & beef soup."[75] Yet the long-term results were limited. Allegations that guards stole supplies and counter-allegations that the U.S. government had sent contraband items stymied USSC efforts.[76]

As in the case of Confederate prisoners, Union prisoners with cash or connections fared better. Captured at Bull Run, James Gillette assured his family from Richmond that he had "plenty to eat," and each meal consisted of a half loaf of bread, meat, sometimes rice, and, in the morning, coffee. With his money, he could buy additional food, and the prisoners built a stove to "roast sweet potatoes and stew tomatoes." While Gillette wanted a change of clothing, he did not ask for money or food, with the exception of chocolate. "You see I am bound to live while the money lasts," he comforted his family. He also knew he was not representative of the whole prison population. For every man who had money, he believed there were nine men who had nothing. Few were as comfortable as Gillette in Confederate prisons even in the early months of the war.[77]

This standard of living for Union officers remained higher than that of enlisted men even late into the war. One well-connected mess of Union officers in late 1863 could count on regular supplements of food and supplies from family and friends. After one messmate received a box, Alonzo Keeler made bread pudding by adding water, salt, eggs, sugar, and condensed milk to their bread ration. Alongside the "butter, bread, bologna & sponge cake," Keeler thought that he had never tasted "a more palatable meal." Supplementing rations became more difficult when Confederate officials restricted boxes at the end of the year. "If you should learn that boxes may be sent again," Keeler wrote, "the same kind of articles will always come in play."[78] A strict reliance on supplemental rations was not sustainable. Henry Taylor solicited clothing and food as soon as he arrived in Richmond. "In the eating line," Taylor wrote that he wanted a ham, cans of butter and chowder, "five pounds coffee, four pounds sugar, onions, pickles, and any thing of substantial fat you can put up." Taylor, like Keeler, received at least one box in 1863; however, the supplies went quickly and food became scarcer as the two made their ways through the Deep South.[79]

Despite increasing scarcity throughout the war, prisoners hoped to preserve food customs, especially on holidays. Officers had the most success. In Richmond in 1863, Nathaniel Rollins and two other officers combined packages from loved ones to amass a Christmas feast. They ate "Boiled Potatoes, Roast Beef, Biscuit & Butter, Dried Apple Sauce, Cheese, Syrup, Chocolate with Sugar & Condensed milk. Apple Dumplings with sauce of sugar & butter. Preserved Pine-apples also pickles, salt & pepper."[80] At other times this came in the form of increased rations. At Fort Delaware in 1864, Francis Boyle wrote that Christmas dinner consisted of "a can of tomatoes and a bread & molasses pudding. The Yankees gave us a *double ration* of bread for breakfast—just about the quantity they ought to give us every day. They did the same generous deed on Thanksgiving Day."[81]

Yet most Union prisoners had lean holidays. Ransom Chadwick bemoaned on July 4, 1864, that the so-called fresh beef was full of maggots and "stunk enough to knock a man over."[82] On Thanksgiving in a Charleston, South Carolina, prison, Alfred Burdick mixed sweet potatoes and meal together and baked them in canteen halves. For Burdick, this "royal feast" made Thanksgiving "a poor one."[83] Good meals required careful planning and effective engagement with the prison marketplace. Union prisoner Jacob Heffelfinger purchased and raised three hens and a rooster. He considered eating one of the hens, but she started laying eggs "just in time to save her life beyond Christmas." Heffelfinger was careful to stretch out his resources, and it wasn't until the middle of January that he killed his productive hen. "She was fat as butter, and made a most delicious stew." Alongside the stew, he purchased sweet potatoes, wheat bread, and cakes to make "an excellent dinner, which almost emptied my pocketbook."[84] The dinner in the making lasted more than two months, but Heffelfinger succeeded in improving the taste of prison rations, if only temporarily, through the market.

Southern sympathizers in the Border States and in the North were more effective at aiding Confederate prisoners. Marcus Toney praised his box, writing that "none but those who have experienced Prison life know how refreshing it is to receive luxuries after being on prison diet."[85] Another prisoner, anticipating ham, pickles, and tobacco, told his parents, "My mouth is watering for them now."[86] Still, senders and recipients knew the dangers of sending valuable supplies. Guards confiscated what mold did not ruin. Courtney Pickett worried that packages would never reach their recipients. "It breaks our hearts nearly," she wrote, "to think of the yanks getting even a biscuit intended for our *gentlemen*."[87] Even after a recipient acknowledged receipt of a package, Pickett had lingering suspicions of the "intolerable thieves" guarding prisoners. She believed that the examination of letters prohibited the recipients from stating that items were missing from the box.[88]

Internal Markets

Alongside mail, markets enabled prisoners to make choices in prison. Once again, prisoners with money or friends held an advantage over others. Confederate soldier Benjamin Farinholt benefited from a wide range of food and drink options in Pennsylvania as part of the invading Army of Northern Virginia. He enjoyed everything from candy and fruit to coffee and whiskey. Although his capture at Gettysburg and initial confinement at Fort Delaware reduced these options, he boasted of his ability to purchase additional food at Johnson's Island. So long as his money lasted amid inflated prices, he could buy ham, cheese, butter, eggs, sugar, molasses, cabbage, beets, onions, and cucumbers.[89]

Union prisoners, alongside Confederate soldiers and civilians, faced hyperinflation as the war went on. In the summer of 1862 on Belle Isle, flour cost $22 a barrel, sugar $1.10 a pound, and bacon $0.75 a pound. William Collin and his messmates bought a barrel of flour, but lost most of it when a "mob" rushed them the next day. Still, they reinvested in flour to make dumplings for themselves and "flapjacks" to sell. After making $2.50 from flapjacks, Collin believed that they could still break even with similar business on subsequent days.[90] Two years later, prices at a prison in Danville showed the effect of scarcity and inflation: flour now cost $215 a barrel, sugar $10.00 a pound, and bacon $6.00 a pound. These prices were a fraction lower than those at Richmond, indicating that prisoners may have been paying in U.S. "greenbacks" rather than Confederate currency.[91]

Prisoners also engaged with the market by making things with their hands that they could sell or trade with outsiders, including the guards and the women who shipped in food. In a way not dissimilar from the bone splitting, prison artisans created value from refuse as well as buttons, shells, and imported material. J. G. Anderson told Anna Miller, another supplier of prisoner needs, that he had become "quite a mechanic in the art of ring making." He promised to send "a specimen of rebel ingenuity."[92] Edward Drummond noted that nearly all the prisoners occupied their time crafting rings and other articles. "It is a curiosity," he discovered, "to see the many articles manufactured: Pipes, Chess Men, Rings, Studs, Sleeve Buttons &c &c,

some of a very fine style."[93] This widespread business offered prisoners an opportunity to make something with their hands to sell or trade for food, tobacco, or other consumer goods.

Many prisoners worked for better rations independently or as parolees for their captors. There were tiers of society that mirrored stratification on the outside: a class of professionals and businessmen; a middling class of skilled workers, artisans, and barbers; and a bottom tier of unskilled laborers.[94] Some paroled prison labor, such as the draining of Foster's Pond at Elmira or cutting wood, could be beneficial to the greater prison population. Others could be detrimental. William H. Smith of Michigan arrived at Andersonville only a few days after it opened and secured himself a place working in the prison hospital. Many Union prisoners placed partial blame for their suffering on paroled prisoners, and Smith was a dangerous person to put in charge of the quinine and medicinal whiskey. Smith and another paroled man "got rather more liquor down than we can hold," he admitted, and "consequently we heave up Jonah." At least his friends were able to share in the barrel of beer that he brewed at the prison in September and October.[95]

While alcohol was available, at least clandestinely, in prison markets, coffee was one of the most desired consumer goods. It was a staple drink for nineteenth-century America, and the stimulating effect of chewing coffee grounds and drinking the beverage also staved off hunger and decreased thirst. A cookbook issued to Union soldiers also stated "the fragrance or aroma" was "the chief virtue of the drink."[96] During the Civil War, there were more recipes for coffee substitutes in the Confederacy than any other consumer good. The Confederate Receipt Book suggested roasting acorns in place of coffee, and civilians substituted parched rye, corn, peanuts, as well as the seeds of watermelon and okra.[97]

Confederate prisoners in the North often had better access to coffee than they did in the South. Thomas Hall could acquire coffee in New York, even if he had to drink it black. He was not used to the taste but it was less burdensome when he considered it was the style in Turkey and China.[98] Union soldiers had more reliable access to coffee in their army, but not as prisoners. Frederic James wrote the poem "Morale" at Andersonville, which dealt with the accusation that prisoners were "straggling coffee drinkers" when captured. James warned would-be stragglers that they would find no coffee in a Confederate prison:

Now Volunteers and substitutes whilst marching in the column,
It behooves each and all of you to take this warning solemn,

Don't leave your ranks on any account or circumstance whatever,
Else you will see, that nabbed you'll be unless you're very clever.

The host of Union prisoners, that swell the number taken,
Are captured by the road side at their coffee and fried bacon.
This fact should well be borne in mind, by all good Union thinkers,
That two out of three, that captured be are straggling coffee drinkers.

The prison fare as served out here, is scanty, poor and bad;
A mite of pork, of meal, one pint, is all that can be had.
Of *Coffee* you'll not get one sup, in this Pinelong Institution,
But foul air and water quite enough to wreck your constitution.[99]

Instead, Union prisoners had to scratch for coffee substitutes like Confederate soldiers and civilians. Prisoners made "conscript" or "crust" coffee from the coals of burnt cornmeal as well as bread crust and rye. They would wait until release for real coffee.[100]

Alongside coffee, tobacco mattered to hungry men. Roger Hanson, a Kentucky lawyer and former state legislator, especially liked Spanish cigars. From Fort Warren, he asked for two boxes of cigars from a friend in Kentucky. "I like a strong cigar," he wrote, and "I have sent to Boston for cigars but they do not send good ones."[101] Tobacco was also nonperishable and easily divisible into smaller units, which made it suitable for use as currency in prison trade. One Confederate prisoner at Elmira admitted that he was "a slave to the 'Indian Weed.'" Another stated he would prefer half rations to being without tobacco, which, like coffee, had the benefit of suppressing the appetite. This prisoner explained that "the tobacco would pacify his stomach for two hours, while the bread would only aggravate it."[102] Not long after eating raw cornmeal at Belle Isle, George Hegeman exclaimed that he was hungry, without rations, and "chewing tobacco to prevent from going mad."[103] Frank Bennett and his messmates lost their appetite for food shortly after Confederates threatened to charge them with stealing cotton and tampering with slaves. Instead of eating, he wrote, "we puffed vigorously at our cigars."[104] For these men, tobacco provided a related but—in their view—superior comfort in the moment to food.

Not all prisoners welcomed the habits of these men. Henri Mugler immigrated from Alsace-Lorraine to America in the 1850s and served in the U.S. Army. He joined a Virginia regiment as a musician in 1861 and deserted to Union lines in 1864, after which he spent the rest of the war as a prisoner. From Elmira, Mugler expressed disgust for African Americans, diehard rebels, and prisoners who begged for food and tobacco. He wrote that such prisoners put "themselves on perfect equality with the negro soldiers begging chews of tobacco from them and trading and conversing with them." He was even more appalled when he discovered that one of the prisoners was chewing a discarded quid of tobacco from a black soldier.[105] Marcus Toney described a similar scene at Elmira. "Until I reached prison I did not know what a slave to habit man was," he wrote. "I have seen men go hungry a day and save their rations and trade them for tobacco. I have seen a prisoner discharge a quid of tobacco from his mouth and another one pick it up, dry and smoke it."[106] There may have been more to the story than Toney preferred to publish. While in prison, Toney had once written to a friend, "I am at present out of Tobacco, and you know very well what it is [like] to abstain as suddenly from a habit which we indulge so much in." He asked his friend for five or ten pounds of smoking tobacco and five pounds of chewing tobacco. His autobiographical omission raises the question of whether Toney may have been the chewed quid smoker.[107]

The more desperate prisoners traded or sold their belongings and nearly any article of clothing for food to eat or sell. Men with extra stamps in Union prisons could sometimes trade them for an entire ration.[108] William Dolphin traded his overcoat for two pounds of tobacco, one pound of sugar, and three dozen biscuits. In a matter of weeks, Dolphin sold his pocketbook and his boots to buy an onion and sweet potatoes, and he shared wheat bread with his messmate, Hubert Smith, who had sold his shoes.[109] Five days after turning twenty years old, Thomas Springer sold a gold ring for four dollars. This allowed him to buy six apples and a loaf of wheat bread, which he traded for a full day's ration of cornbread.[110] Describing the desperation from memory, Allen Abbott recalled, "Watches, knives, rings, jewelry, pocketbooks, anything that could be spared, was sold for rations."[111] Many prisoners effectively consumed their belongings by selling or trading their personal effects for food.

In Southern prisons, where time seemed to stand still, one form of hard currency was in great demand—watches. Union prisoners described metaphorically eating their watches to purchase other articles. Having already "eaten my watch," Hiram Eddy wrote that he could no longer supplement his rations with sugar, coffee, potatoes, or butter.[112] In South Carolina, Jacob Heffelfinger wrote that he and his messmates' eating had temporarily improved because "we are eating up my watch."[113] Prisoners ate their watches by trading them to civilians for food that they ate or sold to others. Nicholas De Graff recalled losing his haversack and canteen to his captors, but he successfully hid a watch he had taken from his brother's body at Shiloh in 1862. "Little did I then think," De Graff wrote, "that it would be parted with within a few months for a pittance of corn meal."[114] Shortly after arriving at Florence, South Carolina, Eugene Sly noted that citizens traded bushels of sweet potatoes for watches.[115]

The hunger that propelled prisoners to swallow their watches also fueled gambling. While few men admitted to gambling, many complained about its omnipresence. For Jonathan Stowe, gambling added to "the noise and confusion of the day" in a Richmond prison. "I have used my utmost influence to check it," Stowe wrote, "but it is useless as they have got a good start and I am met only with jibes and jest so [I] go below to study."[116] Men like Stowe interpreted gambling as a sign of the moral corruption of rougher men, but desperate men gambled to improve their condition. George Albee defended playing poker. "If I lose," he wrote, "I will be no worse off & I may win enough to buy a loaf or two of bread."[117] Henry Tracy took advantage of the gambling in one of Richmond's prisons in 1863 to raffle off his watch. The raffle winner might still resell the watch, and Tracy earned more than he would have by simply selling or trading it.[118]

Switching allegiance was a most extreme form of gambling. Although both Union and Confederate prisoners defected in hopes of improving their material condition, swearing an oath to a recent enemy was most common at the end of the war as a prerequisite for release from Northern prisons. The phrases "swallowing the oath" or "the eagle" were apt metaphors for Southern men taking the oath of allegiance to the United States. Luther Mills recalled a rare nightmare that helped him explain what "swallowing the eagle" meant to Confederate prisoners. In his dream, an "enormous eagle," flying over the stockade, "burst with a loud noise, and thousands upon thousands of little eagles fell into the prison pen. And then every prisoner began to catch the eaglets and to swallow them." Years after the Civil War, Mills claimed to experience "an unpleasant sensation" in his throat when thinking about the oath.[119]

WHETHER SOLICITING FOOD or receiving donations, breaking bones for marrow or carving jewelry, discussing recipes or swallowing the oath, prisoners connected eating with their destiny. Even after chicken thief William Dolphin sold his coat and pocketbook for food, he and the shoeless Hubert Smith lived in hope of a better future. At some point that winter, Dolphin's messmates started gambling, and the result was a web of debt obligations. Willis Van Buren and Smith lost two dinners to Dolphin, who lost an oyster supper to John Burritt and a mince pie to William "Gus" Sipperly. Smith won two pies from Sam Brown and two pies and one dinner from George Boyce, but he and Edwin Graves also lost two gallons of oysters to Dolphin and Burritt. William Wood, a sergeant from a different company of the 2nd New York Cavalry, lost an oyster fry to Smith, Graves, and Dolphin. One day Dolphin and Boyce might be up three pies from Smith. On another day Dolphin would owe Smith and Boyce three lemon pies. Bets flew in all directions and debts mounted.

These men had neither run into some cache of external provisions on Belle Isle nor were they gambling away their rations. The wagers were payable in the future and debts reinforced mutual obligations between men. Smith and Dolphin owed Graves and Wood "all of the chicken Pot pie that we can eat," but Graves and Wood owed the former "mince pie for desert." The stakes also increased as time went on and the loser became included in the winner's payout. Dolphin did not just owe Joseph "Jo" Whiting "all of the oysters" that he could eat, but all "that we can eat." In a similar way, Dolphin came to owe Benedict Wall and Boyce "all of the cheese & molasses cake that we can eat." Sergeant Wood owed Dolphin, Smith, and Thomas Doane "all of the cod fish Balls roast beef bread & coffee [and] butter that we can eat." There were bets for peanuts, dumplings, apples, cans of condensed milk, and potatoes with gravy, but it was also about more than food. Mutual obligations promoted survival and helped these men imagine a future without hunger and with the liberty to exercise civilized taste once again.[120]

Most of the twelve men in Dolphin's circle won a more important prize than the foods Dolphin meticulously recorded. Instead of boarding trains for Andersonville, at least nine were part of a series of small-scale exchanges in March and April 1864. William Downes, released in mid-April, may have been aboard the shipload of emaciated prisoners that shocked Northern households; however, there can be little doubt that all twelve knew hunger at a granular level.[121]

Two of the men were not so lucky. Hubert Smith and John Burritt did not go to City Point with Dolphin and the rest, nor did they live much longer. Smith died in early May 1864 and Burritt followed in death several weeks later. The biographical roster of the regiment recorded no specific cause of death for Smith but did record one for Burritt. Despite the gallons of oysters owed to him by William Dolphin and Hubert Smith, John Burritt died of starvation on Belle Isle.[122]

Epilogue
Sensing through Time

MacKinlay Kantor knew how to evoke the senses.

In an essay for the *New York Times Book Review* in October 1955, Kantor de-scribed how he had "relived the tragedy" of Andersonville in the form of a ghostly encounter. At 4 A.M. in February 1954, he drove from his motel in Americus, Georgia, to "Providence Spring" in the prison park. At that spot, memoirists had recalled a miracle: after they had thirsted for clean water all summer, a flash flood in August 1864 uncovered a hidden spring near the western "deadline" along the prison stockade wall. Parking near that spring, Kantor heard—perhaps suspiciously for February, even in southwest Georgia—the sounds of nature. "Frogs were singing like birds along a tiny water course," he wrote, but after a time his thoughts wandered from the spring to the national cemetery where 13,000 victims of Andersonville lay buried. He thought too of the memorials, especially the Connecticut monu-ment, which depicts a standing Union prisoner from that state, hat in his left hand, stepping forward with a stoic expression of silent endurance. The simple monument was then—and is still now—one of the haunting visual representations of tragedy at Andersonville National Historic Site.[1]

Kantor drove from Providence Spring to the high ridge on the south side of the prison stockade. From that ridge overlooking the entire prison, he con-tinued to hear "that constant spurting symphony of frog voices" from the creek near Providence Spring as well as an owl that "spoke among the un-derbrush." While Kantor thought about the eternal fate of the 50,000 pris-oners and guards, it happened. "I heard them coming," he wrote. "They twitched in a whispering rank from woods at the north," and Kantor watched the dark valley as he heard them march "out into open ground where little circular fences protected the wells and tunnels they had dug—black pits drilled down through colored layers of clay." For those who might think him out of his mind, Kantor doubled down and leaned on his senses as the dis-cerner of truth from fiction. "It was no illusion—I *heard* those soft-footed thousands walking ever closer."

Kantor thought living through two world wars had prepared him for An-dersonville. As a journalist at the end of World War II, he had arrived with the troops who liberated the Buchenwald concentration camp in Germany.

When Kantor began crying at Andersonville that February morning it was not from fear; rather, tears came from the belief that the ghosts of Andersonville "had come to tell me that there must be no compromise." It began to rain, and he felt that "they were touching me, they were all around me, brushing my face and hands, the hair of my head." Almost two years later, after having put the finishing touches on his novel about the prison, Kantor felt "grateful to those many boys I heard walking toward me in the rain," and he hoped that he had kept the pledge to tell the story of Andersonville from their perspective.[2]

Kantor's Pulitzer Prize–winning novel, *Andersonville*, was only loosely based on the real prison. In his novel, the smell of decay emerges as a physical and moral manifestation from the start. Ira Claffey, a yeoman slaveowner near Andersonville, fears in the first scene that decay will infect his potato crop, and Kantor's parallel between rotting nature and rotting humans is at once established. "One bruise, one carelessness, and the rot begins. Decay is a secret but hastening act in darkness; then one opens up the pine bark and pine straw—or shall we say, the Senate?—and observes a visible wastage and smell, a wet and horrid mouldering of the potatoes. Or shall we say, of the men?" Weeks before the first prisoners arrived, Claffey smells something dead at the prison construction site. By late spring, the stench has permeated everything and Captain Henry Wirz has come to the conclusion that the prisoners inside the stockade are not men but bears. The novel reeks with the odor and decivilization of Andersonville.[3]

Or does it? Just as Northern civilians in 1864 could not unsee the emaciated men in *Harper's Weekly*, Kantor could not unsmell the human cost of World War II. The odor of Buchenwald, which Kantor described in 1945 as so overpowering that he could "hardly smell" dinner being cooked, influenced his understanding of the Confederate prison.[4] His use of the senses, especially smell, is perhaps too compelling. After opening his book years ago, I put it back on the shelf for fear of conflating Kantor's olfactory imagination and my own research. Part of this hesitation came from historian William Marvel's sober warning: "Few Civil War novels are so captivating," Marvel writes, "and perhaps none has done quite so much to distort the history of a particular event."[5] While Andersonville has been controversial since 1864, and much distortion has come from Confederate apologists, Marvel is right to criticize Kantor's use of historical evidence.[6] As a novelist, though, Kantor had different obligations than a historian. A novelist must write a compelling story; a historian must show evidence that someone in the past saw, smelled, heard, tasted, or felt something. Kantor's *Andersonville* reeks, just not of the historical Andersonville.

Kantor's olfactory time capsule suggests both the power and the limitations of sensory history. Studying the senses humanizes and individualizes people in the past. It does not humanize in the crude sense of the term: people in the past, whether men or women, enslaved or free, were fully human, and no modern scholar can make them any more or less so. Attention to the senses can demystify prisoners by foregrounding their humanity and their capacity to feel and to think without stereotyping prisoners in tidy ideological categories. Whether at Andersonville or Belle Isle or Point Lookout or Elmira, prisoners came from across the United States and around the world. While prisoners shared similarities and differences of background and lived experience, they all witnessed the world through some combination of the five senses. Thankfully for historians, they also expressed these sensory experiences through writing.

Even individual experiences have histories. Historians of memory have long pointed out that remembering is a process of creating rather than simply a mechanism of storing and recalling bits of information. Prisoners adjusted their memories of the past to meet the needs of the present, and their sensory experiences were part of that ever-changing process. Remembering involves two contexts separated by time, whether the experience was fifty minutes or fifty years ago. Robert Bingham, profiled in the introduction of Chapter 1, left at least two records of captivity. He began his two-volume diary at Fort Norfolk on June 30, 1863, beginning from memory with the skirmish on the South Anna River that had occurred four days earlier. The second, much shorter account came in the form of a letter in March 1923, three months before the sixtieth anniversary of his capture. Both accounts were explicitly written to women: in 1863 it was his wife, and his writing exercise helped Bingham preserve his sense of manhood in captivity; in 1923 it was Bingham's granddaughter. A brief comparison of Bingham's senses in the 1863 journal and in the 1923 letter suggests that time and context affected the same event. The similarities, the discrepancies, the mentions, and the omissions all show that Robert Bingham continued to process his capture and imprisonment. His captivity experience did not stop evolving when he was exchanged.[7]

Bingham's capture looked, sounded, and felt different in 1863 and 1923. Four days after the skirmish, Bingham recalled it as a "painful" and "humiliating" day in which his men "fired badly" and he surrendered after the loss of one man. The most humiliating moment came in surrendering his pistol.

Although he was numb and "felt nothing" at the moment of capture, being stripped of his pistol—which he had used to impress women—and the curses of the officer demanding it "brought me to myself and I felt it most keenly."[8] In 1923, Bingham emphasized the killing and the dying. This time his men did "excellent target practice" on Union cavalry and he recounted holding a dead teenager, Isiah Cash, "and felt and heard the broken bones scrape against each other like a crushed egg shell." There was no mention of a pistol or his humiliation in 1923.[9]

When Bingham recalled his travel as a prisoner to Fort Norfolk in 1923, he emphasized greater comfort than he had during the war. In 1863, Bingham had written that "all the *fighting* men treated us *well*," but he was so insulted by the words of a "brutish" officer that Bingham spiraled into a numb, "comatose state" until reaching the fort. Sixty years later, at the height of white sectional reconciliation, Bingham recalled that "both officers and privates treated us like brothers" and that they were enemies on the battlefield "only technically." Their captors "divided their last crust with us, and expressed great regret that they did not have more food to share with us."[10]

The sensory environment of Fort Norfolk contained more similarities across the chasm of six decades, and where it differed in sensory detail the overarching themes aligned. In 1863, Bingham found the rooms damp, the floors rotten, and "the stench of the privy almost intolerable," and prisoners knocked out bricks in hopes of creating a draft. He derived some comfort from watching the sunset across the bay, from a draft of air that came up the steps, and from the novel *Shirley, A Tale*. The latter read to Bingham like the fresh air he could not breathe because it had a "style as clear & pure as a mountain atmosphere after the rain." In those early days, Bingham also learned prisoner self-care: how to scrub his shirt, drawers, and socks in a washtub. He listened skeptically to salutes fired on the Fourth of July. They sounded like "a mockery." Other days passed with "perfect monotony," and the lack of quietude on Sundays bothered his ears.[11]

While Bingham noted in 1863 that he was being held as a hostage under the threat of execution, he elaborated sixty years later. The U.S. government had selected hostages to pressure the Confederate government and the state of Alabama not to carry out a threat to execute Union prisoners accused of promoting slave rebellions.[12] While Bingham, from the distance of sixty years, thought the U.S. retaliation policy proper, that knowledge offered little comfort in the physical conditions of captivity. Bingham and sixteen other men were kept in a crowded room with a single window. "The Black Hole of Calcutta could hardly have been worse," he wrote, and the heat compelled the prisoners to go nude. Their food, which went unmentioned in his diary, consisted of "sour loaf bread, rancid pickled beef and 'tea' made of the leaves of blackberry bushes." Bingham credited the "excellent cistern water" for the good health of the room. Although most of Bingham's two-volume diary concerned his experience at Johnson's Island, the letter to his granddaughter condensed time after Fort Norfolk. He mentioned only making jewelry, reading Charles Dickens's novels, and switching places with a sick prisoner during a special exchange of men unfit for duty.[13]

Robert Bingham had forgotten or chose not to recall the stench of the privy, the sounds of Sunday or the Fourth of July, the sight of the bay, or the feeling of washing clothes, but he did remember the feeling of confinement and the taste of the bread, rancid beef, and the blackberry tea. Bingham also neglected to mention Della, a grandmother Henrietta never met, but whose name and love had been so important to him that he wrote nearly every day in a journal she would only see in the future. Although separated by sixty years, both accounts used the senses to explain a complicated experience. They were both accurate to the extent that they helped Bingham convey what he wanted to express at a specific time and place in his life. Neither was more authentic than the other, and both reflected different concerns and underlying motivations. Still, in both cases, Bingham used the senses to explain his perseverance to important women in his life.

IN WRITING *Living by Inches*, I have come to know Andersonville on a more intimate level than other prisons. A friend promised—or warned—that whatever I thought about the Civil War, Andersonville would change that. He was right. Understanding Andersonville meant wringing out the last bit of nostalgia for the American Civil War left over from my childhood. During my first visit as a researcher in the summer of 2011, I found the writings of William Peabody, Samuel Foust, and others so disturbing that I canceled social plans in Atlanta and began a six-hour drive home as soon as the library closed. I kept returning in the summers to come. In June 2015, amid the Confederate flag debates renewed after the racially motivated mass shooting at Mother Emanuel A.M.E. church in Charleston, I moved from South Carolina to southwest Georgia to work at Andersonville as a seasonal park ranger. In 2016, when Georgia Southwestern State University hired me as an assistant professor, fate again prolonged my stay near Andersonville.

My most inspiring week at Andersonville came in 2013, two years after my first visit and two years before my return as a park ranger. After receiving a travel grant from the Friends of Andersonville, I spent five days at the

Andersonville library and five nights alone in the guest cottage located between the prison and the cemetery. At 5:00 P.M. each day, park rangers closed me inside the modern gates. It rained almost every day, and even before the handful of visitors and the staff left, the park had a palpable feeling of emptiness, like a ruin or a ghost town. The quietude of being alone at Andersonville became a penetrating silence.

My time at Andersonville was its own sensory experience, albeit a twenty-first-century one that contrasts sharply with that of the prisoners in 1864 or Kantor in 1954. I had a peculiar feeling of elation when first returning. This made me feel some guilt. When Samuel Gibson, David Kennedy, and William Peabody walked through Andersonville's wooden gates in 1864, all three had begun some of the worst days of their lives. Yet I entered the park as a privileged guest, and that knowledge highlighted the distance separating me from the prisoners I was studying. Each evening I stepped out into what seemed like endless thunderstorms and took walks, learning every inch of the park. What could be said about the smells, sounds, sights, tastes, and touches after 149 years? How, if at all, could my own sensory experiences explain the assumptions and methodology underlying my project? What did my complete liberty to roam the park feel like, and how can historians uncover the feelings of prisoners? With these questions in mind I set out in the park each evening to put the last of the remaining light to use.

Although I did not relive the tragedy in the way that Kantor describes, my walks emboldened my research and writing. The modern sensory experience reinforced my conviction that if I were to understand Civil War prison experience, I had to process the diaries, letters, official reports, and memoirs in a different way than traditional case studies of individual prisons or policy studies of prisoner management. In deciding to frame captivity through the senses, it also became clear that the subject was not the singular realm of Civil War history, or environmental history, or social history. It is all of these things. When prisoners interacted with their surroundings, myriad entangled experiences, cultural predispositions, and social constructs embedded each smell, sound, taste, feeling, and sight.

My adventures were most rewarding the first evening because my perspective was fresh and my senses most keen. The prison site encompasses a stream, which bisects the open field and separates two ridges that drain into it. Although the original wooden stockade has vanished above the ground's surface, the landscape features two parallel rows of posts that re-create the original perimeter. An outer row marks the fourteen-foot wall that shaped the view of the outside world for prisoners, and an inner row denotes the "dead-line" or "deadline." I thought about etymology while tracing the inner line of posts and touching each one. Historical terms like this one embody the power of metaphor to reveal meaning. A deadline is now what George Orwell has called a "dead metaphor." Between the Civil War and approximately 1920, when deadline earned its modern meaning of "time limit" in the publishing world, the term "deadline" almost exclusively referred to a tangible threat in Civil War prison camps: cross this line and you will die.[14] Time and expanded usage killed the metaphor, and overuse has blunted its power. For fourteen months, this deadline visually partitioned faltering life and certain death. Today, most deadlines are negotiable requests rather than inflexible demands.

Walking along the deadline at Andersonville boosted my confidence that sensory perception provides historians with a way to amplify particular lessons from related fields, particularly about the relationship between humans and the natural world. As with Kantor's frogs in 1954, the sounds of nature in 2013 overpowered all else, broken only by the occasional truck or train in the distance. Rain often muffled the sound of insects, but when it slacked, the summer insects produced a collective buzz in my ears. When this happened, insects were not just the backdrop; they were central to my listening experience, and in the case of mosquitoes, the feeling. At that moment, the presence and magnitude of the sounds and feelings of the natural world were impossible to ignore. I knew a sensory history of prisons would have to wrangle with the power of nature.

Then there was the air, field, and stream. Alongside the sound and feeling of insects, the damp air had an earthy smell and one of recently cut grass. The smell of cut grass is a modern scent because it depends on the cultural desire, technology, and labor to maintain short grass. The green field would have been red clay in 1864. That which did *not* have a distinct odor also piqued my interest: the small, marshy tributary that served as a cistern, a bath, and a gutter for tens of thousands of prisoners. Although Stockade Branch smelled fine, it looked less benign. Red clay, which peeks out from parts of the grassy hillside, also forms the bed of Stockade Branch, giving the odorless water the appearance of a fleshy wound across the landscape. Following the stream out of the prison site and into thick woods, I walked until I found the metal park boundary signs. Then I turned back because the stream had turned into a swamp, and darkness and rain had erased all but the last evening light. That was when the rainy woods became frightening. An unseen owl hooted. In the distance a dog barked and several gunshots rang out. Maybe I imagined the sound of a distant train. In the diminishing light these sounds felt close, too close, and I quickened my pace to high ground that led through one of the three prison hospitals and back to the prison site. Arriving at the cabin in complete darkness I dried off and cooked a "historic" fare of cornbread, abstaining from meat (not in solidarity with my subjects but because I was nearing a hundred meatless days as an aspiring vegetarian).

My own sensory experiences illustrate what sensory history can and cannot do. Rain drenched the skin of prisoners nearly every day in June 1864 as it did mine those evenings of August 2013. A deadline exists now in the exact same place as it did in 1864. Prisoners felt the bite of insects and heard the sounds of trains, gunshots, and dogs. And they did not get half enough to eat. If sensory perception reveals time, place, and culture, it is also limited by those same factors. My deadlines are a linguistic vestige of a word that originated in prison violence but long ago left that context and meaning behind. The prison stream smelled fine to my nose, but I did not dare drink from it. Signs warned me not to drink from Providence Spring because we have as healthy a fear of microorganisms as prisoners had of foul-smelling air. The sounds of gunshots and dogs, though a worrying welcome to southwest Georgia, did not carry me back to the thoughts of a runaway slave or prisoner. Although the physical sounds may have some similarities to the past, the perception of those sounds depends on time and place and person. I cannot shed my own historical skin and put on that of a runaway slave or fugitive Union prisoner any more than Samuel Gibson or David Kennedy could fly like a bird out of Andersonville.

Notes

Abbreviations

ALDAH	Alabama Department of Archives and History, Montgomery, Ala.
ANHS	Andersonville National Historic Site, Andersonville, Ga.
BHLUM	Bentley Historical Library, University of Michigan, Ann Arbor, Mich.
CMLSC	Confederate Memorial Literary Society Collection, under the management of the Virginia Historical Society, Richmond, Va.
CTHS	Connecticut Historical Society, Hartford, Conn.
CWMC	Civil War Miscellaneous Collection
CWTI	*Civil War Times Illustrated* Collection
DEPA	Delaware Public Archives, Dover, Del.
DU	Duke University, Durham, N.C.
FHS	Filson Historical Society, Louisville, Ky.
FLSA	Florida State Archives, Tallahassee, Fla.
GC	Gettysburg College, Gettysburg, Pa.
HC	Hillsdale College, Hillsdale, Mich.
HSPA	Historical Society of Pennsylvania, Philadelphia, Pa.
INHS	Indiana Historical Society, Indianapolis, Ind.
KYHS	Kentucky Historical Society, Frankfort, Ky.
LC	Library of Congress, Washington, D.C.
LVA	Library of Virginia, Richmond, Va.
MAHS	Massachusetts Historical Society, Boston, Mass.
MARBL	Manuscripts, Archives, and Rare Books Library, Emory University, Atlanta, Ga.
MDHS	Maryland Historical Society, Baltimore, Md.
MNHS	Minnesota Historical Society, St. Paul, Minn.
MSDAH	Mississippi Department of Archives and History, Jackson, Miss.
NARA	National Archives and Records Administration, Washington, D.C.
OHHC	Ohio History Connection, Columbus, Ohio
PHSC	Peoria Historical Society Collection, Bradley University, Peoria, Ill.
SCL	South Caroliniana Library, University of South Carolina, Columbia, S.C.
SHC	Southern Historical Collection, University of North Carolina, Chapel Hill, N.C.
TNSLA	Tennessee State Library and Archives, Nashville, Tenn.
UAL	University of Alabama, Tuscaloosa, Ala.
UIL	University of Illinois, Urbana-Champaign, Ill.
UIAL	University of Iowa Libraries, Iowa City, Iowa
UMD	University of Maryland, College Park, Md.
USAHEC	United States Army Heritage and Education Center, Carlisle, Pa.

UTN University of Tennessee, Knoxville, Tenn.
UVA University of Virginia, Charlottesville, Va.
UVT University of Vermont, Burlington, Vt.
VAHS Virginia Historical Society, Richmond, Va.
VTHS Vermont Historical Society, Barre, Vt.
WIHS Wisconsin Historical Society, Madison, Wis.
WMU Western Michigan University, Kalamazoo, Mich.
WVU West Virginia University, Morgantown, W. Va.

Introduction

1. Samuel J. Gibson Diary, April 25 and 26, 1864, Samuel J. Gibson Diary and Correspondence, LC; 1860 U.S. Census, Armstrong County, Pa., population schedule, Washington, 686 (stamped), dwelling 1756, family 1679, S. J. and Rachel Gibson; digital image, *Ancestry.com* (http://ancestry.com); citing NARA microfilm publication M653, roll 1070.

2. Gibson Diary, May 1, 1864, Gibson Diary and Correspondence, LC.

3. Hoock, *Scars of Independence*, 186, 211.

4. Gibson Diary, May 4–6, August 21, 27, 1864, Gibson Diary and Correspondence, LC. On personal or "self-care," see Meier, *Nature's Civil War*, 2–7.

5. Gibson Diary, August 26, 1864, Gibson Diary and Correspondence, LC; Foote, *Gentlemen and the Roughs*, 16.

6. Gibson Diary, May 8–9, July 30, 1864, Gibson Diary and Correspondence, LC.

7. Gibson Diary, May 14, 18, 1864, Gibson Diary and Correspondence, LC.

8. Gibson Diary, July 28, August 12, 1864, Gibson Diary and Correspondence, LC.

9. Gibson Diary, December 23, 1864, Gibson Diary and Correspondence, LC.

10. Whitman, *Specimen Days*, 70.

11. Classen, "Foundations for an Anthropology of the Senses," 401–12; Classen, Howes, and Synnott, *Aroma*; Howes, "Can These Dry Bones Live?," 442–51; Howes, *Varieties of Sensory Experience*; Howes, *Empire of the Senses*; Ackerman, *A Natural History of the Senses*; Corbin, *Foul and the Fragrant*.

12. On cornbread, see chapter 5 of this book. On odor, see Smith, *How Race Is Made*, 12–16. Much of sensory history has focused on the changing hierarchy of the senses. For sensory historians, this book demonstrates the persistence and value of the "lower senses" in the increasingly visual cultures of the nineteenth century. See McLuhan, *Gutenberg Galaxy*, 26; McLuhan, "Inside the Five Sense Sensorium," 43–52; Classen, "The Witches Senses," 70–84; Stewart, "Remembering the Senses," 59–69; Roberts, "Death of the Sensuous Chemist," 106–27.

13. For overviews of these debates, see Gillispie, *Andersonvilles of the North*, 51–68; Sanders, *While in the Hands of the Enemy*, 1–6.

14. Edwin Stanton to Benjamin Butler, November 17, 1863, United States War Department, *The War of the Rebellion: A Compilation of the Official Records of the Union and Confederate Armies* [hereafter *Official Records*], Ser. II, Vol. 6: 528, 532–34; Speer, *Portals to Hell*, 114.

15. On African American prisoners, see Newhall, "'This Is the Point on Which the Whole Matter Hinges.'" On women, see Zombek, *Penitentiaries, Punishment, and Military Prisons*, 157–77.

16. Smith, *Smell of Battle*, 1–3.

17. Charles H. Blinn Diary, April 17, 1862, UVT; William H. Haigh to "My Dear Kate," June 1, 1865, William H. Haigh Papers, MS 02649-z, SHC; Smith, *Smell of Battle*, 73; Wiley, *Life of Johnny Reb*, 71–72; Hess, *Union Soldier in Battle*, 15–28, 143–57; Warren, *Rebel Yell*.

18. Hess, *Union Soldier in Battle*, 15–28; Smith, *Smell of Battle*, 75–77; Smith, *Listening to Nineteenth-Century America*, 199–200; Faust, *Republic of Suffering*, 128; Nelson, *Ruin Nation*, 161–75; Berry, "When Metal Meets Mettle," 12–21; Berry, *Weirding the War*, 2; Adams, *Living Hell*.

19. Faust, *Republic of Suffering*, 92–98; Davis, *Taste for War*, 15, 22–25; White and White, *Sounds of Slavery*, 187–89; Smith, *Listening to Nineteenth-Century America*, 238–46; Kytle and Roberts, *Denmark Vesey's Garden*, 41–48; McWhirter, *Battle Hymns*; Manning, *Troubled Refuge*, 8; Foner, *Reconstruction*, xxi.

20. Wiley, *Life of Johnny Reb*, 150–59, 164–66, 170–71; Linderman, *Embattled Courage*, 97–99, 122, 129–33, 165, 242, 253; Meier, *Nature's Civil War*, 2; Glatthaar, *March to the Sea and Beyond*; Daniel, *Soldiering in the Army of Tennessee*; Frank and Reaves, "*Seeing the Elephant*"; Logue, *To Appomattox and Beyond*; Mitchell, "'Not the General but the Soldier,'" 81–95.

21. Phillips, "Battling Stereotypes," 1407, 1416.

22. Berry, "When Metal Meets Mettle," 16; Scarry, *Body in Pain*, 3–11.

23. Phillips, "The Grape Vine Telegraph," 753–88; Phillips, *Diehard Rebels*; Drake, *The Blue, the Gray, and the Green*, 9, chs. 7–10; Brady, *War upon the Land*; Bell, *Mosquito Soldiers*; Ouchley, *Flora and Fauna*; Fiege, *Republic of Nature*, 199–227; Brady, "From Battlefield to Fertile Ground," 305–21.

24. Sanders, *While in the Hands of the Enemy*, 1; McPherson, *Battle Cry of Freedom*, 802–3; Hesseltine, *Civil War Prisons*, 2. Timing mattered. According to two economists, Union prisoners captured before July 1863 died at a rate of approximately 4 percent and those captured after that month died at a rate of 27 percent. Costa and Kahn, "Surviving Andersonville," 1468.

25. Hesseltine, *Civil War Prisons*; Speer, *Portals to Hell*.

26. Sanders, *While in the Hands of the Enemy*, 1; Cloyd, *Haunted by Atrocity*; Pickenpaugh, *Captives in Gray*; Pickenpaugh, *Captives in Blue*.

27. Hiram Eddy Diary, 1861–1862, memoranda pages, Hiram Eddy Papers, MS 78637, CTHS; Pickenpaugh, *Captives in Blue*, 18–22. On mobility in the Civil War, see Sternhell, *Routes of War*.

28. Speer, *Portals to Hell*, 9–10; Winslow and Moore, *Camp Morton*; Frohman, *Rebels on Lake Erie*; Gray, *Business of Captivity*; Levy, *To Die in Chicago*; McAdams, *Rebels at Rock Island*; Pickenpaugh, *Camp Chase*; Pickenpaugh, *Johnson's Island*; Futch, *History of Andersonville Prison*; Marvel, *Andersonville*; Davis, *Ghosts and Shadows of Andersonville*; Bryant, *Cahaba Prison*; Fetzer and Mowday, *Unlikely Allies*.

29. Hesseltine, *Civil War Prisons*, 1–6; Pickenpaugh, *Johnson's Island*, 101–4.

30. Hesseltine, *Civil War Prisons*, 34–44, 55–68; Pickenpaugh, *Captives in Gray*, 1–42; Pickenpaugh, *Captives in Blue*, 1–3, 15–34.

31. Witt, *Lincoln's Code*, 230–49, 254–64; Hesseltine, *Civil War Prisons*, 30–33; Sanders, *While in the Hands of the Enemy*, 116–17; Gillispie, *Andersonvilles of the North*, 85–95.

32. Witt, *Lincoln's Code*, 254–64; Pickenpaugh, *Camp Chase*, 47–61; Pickenpaugh, *Captives in Blue*, 57–74.

33. Hesseltine, *Civil War Prisons*, 93–114; Pickenpaugh, *Captives in Gray*, 61; Gillispie, *Andersonvilles of the North*, 85–95; Sanders, *While in the Hands of the Enemy*, 145–62.

34. Williams and Kutzler, *Prison Pens*, 10–29.

35. Alonzo Merrill Keeler Diary, September 1863–1864, Keeler Family Papers, BHLUM.

36. Hesseltine, *Civil War Prisons*, vii; Gillispie, *Andersonvilles of the North*, 3; Pickenpaugh, *Captives in Gray*, 98–99; Sternhell, "Afterlives of a Confederate Archive," 1027.

37. Gibson Diary, June 12, 1864, Gibson Diary and Correspondence, LC; Samuel J. Gibson to "My Dear Wife," June 12, 1864, Gibson Diary and Correspondence, LC. On censorship, see Gray, *Business of Captivity*, 109–10; Pickenpaugh, *Captives in Gray*, 98–100; Pickenpaugh, *Camp Chase*, 36.

38. Hesseltine, *Civil War Prisons*, 233, 243, 248–50, 262. William Marvel has shown that many famous prison "diaries" are unreliable. Marvel, *Andersonville*, 172, 256–57 fn47, 257 fn55, 323–26. James Gillispie demonstrates that much of the modern literature on Northern prisons echoes Lost Cause interpretations. Gillispie, *Andersonvilles of the North*, 60–62. See, for example, Horigan, *Elmira*; Beitzell, *Point Lookout*; Burnham, *So Far from Dixie*; Hall, *Den of Misery*; Joslyn, *Immortal Captives*.

39. Sternhell, "Afterlives of a Confederate Archive," 1037–41; Brundage, *Southern Past*, 105–21; Fabian, *Unvarnished Truth*, 124. Friends of Eugene Forbes, for example, published his wartime diary in 1865. While the dead man's diary was one way of establishing the "unvarnished truth," Forbes had been an apprentice in a printing house and his colleagues published the book. Fabian, *Unvarnished Truth*, 124; Reynolds and Seal, *All for the Flag*, 3–4. On the persistence of bitter divisions, see Blight, *Race and Reunion*, 152–54; Cloyd, *Haunted by Atrocity*, chs. 1–3; Gillispie, *Andersonvilles of the North*, chs. 1–2; Gardner, "Andersonville and American Memory," 180–96.

40. Robert Bingham Diary, Vol. 1, front cover verso, Robert Bingham Papers, Folder 3, MS 03731-z, SHC; Haigh to "My Dear Kate" [a diary written as a letter], May 24, 1865, Haigh Papers, SHC; William T. Peabody Diary, June 20, 22, 1864, ANHS.

41. Gibson Diary, May 24, October 17, 1864, Gibson Diary and Correspondence, LC. On prisoners' views of race, see Robins, "Race, Repatriation, and Galvanized Rebels," 117–40.

Chapter One

1. Robert Bingham Diary, Vol. 1, June 30, July 24, 26, 27, 1863, Robert Bingham Papers, Folder 3, MS 03731-z, SHC; *Official Records*, Ser. II, Vol. 8: 991.

2. Berry, *All That Makes a Man*, 181.

3. Bingham Diary, Vol. 1, July 30, 1863, Bingham Papers, Folder 3, SHC.

4. Lincoln, *Collected Works*, Vol. 4: 438, White, *Midnight in America*, 1–7; Wells, *Civil War Time*, 45, 52; [United States War Department], *An Act, Establishing Rules and*

Articles for the Government of the Armies of the United States, 24; Confederate States of America, War Department, *Articles of War*, 10.

5. Baldwin, *In the Watches of the Night*, 6–7; Ekirch, *At Day's Close*, 15–17, 19–22, 28–30, 31–74, 257–58; Palmer, *Cultures of Darkness*, 6; Stansell, *City of Women*, 59–62; White, *Ar'n't I a Woman?*, 134–35; Tocqueville, *Democracy in America*, 252, 252fn.

6. Bouman, "Luxury and Control," 17; Nead, *Victorian Babylon*, 83–84. Constance Classen argues that in the Middle Ages, night was "the realm of touch, when sight failed and the tactile senses attained their full potential." *The Deepest Sense*, 11.

7. O'Brien, *An Evening When Alone*, 80.

8. Smilor, "Personal Boundaries in the Urban Environment," 29.

9. McCord, *Statutes at Large of South Carolina*, 7:410; Johnson, *River of Dark Dreams*, 232–33; Melbin, *Night as Frontier*, 36–37; Scott, *Domination and the Arts of Resistance*, 121.

10. Smith, *Mastered by the Clock*, 145–46.

11. Marks, *Southern Hunting*, 22, 27; Camp, *Closer to Freedom*, 24–25.

12. Rachel Blanding to Hannah Lewis, July 4, 1816, William Blanding Papers, Folder 1, SCL.

13. Woodward, *Mary Chesnut's Civil War*, 211; Smith, *Hearing History*, 373.

14. White, *Midnight in America*, 10–19.

15. Charles Holbrook Prentiss Diary, March 19, 1863, Letters and Diaries, CWMC, USAHEC.

16. George E. Albee Diary, June 20, 1864, MS 41695, LVA.

17. John M. Follett to his parents, June 19, 1864, quoted in Ouchley, *Flora and Fauna*, 151.

18. [Gunn], *Gunn's Domestic Medicine*, 143.

19. Virgil S. Murphey Diary, n.d., 15, MS 00534-z, SHC.

20. James A. Bell to "My Dear Brother," September 30, 1862, Bell Papers, DEPA.

21. Jacob Heffelfinger Diary, June 28–30, July 3, 6, 9, 14, 1862, CWTI, Box 14, USA-HEC; Berry, "When Metal Meets Mettle," 16.

22. Aza Hartz [George McKnight], "My Love and I," in John Thomas Parker Commonplace Book, 1859–1865, MSS 5:5 P2264:1, VAHS; Ellinger, *Southern War Poetry*, 43–44; Frohman, *Rebels on Lake Erie*, 146.

23. George Marion Shearer Diary, November 2–21, 1864, Cash Account, March [November] 1864, MS C0080, Digital Collections, UIAL. When Shearer arrived at Andersonville, he foraged for similar means of shelter in early January 1865.

24. George Clarkson Diary, December 26, 1864, ANHS. See also Ames, "A Diary of Life in Southern Prisons," 12; Robins, *They Have Left Us Here to Die*, 66. On burrowing, see Burson, *Race for Liberty*, 34–35; Francis A. Dawes Diary, December 26, 1864, CWTI, Box 9, USAHEC.

25. 1850 U.S. Census, Susquehanna County, Pa., population schedule, Borough of Montrose, 184B (stamped), dwelling 72, family 92, Joseph Krause, Mary Ann Krause, Joseph Franklin Krause; digital image, *Ancestry.com* (http://ancestry.com); citing NARA microfilm publication M432, roll 829; Franklin J. Krause Diary, June 1–August 30, 1864, Andersonville Civil War Diary, MS 14096, UVA.

26. Krause Diary, June 13, July 18, August 30, 1864, Andersonville Diary, UVA.

27. Dougherty, *Prison Diary*, 4.

28. Bingham Diary, Vol. 1, July 30, 1863, Bingham Papers, Folder 3, SHC.

29. Francis Boyle Diary, October 18, 1864, Francis A. Boyle Books, MS #1555-z, SHC; Gray, *Business of Captivity*, 108.

30. Samuel J. Gibson Diary, September 30, 1864, Samuel J. Gibson Diary and Correspondence, LC; Elvira A. Fulton McKee, Pension File, for late husband Cyrus K. McKee (103 Pennsylvania Infantry, Company B), certificate no. 83166, RG 15, "Case Files of Approved Pension Applications of Widows . . . ," NARA.

31. Boyle Diary, March 5, 1865, Boyle Books, SHC.

32. Samuel L. Foust Diary, July 9, 22, August 2, September 18, October 23, November 17, 1864, ANHS.

33. Clarkson Diary, July 2, 1864, January 11, 1865, ANHS.

34. "Name Index to Register of Federal Prisoners of War Admitted to the Hospital at Andersonville, Georgia, February 1864–April 1865," entry for Robert Shellito, RG 249, M1303, roll 2; William W. Seeley Diary, memoranda section, ANHS; [Atwater and Barton], *A List of the Union Soldiers*, 58.

35. William Dolphin Diary, February 26, 1864, Civil War Union Diary, MSS 15813, UVA.

36. Thomas W. Springer Diary, September 28, October 1, 1864, MS 7093-v, UVA; Krause Diary, memoranda pages, Andersonville Diary, UVA. James Eberhart began writing in Springer's diary in the final months of the latter's life. Eberhart also seems to have copied Springer's entries into his own diary. Thus, Springer's entries were (unknowingly) published as Eberhart's own in the twentieth century. See McLaughlin, "Diary of Salisbury Prison by James W. Eberhart," 211–51.

37. James Burton Diary, September 17, 1864, MS #120, MARBL, EU.

38. Bryan and Lankford, *Eye of the Storm*, 214.

39. Samuel E. Grosvenor Diary, May 6, 1864, MS 81588, CTHS; John A. Baer Diary, August 9, 1864, ANHS; Marvel, *Andersonville*, 95–98.

40. Frank T. Bennett, "Narrative of Lieut. Col. F. T. Bennett," 15, Frank T. Bennett Papers, RL.30205, DU. Bennett's original diary was written in the margins of the novel *Lotus-Eating: A Summer Book*. Frank T. Bennett Diary, 1862, MS 3041, HSPA. One or two centuries earlier, this would have been less shocking. See Boynton, "The Bed-Bug and the 'Age of Elegance,'" 15–31; Sarasohn, "'That Nauseous Venomous Insect,'" 513–30; Ekirch, "Sleep We Have Lost," 353–55; Southall, *A Treatise on Buggs*, 9.

41. Stephen Minot Weld Diary, August 6, 1864, MS N-2378, MAHS.

42. George F. Gill Diary, January 22, 1863, MS A G475, FHS; Robins, *They Have Left Us Here to Die*, 86–87.

43. Jones, "Investigations upon the Diseases," in [United States Sanitary Commission], *Sanitary Memoirs*, Vol. 1: 497–98; Crawford, *Deadly Companions*, 153; John B. Kay Diary, August 25, 1864, John B. Kay Papers, MS 851695Aa1, BHLUM.

44. Alonzo Merrill Keeler Diary, October 14, 1864, Keeler Family Papers, BHLUM.

45. Jacob Heffelfinger Diary, September 19, 20, 1864, CWTI, Box 14, USAHEC.

46. Bryan and Lankford, *Eye of the Storm*, 171.

47. Buck, "A Louisiana Prisoner-of-War," 238.

48. Baldwin, "How Night Air Became Good Air," 412–17.

49. Nightingale, *Notes on Nursing*, 19.

50. William Duncan Wilkins Diary, August 16, 1862, William Duncan Wilkins Papers, MSS 61935, LC. See also Hartmann, "My Libby Prison Diary," 77–113.

51. [James H. Franklin], "Prison Diary Fort Delaware and Point Lookout," 5, undated [July 1863], CMLSC, VAHS.

52. [Franklin], "Prison Diary," 7, undated [July 1863], CMLSC, VAHS.

53. Grosvenor Diary, May 6, 1864, MS 81588, CTHS; House Special Committee, *Report on the Treatment of Prisoners*, 57. See also Vaughter, *Prison Life in Dixie*, 56–57; Urban, *My Experiences*, 537.

54. Frost, *Camp and Prison Journal*, 25.

55. Flinn, "A Southern Solder Boy's Story of Some Things He Saw and Heard & Felt in a Northern Prison," 1893, J. William Flinn Papers, SCL.

56. Smith, *Listening to Nineteenth-Century America*, 35–37, 138–40. See also Hindus, *Prison and Plantation*; Ignatieff, *A Just Measure of Pain*; Zombek, *Penitentiaries, Punishment, and Military Prisons*, 3–21.

57. Henry M. Lazelle to William Hoffman, December 31, 1862, *Official Records*, Ser. II, Vol. 5: 132–33.

58. A. M. Clark, "Report of Inspection of the prisoners of war hospital at U.S. Military Prison, Alton, Ill.," October 15, 1863, *Official Records*, Ser. II, Vol. 6: 392; Clark, "Report of the Inspection of the Gratiot and Myrtle Street Prisons and Hospital at Saint Louis, Mo.," October 18, 1863, *Official Records*, Ser. II, Vol. 6: 404–5; Clark, "Report of Inspection of McLean Barracks," October 29, 1863, *Official Records*, Ser. II, Vol. 6: 443; Clark, "Report of Inspection of Camp Chase and Hospital Near Columbus, Ohio," October 31, 1863, *Official Records*, Ser. II, Vol. 6: 479–80; A. M. Clark, "Report of Inspection of the Hammond U.S. General Hospital at Point Lookout, Md.," December 17, 1863, *Official Records*, Ser. II, Vol. 6: 740–41.

59. Gray, *Business of Captivity*, 18.

60. Thomas P. Turner, "Rules and Regulations of the C.S. Military Prisons," undated, RG 294, NARA, reproduced online at Michael D. Gorman, "Civil War Richmond," www.mdgorman.com.

61. Winslow and Moore, *Camp Morton*, 28. See also Toney, *Privations of a Private*, 94; Vaughter, *Prison Life in Dixie*, 69–70; Cavada, *Libby Life*, 46–47; Sprague, *Lights and Shadows*, 44; Wilkeson, *Turned Inside Out*, 221.

62. R. Lamb, Instructions to prison guards, April 1, 1864, *Official Records*, Ser. II, Vol. 7: 1.

63. Turner, "Rules and Regulations." Similar regulations existed for Point Lookout. C. H. Lawrence, General Orders No. 10, April 18, 1864, *Official Records*, Ser. II, Vol. 7: 66–68; Rules and Regulations for General Hospital #21, n.d., Ser. III, Confederate States of America Medical Records, 1861–1865 Collection, M217, McCain Library and Archives, University of Southern Mississippi, reproduced online at Michael D. Gorman, "Civil War Richmond," www.mdgorman.com.

64. "Proceedings of a Court of Inquiry," May 16, 1862, *Official Records*, Ser. II, Vol. 3: 580, 581, 578–86; Estabrook, *Wisconsin Losses in the Civil War*, 175; Thompson, "'Dying Like Rotten Sheepe,'" 7–10.

65. Peter Zinn to Joseph Darr Jr., November 21, 1862, Camp Chase, Ohio, *Official Records*, Ser. II., Vol. 5: 139.

66. Wilkeson, *Turned Inside Out*, 215, 222, 230; Toney, *Privations of a Private*, 105.

67. John L. Hoster Diary, July 4, 1864, MS #464, MARBL, EU.

68. Henry H. Stone Diary, July 14, 1864, ANHS. See also Krause Diary, July 14, 1864, Andersonville Diary, UVA.

69. Ulysses S. Grant to J. A. McClernand, February 17, 1862, *Official Records*, Ser. II, Vol. 3: 272.

70. William Hoffman to M. C. Meigs, March 10, 1862, *Official Records*, Ser. II, Vol. 3: 367.

71. William S. Pierson to William Hoffman, October 17, 1863, *Official Records*, Ser. II, Vol. 6: 391.

72. Henry Dysart Diary, May 19, 1862, Battle of Pea Ridge, Arkansas Civil War Diary, UIAL.

73. Niccum, "Documents," 282.

74. Jesse E. Watson Affidavit, December 8, 1863, *Official Records*, Ser. II, Vol. 6: 674. See also James T. Wells, "Diary of a Confederate Soldier and Recollections of a Federal Prison during the War," 28–29, James T. Wells Papers, SCL; Toney, *Privations of a Private*, 87.

75. James McCaggen Mayo Diary, August 23, 1863, LC.

76. Albee Diary, September 19, 1864, LVA.

77. Frost, *Camp and Prison Journal*, 24, 30. A civilian prisoner described a similar experience at the Old Capitol Prison in Washington, D.C. William F. Broaddus Diary, August 4, 1862, MS 22466, LVA.

78. Thomas Lafayette Beadles Diary, January 20, 1864, MS Z 2021.000, MDAH.

79. Beadles Diary, March 21, 1865, MDAH; William H. Haigh to "My Dear Kate," June 1, 1865, William H. Haigh Papers, MS #2649-z, SHC. At Johnson's Island, the "Rebel Thespians" offered entertainment and implicit political commentary on the war. See "Island Minstrels," Joseph Mason Kern Papers, Folder 2, MS 03536-z, SHC. Prisoners held similar events at Point Lookout. Pierson, *Diary of Bartlett Yancey Malone*, 55.

80. Wilkins Diary, September 3, 1862, Wilkins Papers, LC.

81. Kay Diary, October 16, 1863, Kay Papers, BHLUM; Keeler Diary, October 7, 8, 1863, Keeler Family Papers, BHLUM; Browne, *Four Years in Secessia*, 265.

82. Haigh to "My Dear Kate," June 1, 1865, Haigh Papers, SHC.

83. Lewis C. Bisbee Diary, January 23, 1864, Lewis C. Bisbee Papers, MS P1268, MNHS; see also Heffelfinger Diary, September 13 and 15, 1864, CWTI, Box 14, USAHEC.

84. Heffelfinger Diary, May 10, 1864, CWTI, Box 14, USAHEC.

85. Robert H. Kellogg Diary, May 9, 1864, Robert H. Kellogg Papers, MS 68013, CTHS; Helmreich, "Diary of Charles G. Lee," 17.

86. Kay Diary, November 24, 1863, Kay Papers, BHLUM.

87. Kay Diary, October 17, 1863, January 10, 1864, BHLUM.

88. Murphey Diary, undated entry, 26–27, SHC. Julius H. Brown wrote that dreams illustrated the fact that "the Rebels could not fetter the spirit." Browne, *Four Years in Secessia*, 267; White, *Midnight in America*, 27–30, 37–41.

89. Bingham Diary, Vol. 1, September 5, 1863, Bingham Papers, Folder 3, SHC.

90. Bingham Diary, Vol. 2, November 11, 12, 1863, SHC.

91. Bell, "Notes and Documents," 174.

92. Eugene R. Sly Diary, November 30, December 1, 1864, United States Civil War Collection, WMU.

93. Elisha Rice Reed Diary, January 26, 29, 1862, Elisha Rice Reed Papers, Wis Mss 115S, WIHS. Nearly every detailed prison dream remarks on the letdown of waking up. Haigh to "My Dear Kate," May 29, 1865, Haigh Papers, SHC.

94. William H. Tillson Diary, n.d., 1, MS 05007-z, SHC.

95. Milton Woodford to sister, October 28, 1862, Camp Parole, Maryland, Churchill and Woodford Family Papers, MS 78279, Folder 5, CTHS. See also Milton Woodford Diary, January 4, 1863, Woodford Family Papers, CTHS.

96. Bierce, *Tales of Soldiers and Civilians*, 16.

Chapter Two

1. William Duncan Wilkins Diary, August 12, 1862, Wilkins Duncan Wilkins Papers, MSS 61935, LC; Hartmann, "My Libby Prison Diary," 77, 80–81.

2. Wilkins Diary, August 12, 13, 14, 1862, Wilkins Papers, LC.

3. Wilkins Diary, August 15, 1862, LC.

4. James A. Bell to "My Dear Brother," September 30, 1862, Bell Papers, DEPA.

5. Wilkins Diary, August 26, September 6, 1862, Wilkins Papers, LC.

6. Wilkins Diary, September 24, 1862, LC.

7. Meier, *Nature's Civil War*, 2; Brown, *Foul Bodies*, 294–300.

8. On intersensoriality, see Howes, *Sensual Relations*.

9. "The Senses — Smell," *Harper's New Monthly Magazine* 12, no. 70 (March 1856), 494, 495, 496, 497, 499; "The Senses — Sight," *Harper's New Monthly Magazine* 12, no. 72 (May 1856), 801–7.

10. Rosen, "'Knowing' Industrial Pollution," 567–68; Corbin, "Urban Sensations," 55–67; Valencius, *Health of the Country*, 85–158; E. H. Barton, "Sanitary Map of the City of New Orleans," in Sanitary Commission, *Report of the Sanitary Commission*, xvi, 211–12. On smell, landscape, and health, see also Mitman, "In Search of Health," 184–210; Rosen, "'Knowing' Industrial Pollution," 565–97; Rosen, "Noisome, Noxious, and Offensive Vapors," 67–82.

11. Brown, *Foul Bodies*, 297.

12. Gower and Allen, *Pen and Sword*, 599.

13. Wilkins Diary, August 16, 1862, Wilkins Papers, LC.

14. George William Brown to George C. Schattuck, November 19, 1862, George W. Brown Collection, MS 2398, MDHS.

15. Brown to Schattuck, November 19, 1862, Brown Collection, MDHS.

16. William H. Davis Diary, May 18 and 19, 1863, William H. Davis Papers, MS #301, MARBL, EU.

17. Charles B. Stone Diary, February 21, 1863, UVT.

18. Frank T. Bennett, "Narrative of Lieut. Col. F. T. Bennett," 13, 80, Frank T. Bennett Papers, RL.30205, DU.

19. His letters were smuggled out of prison. Hiram Eddy to his wife, May 2, 1862, Hiram Eddy Papers, MS 78637, CTHS; Pickenpaugh, *Captives in Blue*, 37.

20. Jonathan P. Stowe Diary, October 26, November 15, 1861, CWTI, Box 26, USAHEC; *Richmond Enquirer*, January 13, 1862; James McCaggen Mayo, September 12, 1863, LC; James B. Irvine Diary, March 8, 1865, ALDAH; Gerold, "Why Do Gentlemen Smoke?" in Beaudry, *Libby Chronicle*, 25; Lane, "'A Marvel of Taste and Skill,'" 50–51, 169–70.

21. House Special Committee, *Report on the Treatment of Prisoners*, 81; Sabre, *Nineteen Months a Prisoner*, 91–92; Ransom, *John Ransom's Diary*, 112; Marvel, *Andersonville*, 323.

22. Samuel J. Gibson Diary, May 4, 6, 1864, Gibson Diary and Correspondence, LC.

23. John L. Hoster Diary, June 20, 1864, MS #464, MARBL, EU. See also James E. Wenrick Diary, August 6, 1864, AM 66954, HSPA.

24. William Lloyd Tritt Diary, June 14, 17, 1864, M92-141, WIHS.

25. Schiller, *A Captain's War*, 154.

26. Gower and Allen, *Pen and Sword*, 608.

27. Wilkins Diary, August 28, September 5, 1862, Wilkins Papers, LC.

28. Alonzo Tuttle Decker Diary, n.d., ANHS. See also Franklin J. Krause Diary, June 20, 1864, Andersonville Civil War Diary, MS 14096, UVA.

29. Helmreich, "Diary of Charles G. Lee," 22.

30. Samuel E. Grosvenor Diary, June 5, 1864, MS 81588, CTHS. See also Unknown Diary, October 14, 1864, ANHS.

31. Robert H. Kellogg Diary, June 4, September 12, 1864, Robert H. Kellogg Papers, MS 68013, CTHS. Officers at the city jail, however, disagreed. Edmund E. Ryan Diary, September [no day], 1864, PHSC.

32. John S. Ward to Louis Wigfall, "My Dear Sir," April 21, 1862, Camp Chase, Ohio, Papers, Folder 10, VAHS.

33. Gower and Allen, *Pen and Sword*, 659.

34. Frost, *Camp and Prison Journal*, 29.

35. Henry L. Stone to "Dear Cousin Melia," December 5, 1863, Henry Stone Papers, KYHS. See also Ryan Diary, September 28, 1864, PHSC.

36. Nightingale, *Notes on Nursing*, 16fn.

37. James J. Higginson to "Dearest Daddy," November 18, 1862, Higginson Family Papers II, Box 3, MS N-1398, MAHS.

38. Higginson to "My Dear Fellow," November 13, 1863, Higginson Family Papers II, Box 3, MAHS.

39. L. A. Hendrick, "Captivity in Rebeldom," *New York Herald*, January 30, 1864. See also Browne, *Four Years in Secessia*, 242.

40. Gower and Allen, *Pen and Sword*, 599. See also Charles Holbrook Prentiss Diary, March 25, 1863, Letters and Diaries, CWMC, USAHEC.

41. Dennison, *Dennison's Andersonville Diary*, 40.

42. Prentiss Diary, March 27, 1863, Letters and Diaries, CWMC, USAHEC.

43. Eugene R. Sly Diary, May 25, June 21, 1864, United States Civil War Collection, WMU; 1860 U.S. Census, Will County, Ill., population schedule, Lockport, 54, dwelling 499, family 436, Seneca Sly, Eugene Sly; digital image, *Ancestry.com* (http://ancestry

.com); citing NARA microfilm publication M653, roll 238. See also Dennison, *Dennison's Andersonville Diary*, 51.

44. Nightingale, *Notes on Nursing*, 10, 14.

45. Stillé, *History of the Sanitary Commission*, 33; Livermore, *My Story of the War*, 202–3; Humphreys, *Marrow of Tragedy*.

46. "Draft of Sanitary Commission Report No. 19, Camp Inspection Returns," in Geier, Orr, and Reeves, *Huts and History*, 17–25.

47. Henry M. Lazelle to William Hoffman, June 25, 1862, *Official Records*, Ser. II, Vol. 4: 67–68, 68–74. On Lazelle's exchange as a prisoner, see *Official Records*, Ser. II, Vol. 3: 204.

48. Henry W. Bellows to William Hoffman, June 30, 1862, *Official Records*, Ser. II, Vol. 4: 106; see also B. McVickar to Col. J. H. Tucker, June 30, 1862, *Official Records*, Ser. II, Vol. 4: 107–8.

49. William Hoffman to Montgomery C. Meigs, July 1, 1862, *Official Records*, Ser. II, Vol. 4: 110.

50. Melosi, *Sanitary City*, 91, 92–93. See also Tarr, *Search for the Ultimate Sink*, 8–13, 113–22; Montgomery C. Meigs to William Hoffman, July 5, 1862, *Official Records*, Ser. II, Vol. 4: 129; Hoffman to Meigs, July 10, 1862, *Official Records*, Ser. II, Vol. 4: 166; Tarr, "Urban Pollution: Many Long Years Ago," 64–69; Inglis, "Sewers and Sensibilities," 105–30.

51. William Hoffman to Col. J. H. Tucker, July 9, 1862, *Official Records*, Ser. II, Vol. 4: 162; Hesseltine, *Civil War Prisons*, 181.

52. Hoffman to Col. J. H. Tucker, August 1, 1862, *Official Records*, Ser. II, Vol. 4: 324.

53. Henry M. Lazelle to William Hoffman, *Official Records*, July 13, 1862, Ser. II, Vol. 4: 198–200.

54. Henry M. Lazelle to William Hoffman, July 28, 1862, *Official Records*, Ser. II, Vol. 4: 304.

55. Henry M. Lazelle to William Hoffman, August 4, 1862, *Official Records*, Ser. II, Vol. 4: 342.

56. "Whitewashes," *Highland Weekly News* (Hillsboro, Ohio), May 7, 1863.

57. Curtis R. Burke Journal, September 10, 1863, #M 0903, INHS.

58. Joseph K. Barnes letter to Brig. Gen. W. A. Hammond, August 28, 1863, *Official Records*, Ser. II, Vol. 6: 235.

59. A. P. Caraher to A. J. Johnson, April 29, 1864, *Official Records*, Ser. II, Vol. 7: 99.

60. Thomas Hun and Mason F. Cogswell, enclosed in William H. Van Buren to Edwin M. Stanton, May 10, 1863, *Official Records*, Ser. II, Vol. 5: 588.

61. William F. Swalm to J. H. Douglas, November 13, 1864, *Official Records*, Ser. II, Vol. 6: 578.

62. Humphreys, *Marrow of Tragedy*, 252–62.

63. Sanitarians had also promoted flowers, though they did not trust the smell of lilies. Nightingale, *Notes on Nursing*, 60.

64. Gray, *Business of Captivity*, 48; Eugene F. Sanger to Lieut. Lounsbury, enclosed in S. Eastman to William Hoffman, August 17, 1864, *Official Records*, Ser. II, Vol. 7: 604–5; Pickenpaugh, *Captives in Gray*, 207.

65. Gray, *Business of Captivity*, 48, 152; Gillispie, *Andersonvilles of the North*, 199–200; *Official Records*, Ser. II, Vol. 7: 1003–5, 1093; Pickenpaugh, *Captives in Gray*, 213.

66. *Richmond Enquirer*, July 14, 1862; Rosen, "'Knowing' Industrial Pollution," 567–73; see also Rosen, "Noisome, Noxious, and Offensive Vapors," 49–82.

67. *Richmond Examiner*, September 24, 1862. After the war, John Ransom recalled that "the stench" from Belle Isle prevented civilians from coming to gawk at the prisoners. Ransom, *John Ransom's Diary*, 108.

68. "City Intelligence. The Libby Prison and Its Contents," *Richmond Enquirer*, February 2, 1864.

69. John Wilkins to John H. Winder, September 5, 1863, *Official Records*, Ser. II, Vol. 6: 262–63; Isaac H. Carrington to John Winder, November 18, 1863, enclosed in Robert Ould to Solomon A. Meredith, November 21, 1863, *Official Records*, Ser. II, Vol. 6: 544–48.

70. G. William Semple to William A. Carrington, March 6, 1864, enclosed in Carrington to Winder, March 23, 1864, *Official Records*, Ser. II, Vol. 6: 1087.

71. William A. Carrington to John Winder, March 23, 1864, *Official Records*, Ser. II, Vol. 6: 1085. See also Sanders, *While in the Hands of the Enemy*, 192.

72. T. P. Atkinson, John W. Holland, and E. J. Bell to James A. Seddon, enclosure in T. P. Atkinson to James A. Seddon, January 2, 1864, *Official Records*, Ser. II, Vol. 6: 888–89.

73. E. J. Eldridge to Lamar Cobb, May 6, 1864, enclosed in Howell Cobb to S. Cooper, May 5, 1864, *Official Records*, Ser. II, Vol. 7: 120–21; Walter Bowie to R. H. Chilton, May 10, 1864, *Official Records*, Ser. II, Vol. 7: 137; Thomas P. Turner to John H. Winder, May 25, 1864, *Official Records*, Ser. II, Vol. 7: 167.

74. Isaiah H. White to Captain Bowie, May [no date], 1864, *Official Records*, Ser. II, Vol. 7: 125.

75. Isaiah H. White, "Sanitary Report," June 30, 1864, *Official Records*, Ser. II, Vol. 7: 426.

76. Isaiah H. White to "Colonel Chandler," August 2, 1864, *Official Records*, Ser. II, Vol. 7: 525; Isaiah H. White to John H. Winder, August 6, 1864, *Official Records*, Ser. II, Vol. 7: 558.

77. Walter Bowie to R. H. Chilton, May 10, 1864, *Official Records*, Ser. II, Vol. 7: 136; Futch, *Andersonville Prison*, 11–29; Marvel, *Andersonville*, x–xi.

78. Henry Wirz to John H. Winder, September 24, 1864, *Official Records*, Ser. II, Vol. 7: 758–59.

79. "Morning Reports of Federal Prisoners of War Confined at Andersonville Prison, Georgia, 1864–1865," Record Group 249, Records of the Commissary General of Prisoners, 1861–1865, M1303, roll 6; Pickenpaugh, *Johnson's Island*, 10, 104; Speer, *Portals to Hell*, 327.

80. Jones, "Observations upon the Diseases," *Official Records*, Ser. II, Vol. 8: 593, 599; Jones, "Investigations upon the Diseases," *Sanitary Memoirs*, 1:495, 506.

81. Jones, "Investigations upon the Diseases," *Sanitary Memoirs*, 1:507.

82. Louis Manigault to "Ma Chere Femme," September 18, 1864, Louis Manigault Family Papers, LC.

83. Hoster Diary, June 20, 1864, MARBL, EU; Urban, *My Experiences*, 558. Vaughter, *Prison Life in Dixie*, 65–68; Marvel, *Andersonville*, 179–80, 182–87.

84. Andrews, *War-Time Journal*, 64, 78.

85. House Special Committee, *Report on the Treatment of Prisoners*, 81.

86. U.S. Congress, *The Trial of Henry Wirz*, 117–18, 124, 127, 742.

Chapter Three

1. William H. Haigh to "My Dear Kate," May 24, 1865, William H. Haigh Papers, MS #2649-z, SHC.

2. Foote, *Gentlemen and the Roughs*, 48.

3. 1860 U.S. Census, Cumberland County, N.C., population schedule, Fayetteville, 257A (stamped), dwelling 1221, family 1157, William H. Haigh; digital image, *Ancestry.com* (http://ancestry.com); citing NARA microfilm publication M653, roll 894; Haigh to "My Dear Kate," May 24, 1865, Haigh Papers, SHC.

4. Haigh to "My Dear Kate," May 24, 1865, Haigh Papers, SHC.

5. "The Senses—Touch," *Harper's New Monthly Magazine* 12, no. 68 (January 1856), 179.

6. On the environmental history of the Civil War, see Drake, *The Blue, the Gray, and the Green*; Nelson, *Ruin Nation*; Brady, *War upon the Land*; Meier, *Nature's Civil War*; Bell, *Mosquito Soldiers*; Ouchley, *Flora and Fauna*; Fiege, *Republic of Nature*, 199–227.

7. On touch, see Classen, *The Deepest Sense*; Smith, *Sensing the Past*, 93–116; Jenner, "Tasting Lichfield, Touching China," 647–70. Touch has been explored most frequently in the history of medicine. See essays by Roy Porter, "The Rise of the Physical Examination," and Sander Gilman, "Touch, Sexuality, and Disease," in Bynum and Porter, *Medicine and the Five Senses*, 179–97, 198–24. On lice, see Reed, Light, Allen, and Kirchman, "Pair of Lice Lost or Parasites Regained," 1–11; Zinsser, *Rats, Lice, and History*, 170–74.

8. Brumgardt, *Civil War Nurse*, 115–16.

9. Meier, *Nature's Civil War*, 2, 100–104; Brown, *Foul Bodies*, 305–20; Watson, "The Man with the Dirty Black Beard," 1–26.

10. Zinsser, *Rats, Lice, and History*, 185–88; Thomas, *Man and the Natural World*, 57–58.

11. Brown, *Foul Bodies*, 138–40, 150; Wesley, *Works of John Wesley*, 12:248.

12. [Wood], *History of Insects*, 13–14; Kirby, *On the Power, Wisdom and Goodness of God*, 2:316; Sims, *Story of My Life*, 69.

13. Works Progress Administration, Federal Writers Project: *Slave Narrative Project*, Vol. 2, *Arkansas*, Part 7, interview with Clara Walker, 22; Vol. 4, *Georgia*, Part 2, interview with Charlie Hudson, 227; Vol. 4, *Georgia*, Part 1, interview with Della Briscoe, 132; Vol. 11, *North Carolina*, Part 1, interview with Lindsey Faucette, 305. See also Vol. 4, *Georgia*, Part 3, interview with Henry Rogers, 222.

14. Curran, *John Dooley*, 142–43; de Wolfe, *Touched by Fire*, 53; Daniel, *Soldiering in the Army of Tennessee*, 17.

15. [United States War Department], *Revised United States Army Regulations*, 21–22; Foote, *Gentlemen and the Roughs*, 48.

16. Charles Ackley to "Dear Wife," January 3, 1865, Charles Thomas Ackley Letters to His Wife, MSC0541, UIAL. See also Ackley to "Dear Wife," June 2, 1864, Ackley Letters, UIAL.

17. Herbert E. Carpenter to "Dear Friend Martin," January 25, 1863, Herbert E. Carpenter letter, MS 38835, LVA; 1860 U.S. Census, Middlesex County, Conn., population schedule, East Hampton, 634, 635, 637, 648, 649 (stamped), dwellings 961, 971, 981, 1–75 1084, families 224, 234, 247, 351, 361, Newell Root, Gilbert West, Hubert Carpenter, Frederic Nichols, Leander Rich; digital image, *Ancestry.com* (http://ancestry.com); citing NARA microfilm publication M653, roll 83; 1860 U.S. Census, Hartford County, Conn., population schedule, East Hartford, 12 (stamped), dwelling 70, family 83, Martin Roberts, Ira T. Roberts; digital image, *Ancestry.com* (http://ancestry.com); citing NARA microfilm publication M653, roll 79.

18. Henry T. Sellow to "Kind Friend Martin," February 27, 1863, Martin L. Roberts Letters, MS 42191, LVA; Carpenter to "Dear Friend Martin," January 25, 1863, Carpenter Letter, LVA; Meier, "The Man Who Has Nothing to Lose," 86. On discipline, cleanliness, and manhood, see Foote, *Gentlemen and the Roughs*, 47–51.

19. "Letter from Captain Baker," enclosure in John A. Kennedy to W. H. Seward, July 10, 1861, *Official Records*, Ser. II, Vol. 3: 37.

20. Thomas T. Tunstall to W. H. Seward, April 23, 1862, *Official Records*, Ser. II, Vol. 3: 474.

21. Williams and Kutzler, *Prison Pens*, 122.

22. Osborn, "Writings of a Confederate Prisoner of War," 82–84.

23. Stephenson and Davis, "Civil War Diary of William Micajah Barrow," 713, 721, 726.

24. Gower and Allen, *Pen and Sword*, 252, 253, 255, 269, 599.

25. James L. Cooper Memoir, 13, Civil War Collection, Box 12, Folder 11, TNSLA.

26. Elisha Rice Reed Diary, January 15, 1862, Elisha Rice Reed Papers, Wis Mss 115S, WIHS.

27. Niccum, "Documents," 284.

28. Jacob Heffelfinger Diary, July 9, 1862, CWTI, Box 14, USAHEC.

29. Anonymous Diary, August 13, 1864, "Diary of a Union P.O.W. (Captain Thompson?)," Hench Papers pertaining to the Civil War, 1861–1865, MS 8474-u, UVA.

30. George C. Parker to family, October 16, 1862, George C. Parker Letters, CWTI, Box 21, USAHEC. See also Anonymous Diary, 1863, of the 18th Conn. Infantry, no pp; "Army Life and Prison Experience," 12, MS 0290, UTN.

31. James A. Bell to "My Dear Brother," September 30, 1862, Bell Papers, DEPA; Brown, *Foul Bodies*, 364. On conditions in 1864, see Ellery H. Webster Diary, June 25, 1864, UVT.

32. "Humors of Prison Life," *Richmond Enquirer*, January 4, 1862; *New York Times*, March 4, 1862; Speer, *Portals to Hell*, 25; Fairchild, *History of the 27th Regiment N.Y. Vols.*, 203.

33. Jennings, "Prisoner of the Confederacy," 314.

34. John Harrold, *Libby, Andersonville, Florence*, 34. See also George Clarkson Diary, June 21, 1864, ANHS. After the Civil War, John Ransom recalled the Pemberton Prison in a similar way. "The lice are very thick. You can see them all over the floors,

walls, &c. in fact everything literally covered with them; they seem much larger than the stock on Belle Isle and a different species." Ransom, *John Ransom's Diary*, 45.

35. [James H. Franklin], "Prison Diary Fort Delaware and Point Lookout," 8, August 1, 1863, CMLSC, VAHS.

36. Robert Bingham Diary, Vol. 1, August 11, 28, 1863, Robert Bingham Papers, Folder 3, MS 03731-z, SHC.

37. [Franklin], "Prison Diary," 8, August 1, 1863, CMLSC, VAHS.

38. Mary M. Stockton Terry Diary, August 1, 1864, Mss5:1 T2795:1, VAHS. See also Heslin, "The Diary of a Union Soldier," 239–40.

39. Frederic A. James Diary, February [no day], 1864, Frederic Augustus James Papers, MS N-2346, MAHS.

40. Witt, *Lincoln's Code*, 332.

41. Pickenpaugh, *Camp Chase*, 20.

42. George W. Pennington to Ruth A. Pennington," May 15, 1863, George W. Pennington Diary and Letters, MS #20, Civil War Collection, Union Documents, Box 20, Folder 9, MARBL, EU.

43. "Our Army Correspondence," Muscatine (Iowa) *Weekly Journal*, May 23, 1862, 4; "Our Falmouth Correspondence," *New York Herald*, December 3, 1862, 5.

44. "The Song of Belle Island," Newell Burch Diary, vii–viii, SC 248, WIHS.

45. Pickenpaugh, *Camp Chase*, 31, 42, 109; Gillispie, *Andersonvilles of the North*, 78, 136; William J. Hine Diary, February 11, 1865, Civil War Collection, Box 6, Folder 13, TNSLA; Franklin J. Krause Diary, memoranda pages, Andersonville Civil War Diary, MS 14096, UVA; Henry Stone to "Dear Jim," Camp Douglas, August 19, 1863, Stone Family Papers, MMS 16, KYHS; De Witt C. Spaulding Diary, May 11, 1864, #9631Aa2, BHLUM.

46. Haigh to "My Dear Kate," May 24, 1865, Haigh Papers, SHC; Gillispie, *Andersonvilles of the North*, 136.

47. Bingham Diary, Vol. 1, August 11, September 27, 1863, Bingham Papers, Folder 3, SHC.

48. Frohman, *Rebels on Lake Erie*, 16; Gray, *Business of Captivity*, 33, 105; Williams and Kutzler, *Prison Pens*, 126; *Official Records*, Ser. II, Vol. 6: 740, 1004.

49. Henry B. Sparks Diary, April 21, 1864, #SC 0020, INHS; Krause Diary, memoranda pages, Andersonville Civil War Diary, MS 14096, UVA; Frank Jennings Reminiscences, CWTI, Box 16, USAHEC; Futch, *History of Andersonville Prison*, 19; *Official Records*, Ser. II, Vol. 7: 121, 124, 136.

50. Jonathan P. Stowe Diary, November 28, 1861, CWTI, Box 26, USAHEC.

51. Heffelfinger Diary, December 19, 1862, May 9, August 11, 1864, CWTI, Box 14, USAHEC.

52. [Franklin], "Prison Diary," 10, August 1, 1863, CMLSC, VAHS.

53. John A. Baer Diary, July 12, 1864, ANHS.

54. Krause Diary, August 29, May 27–August 29, 1864, Andersonville Diary, UVA.

55. James Diary, August 15, 22, 1864, James Papers, MAHS.

56. *Rochester Daily Union and Advertiser* (Rochester, New York), August 12, 1864; Gray, *Business of Captivity*, 23; Gray, "Captivating Captives," 16–32.

57. Bingham Diary, Vol. 1, July 9, 11, 12, September 27, 1863, Bingham Papers, MS #3731-z, Folder 3, SHC.

58. Asa Dean Mathews Diary, July 12, 14, 1864, MSA 371:12, VTHS.

59. James to "My Dear Wife," January 22, 1864, James Papers, MAHS; James Diary, February [no day], 1864, March 4, 1864, July 16, 27, 1864, James Papers, MAHS.

60. Parker to family, October 16, 1862, Parker Letters, Letters and Diaries, CWTI, Box 21, USAHEC; McLaughlin, "Diary of Salisbury Prison by James W. Eberhart," 243.

61. William J. Flowers to "Friend Isham," October 11, 1862, Hubbard Family Papers, UVT.

62. William T. Peabody Diary, June 27, 1864, ANHS.

63. Charles B. Stone Diary, February 22–25, 1863, UVT; James Diary, February [no day], 1864, James Papers, MAHS; Haigh to "My Dear Kate," May 24, 1865, Haigh Papers, SHC.

64. Parker to family, October 16, 1862, Parker Letters, Letters and Diaries, CWTI, Box 21, USAHEC. See also Anonymous Diary, 1863, of the 18th Conn. Infantry, no pp., CTHS; "Army Life and Prison Experience of Major Charles G. Davis," 12, UTN.

65. Stone Diary, February 22, 1863, UVT.

66. William T. Wilson Diary, June 23, 24, 1864, OHHC.

67. Reynolds and Seal, All for the Flag, 177, 184.

68. Henry Van der Weyde, "Prison Realities," ca. 1864 and Weyde, "Flanking the Enemy," ca. 1864, LVA. The original is at the Danville Museum of Fine Arts and History, Danville, Virginia.

69. John Jacob Omenhausser, "A Lady Visitor Come to Camp to See the Sights." John Jacob Omenhausser, Civil War sketchbook, Point Lookout, Maryland, 1864–1865, UMD.

70. Mathews Diary, July 14, 1864, VTHS.

71. Stone Diary, February 28, March 2, 1863, UVT.

72. George Harry Weston Diary, October 5, 14, 1863, RUB Bay 0037:06, DU.

73. "Register of Enlistments in the United States Army, 1798–1914," M233, roll 198, NARA.

74. William Duncan Wilkins Diary, September 5, 1862, William Duncan Wilkins Papers, MS S61935, LC.

75. James Harsen Sawyer Record Book, 106, MS 96780, CTHS. See also Kelley, What I Saw and Suffered, 26; Horace Smith Diary, July 26, 1864, SC 504, WIHS; William Lloyd Tritt Diary, February 16, 1864, M92-141, WIHS. See also McLaughlin, "Diary of Salisbury Prison by James W. Eberhart," 243.

76. Sawyer Record Book, 106, CTHS; Anonymous Diary, 1863, of the 18th Conn. Infantry, June 24, 1863, CTHS.

77. Nehemiah Solon Diary, June 1, 1864, MS 78606a, CTHS.

78. Bryan and Lankford, Eye of the Storm, 170.

79. Smith Diary, August 15, 1863, WIHS. See also Dougherty, Prison Diary, 43; Bryan and Lankford, Eye of the Storm, 228; Jennings, "Prisoner of the Confederacy," 315.

80. Curtis, History of the Twenty-Fourth Michigan, 434–35.

81. Solon Diary, May 28, 1864, CTHS. See also Alonzo Tuttle Decker Diary, August 23, 1864, ANHS; Mahood, Charlie Mosher's Civil War, 240.

82. Ransom, John Ransom's Diary, 11, 51, 80.

83. Genoways and Genoways, *Perfect Picture of Hell*, 31.

84. Jonathan Boynton Memoirs, 28, Box 13, Folder 11, Letters and Diaries, CWMC, USAHEC. See also Frederick E. Schmitt Reminiscence, ca. 1914, 4, Micro 337, WIHS; A. A. Van Vlack, "A Glimpse of Life in a Rebel Prison in 1864 & 1865," Van Vlack Family Papers, Box 1, #89210, BHLUM.

85. Stephen Alfred Forbes Diary, July 10, 1862, Stephen Alfred Forbes Papers, IHLC MS 815, UIUC; Forbes, *The Insect, the Farmer*, 2–3; Russell, *War and Nature*, 23.

Chapter Four

1. Urban, *My Experiences*, 519–20; Stephen Minot Weld Diary, August 13, 1864, MS N-2378, MAHS; U.S. Sanitary Commission, *Narrative of Privations*, 163; William Lloyd Tritt Diary, July 4, 1864, M92-141, WIHS.

2. David Kennedy Diary, June 22, August 9, 17–18, 1864, MS P519, MNHS. 1860 U.S. Census, Shelby County, Ohio, population schedule, Clinton Township, 498B (stamped), dwelling 455, family 455, Edison S Kilburn, David Kenedy [*sic*]; digital image, *Ancestry.com* (http://ancestry.com); citing NARA microfilm publication M653, roll 1036. Kennedy instructed that, if found, his diary should be returned to E. S. Kilburn. On the furlough myth, see Marvel, *Andersonville*, 158.

3. Kennedy Diary, February 7, April 24, May 8, May 15, June 26, 1864, MNHS. On Sundays and Christian manhood, see Foote, *Gentlemen and the Roughs*, 21–22.

4. Kennedy Diary, May 2, July 19, August 19, 1864, memoranda section, MNHS; [Atwater and Barton], *A List of the Union Soldiers*, 44–50.

5. Kennedy Diary, September 5, 7, 10, 12, 14, 20, 1864, MNHS; Morning Reports of Federal Prisoners of War Confined at Andersonville Prison, Georgia, 1864–1865, Record Group 249, Records of the Commissary General of Prisoners, 1861–1865, M1303, roll 6; Marvel, *Andersonville*, 198–203.

6. Francis A. Boyle Diary, May 12, 1864, Francis A. Boyle Books, MS #1555-z, SHC. For listening as part of the experience of soldiers and civilians, see Smith, *Listening to Nineteenth-Century America*, 198–237; Hess, *Union Soldier in Battle*, 15–28, 143–57.

7. Root, *Tramp! Tramp! Tramp! Or, The Prisoners Hope.*

8. Silber, *Songs of the Civil War*, 37; McWhirter, *Battle Hymns*, 168–69. See also George Washington Hall Diary, May 13, 1864, LC; Domschcke, *Twenty Months in Captivity*, 29; Byers, *What I Saw in Dixie*, 4.

9. Campbell, *Civil War Diary*, 21.

10. James McCaggen Mayo Diary, August 7, 1863, LC.

11. George A. Hitchcock Diary, May 16, 1864, MS N-2282, MAHS.

12. Anson Butler to "My Dear Wife," May 25, 1863, Anson R. Butler Letters, MSC0001, UIAL.

13. Marcus Collis Diary, May 8, 1864, ANHS.

14. Robert Kellogg Diary, April 25, 28, 1864, Robert H. Kellogg Papers, MS 68013, CTHS.

15. Levin, *Remembering the Battle of the Crater*, 7; Samuel Henderson Diary, June 10, 1864, ANHS.

16. [James H. Franklin], "Prison Diary Fort Delaware and Point Lookout," 4–5, n.d. [July 1863], CMLSC, VAHS. See also Campbell, *Civil War Diary*, 24.

17. E. L. Cox Diary, July 3 and 4, 1864, Mss5:1C8394:1, VAHS.

18. Smith, *Listening to Nineteenth-Century America*, 67–68; Faust, *Republic of Suffering*, 141; Rable, *Civil Wars*, 117–18.

19. Ripple, *Dancing along the Deadline*, 14.

20. Kelley, *What I Saw and Suffered*, 30.

21. Wood, *Near Andersonville*, 60, 71–82, 79; Davis, "'Near Andersonville,'" 96–105.

22. Alonzo Merrill Keeler Diary, October 8, 9, 1863, Keeler Family Papers, BHLUM.

23. Robert Bingham Diary, July 10, 1863, in Robert Bingham Papers, Folder 3, MS #03731-z, SHC.

24. John A. Baer Diary, August 14, 1864, ANHS.

25. Kellogg Diary, May 8, 1864, Kellogg Papers, CTHS. See also Lewis C. Bisbee Diary, May 25, 1864, Lewis C. Bisbee Papers, MS P1268, MNHS. On reading and listening, see Smith, *Listening to Nineteenth-Century America*, 2.

26. James Burton Diary, May 19, 1864, MS # 120, MARBL, EU.

27. *A Voice from Rebel Prisons*, 15; Toney, *Privations of a Private*, 87–88; George Marion Shearer Diary, January 10, February 2, 4, 1865, MSC0080, Digital Collections, UIAL; James Vance Diary, August 4, 1864, James W. Vance Papers, VFM 1834, OHHC. A typescript is also available at Andersonville National Historic Site.

28. Baer Diary, July 24, 1864, ANHS.

29. Alonzo Merrill Keeler Diary, October 9, 1863, Keeler Family Papers, BHLUM; Cavada, *Libby Life*, 36; Beaudry, *Libby Chronicle*; Fort Delaware Prison Times, 1865, LC.

30. Rath, *How Early America Sounded*, 51–57; Smith, *Listening to Nineteenth-Century America*, 57–58; Wells, *Civil War Time*, 1–7. See also Adam, *Timewatch*; John Urry, "Time, Leisure, and Social Identity," 131–49; "Register of Claims for Lost Personal Property," Record Group 249, Records of the Commissary General of Prisoners, Entry 84, Vol. 1, NARA.

31. John Alexander Gibson Diary, November 29, 1864, Gibson Family Papers, Mss2 G3598 b 1, VAHS; "General Orders No. 90," November 5, 1864, Isaiah H. White Papers, DU. See also Frohman, *Rebels on Lake Erie*, 15.

32. Jacob Heffelfinger Diary, December 13 through December 31, 1862, CWTI, Box 14, USAHEC.

33. Thomas W. Springer Diary, September 19, 20, and 21, 1864, MS 7093-v, UVA. Nearly thirty years later, one prisoner recalled that the "grub call" sounded "like sweet music." Briscoe Goodheart, "Belle Isle Revisited," *National Tribune* (Washington, D.C.), November 10, 1892.

34. Smith, *Listening to Nineteenth-Century America*, 95–103.

35. [Ingraham], *South-West*, Vol. 2: 52, 54.

36. "Bells for Confederate Service," Montgomery (Ala.) *Daily Advertiser*, April 17, 1862.

37. Daniel F. Cooledge Diary, February 2, 23, March 16, June 1, June 8, 1862, MSC 197, VTHS.

38. Cooledge Diary, June 1, June 8, 1862, VTHS; Rable, *God's Almost Chosen Peoples*, 95–97; Smith, *Listening to Nineteenth-Century America*, 202–3, 213–14, 227, 232.

39. Cooledge Diary, June 29, 30, 1862, August 3, 1862, VTHS.

40. Bingham Diary, Vol. 1, July 5, July 12, August 9, 1863, Bingham Papers, Folder 3, SHC; Robert Bingham to Henrietta Bingham, March 14, 1932, Bingham Papers, Folder 1, SHC; Williams, *Intellectual Manhood*, 110; Foote, *Gentlemen and the Roughs*, 42.

41. Arthur Wyman Diary, August 4 and 7, 1864, Letters and Diaries, CWMC, Box 127, Folder 1, USAHEC; William T. Peabody Diary, August 14, 1864, ANHS; Baer Diary, August 14, 1864, ANHS.

42. Peabody Diary, June 5, 1864, ANHS.

43. William Duncan Wilkins Diary, August 18, 1862, William Duncan Wilkins Papers, MSS61935, LC. For entries that reference sound through the monotony of Sunday and other days, see George Clarkson Diary, July 3, 10, 1864, ANHS; Sheldon R. Curtiss Diary, September 11, 1864, ANHS; John Duff Diary, February 19, 1865, ANHS; Burton Diary, July 10, 1864, MARBL, EU; Heslin, "Diary of a Union Soldier," 243, 272.

44. Heffelfinger Diary, July 6, 1862, CWTI, Box 14, USAHEC.

45. Gower and Allen, *Pen and Sword*, 619. See also Franklin J. Krause Diary, July 17, 1864, Andersonville Civil War Diary, MS 14096, UVA; Nehemiah Solon Diary, May 29, 1864, MS 78606a, CTHS; Heslin, "Diary of a Union Soldier," 270.

46. Kennedy Diary, June 12, July 31, 1864, MNHS. See also Wilbur Wightman Gramling Diary, June 19, July 3, 1864, RG 90000, M88-070, Carton 1, Folder 1, FLSA.

47. Asa Dean Mathews Diary, August 28, September 4, 11, 1864, MSA 371:12, VTHS. See also Henry W. Tisdale Diary, May 29, 1864, ANHS. See also Robins, *They Have Left Us Here to Die*, 29.

48. Mary M. Stockton Terry Diary, July 3 and 10, 1864, Mss5:1 T2795:1, VAHS. See also George W. Pennington Diary, May 15, 1864, George W. Pennington Diary and Letters, MS #20, Civil War Collection, Union Documents, Box 20, Folder 9, MARBL, EU.

49. Bisbee Diary, August 14, 1864, Bisbee Papers, MNHS. For prisoner singing and preaching on Sundays, see Tisdale Diary, July 17, 1864, ANHS; Joseph B. Fenton Diary, July 10, 1864, ANHS; Kellogg Diary, April 24, 1864, Kellogg Papers, CTHS; Niccum, "Documents," 277, 280; Helmreich, "Diary of Charles G. Lee," 17. On "captive congregations," see Rable, *God's Almost Chosen Peoples*, 365–69.

50. Baer Diary, July 10, 1864, ANHS. See also Vaughter, *Prison Life in Dixie*, 62; Abbott, *Prison Life in the South*, 55, 68.

51. John Taylor to his mother, August 24, 1864, in Meissner and Meissner, *I Had Rather Lose a Limb and Be Free*, 42. The bylaws of the Christian Association at Fort Delaware required that music open and close each meeting, Christian Association records, 1864–1865, Boyle Books, Folder 2, SHC.

52. Bingham Diary, Vol. 1, September 6, 1863, Folder 3, SHC.

53. "One Hundredth Advance on Richmond," *Richmond Enquirer*, February 9, 1864.

54. John B. Gallison Diary, May 22, 1864, John B. Gallison Papers, MS N-1266, MAHS. See also Byrne, "A General behind Bars," 69, 75.

55. George E. Albee Diary, September 1, 2, and 3, 1864, MS 41695, LVA; Springer Diary, September 1, 2, 3, 6, 7, 16, 17, 21, 1864, UVA; McLaughlin, "Diary of Salisbury

Prison by James W. Eberhart," 220–24; James W. Vance Diary, June 1, 1864, OHHC; Keeler Diary, October 15, 1863, Keeler Family Papers, BHLUM.

56. Smith, "Of Bells, Booms, Sounds, and Silences," 16–18; "Under the Union Guns," *New York Times*, May 10, 1891. See also Urban, *My Experiences*, 607–8.

57. Burton Diary, September 27, 1864, MARBL, EU.

58. "Under the Union Guns," *New York Times*, May 10, 1891. See also Nathanial Rollins to Senator Tim O. Howe, January 26, 1865, and Rollins Diary, July 29–October 5, 1864, Nathaniel Rollins Papers, Wis Mss UW, WIHS.

59. Heffelfinger Diary, September 14, 1864, CWTI, Box 14, USAHEC. See also Luther Guiteau Billings Memoir, 108, Luther Guiteau Billings Articles and Photographs, LC; Kellogg Diary, September 18, 1864, Kellogg Papers, CTHS; John Collins Welch, "An Escape from Prison during the Civil War, 1864," ca. 1868, 3, SCL; Armstrong, "Cahaba to Charleston," 120.

60. Heffelfinger Diary, October 5, 1864, CWTI, Box 14, USAHEC.

61. Franklin, "Prison Diary," November 9, 1864, CMLSC, VAHS; "Island Minstrels," Joseph Mason Kern Papers, Folder 2, MS 03536-z, SHC; William J. Hine Diary, January 4, January 10, 1865, Civil War Collection, Box 6, Folder 13, TNSLA; Libby Prison Minstrels Collection, 1863, Wis Mss 165S, WIHS.

62. William Peel Diary, June 23, 1864, MS Z 1797.000, MDAH; Pickenpaugh, *Johnson's Island*, 48; Sylvester Crossley Diary, January 13, 16, 1865, MS-042, Special Collections, GC; McWhirter, *Battle Hymns*, 169–70.

63. Crossley Diary, January 16, 1865, GC.

64. Green, *Democracy in the Old South*, 111–56. See also Smith, *Listening to Nineteenth-Century America*, 21, 95–96.

65. Thomas Hall to his mother, July 4, 1862, Thomas W. Hall Papers, MS #2390, Box 1, Folder 8, MDHS.

66. James Taswell Mackey Diary, July 4, 1864, CMLSC, VAHS.

67. Bingham Diary, Vol. 1, July 3, 1863, Bingham Papers, Folder 3, SHC. See also Joseph W. Mauck Diary, July 4, 1864, CMLSC, VAHS.

68. Terry Diary, July 4, 1864, VAHS. On the memory of the American Revolution in soldier writings, see McPherson, *For Cause and Comrades*, 18–19, 104–6, 110–13; and McPherson, *What They Fought For*, 6–10, 27–30, 45, 50–51.

69. Niccum, "Documents," 282–83.

70. Eugene R. Sly Diary, July 4, 1864, United States Civil War Collection, WMU. See also Alonzo Tuttle Decker Diary, July 4, 1864, ANHS; Samuel L. Foust Diary, July 4, 1864, ANHS; Collis Diary, July 4, 1864, ANHS; Josephus Hudson Diary, July 4, 1864, ANHS; George M. Hinkley Diary, July 4, 1864, MS #File 1864 April 11, WIHS; John L. Hoster Diary, July 4, 1864, MS #464, MARBL, EU.

71. Mourning on the Fourth of July had antebellum precedents among political dissenters from the Federalists to the radical abolitionists. Waldstreicher, *In the Midst of Perpetual Fetes*, 24–25, 211–14, 350–51.

72. Domschcke, *Twenty Months in Captivity*, 29. See also Rollins Diary, July 4, 1863 and July 4, 1864, WIHS.

73. Heffelfinger Diary, July 4, 1862, CWTI, Box 14, USAHEC; Bisbee Diary, July 4, 1864, MNHS. Prisoners at Salisbury in 1862 drafted a program for their celebration.

Willis Peck Clarke Papers, MSS 114, WIHS. See also "Capt. H. H. Todd," *National Tribune*, February 13, 1908.

74. Pollan and Gilbert, "Camp Ford Diary," 20.

75. Christian L. Kinder Diary, July 4, 1864, ANHS; Kellogg Diary, July 4, 1864, Kellogg Papers, CTHS. For a similar account at Macon, Georgia, see Abbott, *Prison Life in the South*, 78–79; "An Incident of the Late War," *National Tribune*, December 3, 1881.

76. McWhirter, *Battle Hymns*, 41–48.

77. George William Brown to George C. Schattuck, February 19, 1862, George W. Brown Collection, MS 2398, MDHS.

78. Brown to his brother-in-law George C. Schattuck, January 31, 1862, Brown Collection, MDHS.

79. Bingham Diary, Vol. 1, July 12, 1863, Bingham Papers, Folder 3, SHC.

80. White and White, "Listening to Southern Slavery," 247–48. See also Plagg, "Strangers in a Strange Land," 227–84.

81. Reynolds and Seal, *All for the Flag*, 212.

82. Glazier, *The Capture, the Prison Pen, and the Escape*, 154.

83. Manning, *What This Cruel War Was Over*, 13; McWhirter, *Battle Hymns*, 152–55; McPherson, *For Cause and Comrades*, Ch. 9.

84. Hall to his mother, January 1, 1862, Hall Papers, MDHS.

85. Heslin, "Diary of a Union Soldier," 247.

86. Bryan and Lankford, *Eye of the Storm*, 178. See also Cornelius, *Music of the Civil War Era*, 110–14; John J. Sherman, "The Prisoner Who Sang at Belle Isle," *National Tribune*, February 21, 1884; Sherman, "The Song That Was Sung and Belle Isle," *National Tribune*, April 17, 1884.

87. Mayo Diary, August 17, 22, 1863, LC; William N. Davis to father, December 17, 1863, Davis Family Papers, MS C D, FHS; Sabre, *Nineteen Months a Prisoner*, 92.

88. Northup, *Twelve Years a Slave*, 57–58; Johnson, *River of Dark Dreams*, 209–10; Kennedy Diary, May 8, 1864, MNHS; Samuel J. Gibson Diary, May 18, 1864, Samuel J. Gibson Diary and Correspondence, LC.

89. Hiram Eddy to "My dear wife," Salisbury, May 19, 1862, Hiram Eddy Papers, MS 78637, CTHS. See also Alfred D. Burdick Diary, December 16, 1864, Micro 37, WIHS; James Canon Diary, January 13, 1865, WIHS; Tritt Diary, January 21, 1864, WIHS.

90. Charles Chapin Diary, July 4, 5, 1864, quoted in unidentified letter to "My Dear George," February 10, 1865, Charles Chapin Letter, Mss-18 #119, VTHS; Burton Diary, May 16, 1864, MARBL, EU.

91. Frank T. Bennett, "Narrative of Lieut. Col. F. T. Bennett," June 15, 1862, Frank T. Bennett Papers, RL.30205, DU.

92. Charles H. Blinn Diary, June 22, July 4, 1862, UVT.

93. Gower and Allen, *Pen and Sword*, 621.

94. Samuel B. Boyd to "My dear wife," Camp Chase Ohio, March 2, 1865, Samuel B. Boyd Papers, MS 0871, UTN. See also Thomas Lafayette Beadles Diary, April 5, 1864, MDAH.

95. Peel Diary, March 26, 1864, MDAH; Franklin, "Prison Diary," August 9, 1863, CMLSC, VAHS.

96. Frederic A. James to "My Dear Little Nellie," May 6, 1864, Frederic Augustus James Papers, MS N-2346, MAHS; James Diary, March 14, 1864, James Papers, MAHS. [Atwater and Barton], *A List of the Union Soldiers*, 72.

97. John White Scott to his wife, April 6, 1862, John White Scott Papers, LC; Asa Dean Mathews Diary, July 5, 1864, MSA 371:12, VTHS; J. H. H., "Three Days among the Yankee Prisoners," *Macon Telegraph*, June 8, 1864; White and White, *Sounds of Slavery*, 30–31.

98. Faust, *Republic of Suffering*, 21–22.

99. "The Wounded of Two Armies," *Richmond Examiner*, May 18, 1864; Nelson, *Ruin Nation*, 185.

100. William G. Bonsell to Miss Pond, February 3, 1867, John Pond Papers RG 90000, M80-02, Carton 1, Folder 1, FLSA.

101. Lt. Walker, "Half Past Ten O'Clock," Moncure Autograph Album, CMLSC, VAHS. John K. Farris wrote a similar poem, imagining the bad dreams of a mother in Tennessee and the sounds of grief. John K. Farris Diary, MS #343, MARBL, EU.

102. William H. Haigh to "My Dear Kate," June 1, 1865, William H. Haigh Papers, MS 02649-z, SHC.

103. Thornton, "The Prison Diary of Adjutant Francis Atherton Boyle, C.S.A.," 82, 82fn70.

Chapter Five

1. "Abstract from Monthly Returns of the Principal U.S. Military Prisons," December 1862, January 1863, December 1863, and December 1864, *Official Records*, Ser. II, Vol. 8: 988, 993, 999.

2. "For the Chester Standard. A Christmas Dinner at Fort Delaware in 1862," undated newspaper clipping, Esther B. Cheesborough Papers, 1852–1890, SCL. The undated clipping was published sometime after Stonewall Jackson's death in May 1863 because it refers to a relative of "the lamentable Jackson."

3. My confidence in her authorship comes from the existence of a clipping of this article with an accounting of the donations in the Cheesborough Papers, Manuscript Division, SCL. Sutherland, "Rise and Fall of Esther B. Cheesborough," 22, 24, 30–31.

4. "A Christmas Dinner at Fort Delaware," Cheesborough Papers; Esther B. Cheesborough Notebook, 1862–1863, Cheesborough Papers, 1852–1890, SCL.

5. Pickenpaugh, *Camp Chase*, 107–10; Pickenpaugh, *Captives in Gray*, 180–81; Pickenpaugh, *Johnson's Island*, 78–84; Gray, *Business of Captivity*, 88; Springer and Robins, *Transforming Civil War Prisons*, 20–24.

6. Cheesborough Notebook, 1862–1863, Cheesborough Papers, SCL; Gillispie, *Andersonvilles of the North*, 77, 99. See also Catherine Hooper Letters, ARHC. For examples of Southern women helping Union prisoners, see Varon, *Southern Lady, Yankee Spy*.

7. Cheesborough Notebook, 1862–1863, Cheesborough Papers, SCL; Sutherland, "Rise and Fall of Esther B. Cheesborough," 31–33.

8. Gillispie, *Andersonville's of the North*, 96; Sanders, *While in the Hands of the Enemy*, 310; Hesseltine, *Civil War Prisons*, 196–204.

9. "The Senses—Taste," *Harper's New Monthly Magazine* 12, no. 67 (December 1855), 75, 76–77; Flammang, *Taste for Civilization*, 159–61; Brumberg, *Fasting Girls*, 84–94.

10. Flammang, *Taste for Civilization*, 167–68; Korsmeyer, *Making Sense of Taste*, 3, 13–26; See also Korsmeyer, *Taste Culture Reader*; Smith, *Sensing the Past*, 75–91; Savarin, *Physiology of Taste*, 12.

11. Hilliard, *Hog Meat and Hoecake*, 48–51, 63; Taylor, *Eating, Drinking, and Visiting*, 56–60; Harris, *Good to Eat*, 115, 116; Covey and Eisnach, *What the Slaves Ate*. Expressions such as sweet, sour, salty, and bitter were not rigid subcategories of taste until after the microscope identified taste buds in 1867. Flammang, *Taste for Civilization*, 168; Jütte, "The Senses in Philosophy and Science," 132–34.

12. Swedberg, *Three Years with the 92nd Illinois*, 218–19; Ouchley, *Flora and Fauna*, 25.

13. Cashin, "Hungry People in the Wartime South," 161–62; Fiege, "Gettysburg and the Organic Nature," 93–109; Massey, *Ersatz in the Confederacy*; Davis, *Taste for War*; Wiley, *Life of Johnny Reb*, 92.

14. William Dolphin Diary, August 26, 1863, Civil War Union Diary, MSS 15813, UVA.

15. Dolphin Diary, September 5, 7, 8, 9, 1863.

16. Dolphin Diary, September 23, 24, 26, October 10, November 29, 1863.

17. Dolphin Diary, October 4, 12, 30, 31, 1863, November 22–24, 29, 30, December 2, 29, 1863.

18. William S. Tippett Diary, September 17, 1863, MS 39949, reel 2698, LVA; Byron Parsons Diary, October 21, 1864, Byron Parsons Diaries and Related Notes, LC.

19. [James H. Franklin], "Prison Diary Fort Delaware and Point Lookout," 11, n.d. [July 1863], CMLSC, VAHS.

20. Abbott, *Prison Life in the South*, 25–26; Bryan and Lankford, *Eye of the Storm*, 171.

21. Cyprian P. Willcox Diary, November 18, 1844, quoted in Plaag, "Strangers in a Strange Land," 262; Frederick Douglass, "Lecture on Slavery, No. 1 Delivered in Corinthian Hall, Rochester, NY, on Sunday Evening, December 1, 1850," in Foner, *The Life and Writings of Frederick Douglass*, 2:135.

22. Hooker, *Food and Drink in America*, 46–47; Taylor, *Eating, Drinking, and Visiting*, 20–21; Covey and Eisnach, *What the Slaves Ate*, 80–82.

23. John L. Hoster Diary, April 27, 1863, MS #464, MARBL, EU.

24. "Corn Bread," *Indiana State Sentinel* (Indianapolis, Ind.), March 10, 1862.

25. Nathaniel Kenyon Diary, May 25, 1862, MSS.0809, UAL; Alfred D. Burdick Diary, May 19, 1864, Micro 37, WIHS; Niccum, "Documents," 277; Ransom, *John Ransom's Diary*, 81; Davis, *Taste for War*, 95; Edmund E. Ryan Diary, February 21, 1864, PHSC.

26. James Burton Diary, July 23, 1864, MS # 120, MARBL, EU.

27. James W. Vance Diary, July 6, 1864, VFM1834, James W. Vance Papers, OHHC; Franklin J. Krause Diary, July 12, 1864, Andersonville Diary, Andersonville Civil War Diary, MS 14096, UVA; Samuel J. Gibson Diary, June 6, 1864, Samuel J. Gibson Diary and Correspondence, LC.

28. David Kennedy Diary, June 27, July 1, and July 2, 1864, MS P519, MNHS.

29. Roe, *The Melvin Memorial*, 105, 108, 111, 113,117; Eugene R. Sly Diary, June 2, August 9, September 19, November 4, 25, 1864, United States Civil War Collection, WMU. See also Helmreich, "Diary of Charles G. Lee," 23.

30. U.S. Congress, House, Joint Committee, 38th Cong., 1st sess., Report No. 67, *Returned Prisoners*, 23.

31. U.S. Sanitary Commission, *Narrative of Privations*, 182, 186.

32. Smith, *American Archives*, 12–19; Berger, *Sight Unseen*, 43–44; Stauffer, *Black Hearts of Men*, 54.

33. "Further Proofs of Rebel Inhumanity," *Harper's Weekly*, June 18, 1864. Hesseltine, *Civil War Prisons*, 194–200. On the average weight, see Benjamin Apthorp Gould, *Investigations*, 402. On the differences between Northern newspaper representations of Union and Confederate prisons, see Cloyd, *Haunted by Atrocity*, 24–25; House, Joint Committee, *Returned Prisoners*; U.S. Sanitary Commission, *Narrative of Privations*.

34. Hunter, "Warden for the Union," 103, 132, 158–59, 162.

35. William Hoffman to Edwin M. Stanton, May 3, 1864, *Official Records*, Ser. II, Vol. 7, 111.

36. General Orders No. 100, *Instructions for the Government of Armies of the United States in the Field*, Section III, Article 76, *Official Records*, Ser. II, Vol. 5: 676.

37. Witt, *Lincoln's Code*, 39–43; "Prisoners at Annapolis," *New York Times*, May 7, 1864.

38. Confederate States of America Congress, *Report on the Joint Select Committee Appointed to Investigate the Condition and Treatment of Prisoners of War*, 2; United States Sanitary Commission, *Sanitary Memoirs*, 1:647; Louis Manigault to wife, September 18, 1864, Louis Manigault Family Papers, LC; Gillispie, *Andersonvilles of the North*, 35–36.

39. John C. Allen Diary, March 29, 1864, March–June 1864, Ms5:1 AL536:1, VAHS. This was also documented in the Minnesota starvation experiment. Keys et al., *Human Starvation*, 2:833–35, 837.

40. Henry H. Stone Diary, June 8, 20, 29, August 22, 1864, and cash account pages, ANHS.

41. Stone Diary, December 11, 1864, and cash account pages, July 1, July 2, December 9, 1864, ANHS.

42. Heslin, "The Diary of a Union Soldier," 247. See also Winslow and Moore, *Camp Morton*, 123.

43. Riddle, *Dancing along the Deadline*, 12. See also Ransom, *John Ransom's Diary*, 55.

44. William Peabody T. Peabody Diary, July 28, August 1, 1864, ANHS; Ransom, *John Ransom's Diary*, 10.

45. Franklin, "Prison Diary," 8, n.d. [July 1863], CMLSC, VAHS. See also King, *My Experiences*, 29. After twenty-four weeks of semi-starvation, the Minnesota experiment found that 47 percent of participants were "indifferent about the taste of food." Keys et al., *Human Starvation*, 2:824.

46. Horace Smith Diary, July 25, 1863, SC 504, WIHS. See also Stone Diary, August 20, 1864, ANHS. See also *A Voice from Rebel Prisons*, 6. For Libby Prison, see Bryon Parsons Diary, September 1, 8, 1864, Byron Parsons Diary and Related Notes, LC.

47. Frederic A. James Diary, May 14, 1864, Frederic Augustus James Papers, MS N-2346, MAHS.

48. Heslin, "The Diary of a Union Soldier," 242–44.

49. Mettam "Civil War Memoirs," 164. See also D. E. Gordon Diary, January 15, 1865, CMLSC, VAHS.

50. Buck, "A Louisiana Prisoner-of-War, 1863–65," 237–38.

51. Cashin, "Hungry People in the Wartime South," 167; Massey, *Ersatz in the Confederacy*, 62–63; Toney, *Privations of a Private*, 101.

52. Robert Bingham Diary, Vol. 1, August 28, 1863, Folder 3, Bingham Papers, Folder 3, MS 03731-z, SHC; Curran, *John Dooley*, 298. See also Winslow and Moore, *Camp Morton*, 124.

53. Curran, *John Dooley*, 297; Thomas A. Sharpe Diary, October 10, 1864, MS #20, Civil War Collection, Confederate Documents, Box 6, Folder 19, MARBL, EU. See also Pickenpaugh, *Camp Chase*, 110–11; *Fort Delaware Prison Times*, 1865, LC; Barrett, *Yankee Rebel*, 194–95.

54. John Alexander Gibson Diary, December 2, 1864, Gibson Family Papers, VAHS. A prisoner at Elmira wrote that rats "smelt very good while frying." King, *My Experiences*, 42.

55. Marcus Toney Diary and Letter Book, September 16, 1864, Civil War Collection, Box 7, Folder 9, TNSLA. After the war, Toney claimed to have eaten rat. Toney, *Privations of a Private*, 101.

56. Moore, "Illinois Commentary," 458. See also Ransom, *John Ransom's Diary*, 27, 39. See also House Special Committee, *Report on the Treatment of Prisoners*, 36; Keiley, *In Vinculis*, 63.

57. Luther Guiteau Billings memoir, 59, Luther Guiteau Billings Articles and Photographs, LC.

58. Ellis et al., "The Signature of Starvation," 91.

59. Toney Diary and Letter Book, August 15, 1864, Civil War Collection, Box 7, Folder 9, TNSLA.

60. Winslow and Moore, *Camp Morton*, 124; King, *My Experiences*, 45.

61. William Francis Tiemann Memoir, 18–19, 27–29, Mss5:1 T4432:1, VAHS.

62. Thomas Sparrow Diary, Vol. 1, September 2, 1861, Vol. 2, November 7, December 25, 1861, Thomas Sparrow Papers, MS 01878, SHC; Frost, *Camp and Prison Journal*, 28, 29. On table manners, see Elias, *History of Manners*, 105–7; Flammang, *Taste for Civilization*, 103.

63. Thomas Hall to his mother, December 25, 1861, Thomas W. Hall Papers, MS #2390, Box 1, Folder 8, MDHS.

64. Hall to his mother, January 1, 1862, Hall Papers, Box 1, Folder 8, MDHS.

65. Henry M. Warfield to Charles H. Pitts, December 26, 1861, Charles H. Pitts Papers, MS #1389, MDHS.

66. Thomas W. Hall to his mother, February 10, 1862, October 16, 1861, Hall Papers, Box 1, Folder 8, MDHS.

67. Durham, *Confederate Yankee*, 44.

68. George William Brown to Dr. George C. Schattuck, January 31, February 9, 1862, George W. Brown Collection, MS 2398, MDHS.

69. Durham, *Confederate Yankee*, 52–53.

70. Hall to his mother, October 16, 1861, Hall Papers, Box 1, Folder 8, MDHS.

71. Hall to his mother, February 20, 1862, Hall Papers, Box 1, Folder 8, MDHS. See also Gower and Allen, *Pen and Sword*, 604–5.

72. Charles A. Ray to "Dear Father and Mother," April 20, 1862, Camp Chase, Ohio, Papers, Folder 8, Mss3 C15015 a, VAHS.

73. Joseph T. McGehee to I. C. McGeHee [his mother], April 19, 1862, Camp Chase, Ohio, Papers, Folder 6, VAHS.

74. W. M. Smith to J. S. Reynolds, "My Dear Friend," April 20, 1862, Camp Chase, Ohio, Papers, Folder 9, VAHS.

75. Thomas Dekay Kimball Diary, October 31, 1863, Kimball Civil War Collection, HC; Byrne, "A General behind Bars," 62, 67; Bryan and Lankford, *Eye of the Storm*, 173; Heslin, "The Diary of a Union Soldier in Confederate Prisons," 251.

76. Hesseltine, *Civil War Prisons*, 123–24; Byrne, "Libby Prison," 436–38.

77. James J. Gillette to "Dear Parents," August 8, 18, October 2, November 27, December 4, 1861, James Jenkins Gillette Papers, Box 1, Folder 2, LC.

78. Allen and Allen, *"Guest" of the Confederacy*, 77, 95.

79. Henry Clay Taylor to his father, October 1, 1863, Henry Clay Taylor Papers, 1856–1865, SC 311, WIHS.

80. Nathaniel Rollins Diary, December 24, 25, 1863, Nathaniel Rollins Papers, Wis Mss UW, WIHS. See also Ransom, *John Ransom's Diary*, 23; Dougherty, *Prison Diary*, 29–30.

81. Francis A. Boyle Diary, December 25, 1864, Francis A. Boyle Books, MS #1555-z, SHC.

82. Ransom Chadwick Diary, July 4, 1864, MS 4098, MNHS. See also Kennedy Diary, July 4, 1864, MNHS; George M. Hinkley Diary, July 8, 1864, MS #File 1864 April 11, WIHS; Dennison, *Dennison's Andersonville Diary*, 45.

83. Burdick Diary, November 24, December 25, 1864, January 1, 1865, WIHS. See also John Whitten Diary, December 25, 1863, LC; John C. Ely Diary, December 25, 1864, ANHS. For an earlier transcription, see John C. Ely Diary, John C. Ely Papers, VFM 4808, OHHC.

84. Jacob Heffelfinger Diary, November 9, 10, December 16, 1864, January 14, 1865, Box 14, CWTI, USAHEC.

85. Toney to "Mrs. Nash," August 5, 1864, Toney Diary and Letter Book, Civil War Collection, Confederate Collection, Box 7, Folder 9, TNSLA.

86. Ben W. Coleman to "My Dear Parents," December 7, 1863, Benjamin W. Coleman Papers, Civil War Collection, Box 8, Folder 26, TNSLA.

87. Courtney (Heron) Pickett to "Dear Mrs. Battelle," January 8, 1864, Section 1, Folder 2, Finney Family Papers, Mss1 F4974 a 1–20, VAHS; Kimball Diary, March 4, 1864, Kimball Civil War Collection, HC.

88. Pickett to "My Dear Mrs. Battle," March 22, 1864, Section 1, Folder 2, Finney Family Papers, VAHS.

89. Benjamin Lyons Farinholt to "Dear Lelia," July 1, 1863, Benjamin Lyons Farinholt Papers, Mss2F2273b, VAHS; Farinholt to "My Ever Dear Lelia," August 11, 1863, Farinholt Papers, VAHS.

90. William M. Collin Diary, August 22–25, 1862, memoranda pages, William M. Collin Papers, LC. On the market and trading, see also Francis A. Dawes Diary,

December 22, 23, 24, and 25, 1864, CWTI, Box 9, USAHEC; John A. Baer Diary, July 7, 8, 1864, ANHS.

91. Krause Diary, memoranda pages, Andersonville Civil War Diary, MS 14096, UVA; Jones, *A Rebel War Clerk's Diary*, 212.

92. J. G. Anderson to Anna S. Miller, October 10, 1864, Prisoner of War Letter Collection, CMLSC, VAHS. References to ring and jewelry making abound in prison letters and diaries. The lens of material culture is well documented in the archaeological investigations by David R. Bush. See Bush, *I Fear I Shall Never Leave*; Bush, "Interpreting the Latrines," 62–78.

93. Durham, *Confederate Yankee*, 74. On pipes, see Lane, "A Marvel of Taste and Skill."

94. Gray, *Business of Captivity*, 88; Pickenpaugh, *Johnson's Island*, 53–54.

95. William H. Smith Diary, July 6, August 25, December 24, 1864, MSS 13164, UVA; Krause Diary, memoranda pages, Andersonville Diary, UVA.

96. Sanderson, *Camp Fires and Camp Cooking*, 11. Later as a prisoner in Richmond, Sanderson tried to standardize cooking by his standards, but had little success. Sanderson, *My Record in Rebeldom*, 23–37.

97. Taylor, *Eating, Drinking, and Visiting*, 96–97; Massey, *Ersatz in the Confederacy*, 72–73.

98. Hall to his mother, February 10, 1862, Hall Papers, Box 1, Folder 8, MDHS.

99. While prisoners frequently copied other poems, Frederic James is likely the author of "Morale" because his diary contains three drafts of the poem. Frederic Augustus James Diary, memoranda section, MS N-2346, MAHS.

100. Kennedy Diary, June 3, 1864, MNHS; Thomas W. Springer Diary, July 31, August 21, and September 21, 1864, MS 7093-v, UVA.

101. Roger W. Hanson to "Dear General," April 13, 1862, Roger Weightman Hanson Papers, LC.

102. Gray, *Business of Captivity*, 76. On trading possessions, see McLaughlin, "Diary of Salisbury Prison," 220; "The Yankee Prisoners at Andersonville—A Correspondent of the Atlanta Confederacy," *Charleston Mercury*, August 26, 1864. The Minnesota experiment found that smoking cigarettes, chewing gum (up to 40 packs a day), watching others eat, and smelling food brought "vivid vicarious pleasure." Some nonsmokers began smoking. Keys et al., *Human Starvation*, 834–35.

103. Heslin, "Diary of a Union Soldier," 248.

104. Frank T. Bennett, "Narrative of Lieut. Col. F. T. Bennett," 13–14, Frank T. Bennett Papers, RL.30205, DU.

105. Henri Jean Mugler Diary, August 4, 1864, Henri Jean Mugler Diary and Memoir, MS A&M.1335, West Virginia Collection, WVU.

106. Toney, *Privations of a Private*, 96.

107. Toney to [illegible], January 1, 1865, Toney Diary and Letter Book, Civil War Collection, Box 7, Folder 9, TNSLA.

108. George Washington Hall Diary, August 8, September 14, 1864, LC.

109. Dolphin Diary, November 29, December 1, 9, 10, and 29, 1863, Civil War Union Diary, UVA.

110. Springer Diary, September 3, 8, 1864, UVA.

111. Abbott, *Prison Life in the South*, 46.

112. Hiram Eddy to "My own dear Fannie," April 30, 1862, Hiram Eddy Papers, MS 78637, CTHS. This letter, like his others, was smuggled out of Libby Prison. Hiram Eddy to his wife, May 2, 1862, Eddy Papers, CHS; Basile, *Diary of Amos E. Stearns*, 60–61.

113. Heffelfinger Diary, November 9, 1864, CTWI, Box 14, USAHEC.

114. Nichols De Graff Diary [memoir], CWTI, Box 31, USAHEC. See also Coulter, "From Spotsylvania Courthouse to Andersonville," 188, 189.

115. Eugene R. Sly Diary, September 18, 1864, United States Civil War Collection, WMU.

116. Jonathan P. Stowe Diary, November 13, 14, 1861, CWTI, Box 26, USAHEC; Gillispie, *Andersonvilles of the North*, 180.

117. George E. Albee Diary, September 3, 1864, MS 41695, LVA.

118. Henry G. Tracy Diary, July 8, 1863, Henry G. Tracy Papers, MS 77592, CTHS.

119. Luther Rice Mills Reminiscences, 6, 8–9, MS 00512-z, SHC.

120. Dolphin Diary, January–May bills payable, Civil War Union Diary, UVA; see also Henry B. Sparks Diary, March 5, 1864, #SC 0020, INHS; Bingham Diary, Vol. 1, August 18, 1863, Bingham Papers, SHC.

121. State of New York, *Annual Report*, Vol. 2 [1893]: 343, 352, 410–11, 415, 453, 638, 679, 687, 703, 712–13.

122. State of New York, *Annual Report*, Vol. 2: 358, 641.

Epilogue

1. Kantor, "Last Full Measure," 1. I have found no wartime diary that puts a spring there in August 1864. William Marvel's sources on Providence Spring begin with the Wirz trial transcript. He stops short of calling the story a lie, but he notes that locals contested any sort of divine intervention on behalf of their enemies. Marvel, *Andersonville*, 179–80, 288fn.

2. Kantor, "Last Full Measure," 1, 32.

3. Kantor, *Andersonville*, 7, 67, 227. On authentic sensory experiences, see Horwitz, *Confederates in the Attic*, 9–17. One of the few sensory historians to promote recreating consumable sensory pasts is Peter Charles Hoffer, *Sensory Worlds*, 2, 6. On the debate over reproducing and consuming historical sensations and perceptions, see Smith, "Producing Sense, Consuming Sense, Making Sense," 841–58.

4. Smithpeters, "To the Latest Generation," 23–24, 39; Cloyd, *Haunted by Atrocity*, 132–26.

5. Marvel, *Andersonville*, 323.

6. Cloyd, *Haunted by Atrocity*, 115–16.

7. Thelen, "Memory and American History," 1117–29; Robert Bingham Diary, Vol. 1, June 30, 1863, Robert Bingham Papers, Folder 3, MS 03731-z, SHC; Robert Bingham to Henrietta Bingham, March 14, 1923, Bingham Papers, Folder 1, SHC.

8. Bingham Diary, June 30, 1863, Bingham Papers, Folder 3, SHC.

9. Bingham to Henrietta Bingham, March 14, 1923, 2, 4, Bingham Papers, Folder 1, SHC.

10. Bingham Diary, June 30, 1863, Folder 3, SHC; Bingham to Henrietta Bingham, March 14, 1923, 6, Bingham Papers, Folder 1, SHC.

11. Bingham Diary, June 30–July 6, 1863, Bingham Papers, Folder 3, SHC.

12. Bingham Diary, Vol. 1, July 1, 1863, Bingham Papers, Folder 3, SHC; Hesseltine, *Civil War Prisons*, 94–96; Witt, *Lincoln's Code*, 159–60, 162, 226.

13. Bingham to Henrietta Bingham, March 14, 1923, Bingham Papers, Folder 1, SHC.

14. Orwell, "Politics and the English Language," in Orwell, *The Collected Essays*, 4:127–40; *Oxford English Dictionary*, 2nd ed., s.v. "dead-line."

Bibliography

Primary Sources

Manuscript Collections

Andersonville, Georgia
  Andersonville National Historic Site
    John A. Baer Diary
    George Clarkson Diary
    Marcus Collis Diary
    Sheldon R. Curtiss Diary
    Alonzo Tuttle Decker Diary
    John Duff Diary
    John C. Ely Diary
    Joseph B. Fenton Diary
    Samuel L. Foust Diary
    Samuel Henderson Diary
    Josephus Hudson Diary
    Christian L. Kinder Diary
    William T. Peabody Diary
    William W. Seeley Diary
    Henry H. Stone Diary
    Henry W. Tisdale Diary
    Unknown Diary
    James W. Vance Diary
Ann Arbor, Michigan
  Bentley Historical Library, University of Michigan
    John B. Kay Papers
    Alonzo Merrill Keeler Diary
    De Witt. C. Spaulding Diary
    Van Vlack Family Papers
Atlanta, Georgia
  Manuscript, Archives, and Rare Book Library, Emory University
    James Burton Diary
    William H. Davis Diary
    John K. Farris Diary
    John L. Hoster Diary
    George W. Pennington Diary and Letters
    Thomas A. Sharpe Diary

Baltimore, Maryland
  Maryland Historical Society
    George William Brown Collection
    Thomas W. Hall Papers
    Charles H. Pitts Papers
Barre, Vermont
  Vermont Historical Society
    Charles Chapin Letter
    Daniel F. Cooledge Diary
    Asa Dean Mathews Diary
Boston, Massachusetts
  Massachusetts Historical Society
    John B. Gallison Papers
    Higginson Family Papers II
    George A. Hitchcock Diary
    Frederic Augustus James Diary
    Frederic Augustus James Papers
    Stephen Minot Weld Diary
Burlington, Vermont
  University of Vermont
    Charles H. Blinn Diary
    Hubbard Family Papers
    Charles B. Stone Diary
    Ellery H. Webster Diary
Carlisle, Pennsylvania
  Civil War Miscellaneous Collection, United States Army Heritage Education
      Center
    Jonathan Boynton Memoirs
    Charles Holbrook Prentiss Diary
    Arthur Wyman Diary
  Civil War Times Illustrated Collection, United States Army Heritage Education
      Center
    Francis A. Dawes Diary
    Nicholas De Graff Diary
    Jacob Heffelfinger Diary
    Frank Jennings Reminiscences
    George C. Parker Letters
    Jonathan P. Stowe Diary
Chapel Hill, North Carolina
  Southern Historical Collection, Wilson Library, University of North Carolina
    Robert Bingham Papers
    Francis A. Boyle Books
    William H. Haigh Papers
    Joseph Mason Kern Papers

Luther Rice Mills Reminiscences
Virgil S. Murphey Diary
Thomas Sparrow Papers
William H. Tillson Diary
Charlottesville, Virginia
Albert and Shirley Small Special Collections Library, University of Virginia
William Dolphin Diary
Atcheson L. Hench Papers
Franklin J. Krause Diary
William H. Smith Diary
Thomas W. Springer Diary
Columbia, South Carolina
South Caroliniana Library, University of South Carolina
William Blanding Papers
Esther B. Cheesborough Papers
Welch, John Collins. "An Escape from Prison during the Civil War, 1864"
J. William Flinn Papers
James T. Wells Papers
Columbus, Ohio
Ohio History Connection
John C. Ely Diary
James W. Vance Diary
William T. Wilson Diary
Dover, Delaware
Delaware Public Archives
Bell Papers
Durham, North Carolina
Rubenstein Special Collections Library, Duke University
Frank T. Bennett Papers
George Harry Weston Diary
Isaiah H. White Papers
Frankfort, Kentucky
Kentucky Historical Society
Stone Family Papers
Henry Stone Papers
Gettysburg, Pennsylvania
Gettysburg College Special Collections
Sylvester Crossley Diary
Hartford, Connecticut
Connecticut Historical Society
Anonymous Diary, 1863
Hiram Eddy Papers
Samuel E. Grosvenor Diary
Robert H. Kellogg Papers

James Harsen Sawyer Record Book
Nehemiah Solon Diary
Henry G. Tracy Papers
Milton Woodford Papers
Hillsdale, Michigan
  Hillsdale College
    Kimball Civil War Collection [digital collection]
Indianapolis, Indiana
  Indiana Historical Society
    Curtis R. Burke Journal
    Henry B. Sparks Diary
Iowa City, Iowa
  University of Iowa Libraries
    Charles Thomas Ackley Letters [digital collection]
    Anson R. Butler Letters [digital collection]
    Henry Dysart Diary [digital collection]
    George Marion Shearer Diary [digital collection]
Jackson, Mississippi
  Mississippi Department of Archives and History
    Thomas Lafayette Beadles Diary
    William Peel Diary
Kalamazoo, Michigan
  United States Civil War Collection, Western Michigan University
    Eugene R. Sly Diary [digital collection]
Knoxville, Tennessee
  University of Tennessee
    "Army Life and Prison Experience of Major Charles G. Davis"
    Samuel B. Boyd Papers
Little Rock, Arkansas
  Arkansas History Commission
    Catherine Hooper Letters
Louisville, Kentucky
  Filson Historical Society
    Davis Family Papers
    George F. Gill Diary
Madison, Wisconsin
  Wisconsin Historical Society
    Newell Burch Diary
    Alfred Demeterius Burdick Diary
    James Canon Diary
    Willis Peck Clarke Papers
    George M. Hinkley Diary
    Libby Prison Minstrels Collection
    Elisha Rice Reed Papers
    Nathaniel Rollins Papers

Frederick E. Schmitt Reminiscence
Horace Smith Diary
Henry Clay Taylor Papers
William Lloyd Tritt Diary
Montgomery, Alabama
  Alabama Department of Archives and History
    James B. Irvine Diary
Morgantown, West Virginia
  West Virginia Collection, West Virginia University
    Henri Jean Mugler Diary
Nashville, Tennessee
  Tennessee State Library and Archives
    Benjamin W. Coleman Papers
    Thomas L. Cooper Memoir
    William J. Hine Diary
    Marcus Toney Diary and Letter Book
Peoria, Illinois
  Peoria Historical Society Collection, Bradley University Library
    Edmund E. Ryan Diary
Philadelphia, Pennsylvania
  Historical Society of Pennsylvania
    Frank T. Bennett Diary
    James E. Wenrick Diary
Richmond, Virginia
  Confederate Memorial Literary Society Collection (formerly at the Museum of the
      Confederacy), Virginia Historical Society
    [Franklin, James H.] "Prison Diary of Fort Delaware and Point Lookout"
    D. E. Gordon Diary
    James Taswell Mackey Diary
    Joseph W. Mauck Diary
    Prisoner of War Letter Collection
  Library of Virginia
    George E. Albee Diary
    William F. Broaddus Diary
    Herbert E. Carpenter Letter
    Martin L. Roberts Letters
    William S. Tippett Diary
  Virginia Historical Society
    John C. Allen Diary
    Camp Chase, Ohio, Papers
    E. L. Cox Diary
    Gibson Family Papers
    Benjamin Lyons Farinholt Papers
    Finney Family Papers
    John Thomas Parker Commonplace Book

Mary M. Stockton Terry Diary
William Francis Tiemann Memoir
St. Paul, Minnesota
Minnesota Historical Society
Lewis C. Bisbee Papers
Ransom Chadwick Diary
David Kennedy Diary
Tallahassee, Florida
Florida State Archives
Wilbur Wightman Gramling Diary
John Pond Papers
Tuscaloosa, Alabama
University of Alabama, W. S. Hoole Special Collections Library
Nathaniel Kenyon Diary
Urbana-Champaign, Illinois
University of Illinois at Urbana-Champaign
Stephen Alfred Forbes Diary
Washington, D.C.
Library of Congress
Luther Guiteau Billings Memoir
William M. Collin Papers
Fort Delaware Prison Times
Samuel J. Gibson Diary and Correspondence
James Jenkins Gillette Papers
George Washington Hall Diary
Roger Weightman Hanson Papers
Louis Manigault Family Papers
James McCaggen Mayo Diary
Byron Parsons Diaries
John White Scott Papers
John Whitten Diary
William Duncan Wilkins Papers
National Archives and Records Administration
"Morning Reports of Federal Prisoners of War Confined at Andersonville
Prison, Georgia, 1864–1865," Record Group 249, Records of the Commissary
General of Prisoners, 1861–1865, M1303, roll 6
"Register of Claims for Lost Personal Property," Record Group 249, Records of
the Commissary General of Prisoners, Entry 84, Volume 1
"Register of Enlistments in the United States Army, 1798–1914," M233

Newspapers and Periodicals

Charleston Mercury (Charleston, S.C.)
Frank Leslie's Illustrated Newspaper (New York, N.Y.)
Harper's New Monthly Magazine (New York, N.Y)

Highland Weekly News (Hillsboro, Ohio)
Indiana State Sentinel (Indianapolis, Ind.)
Macon Telegraph (Macon, Ga.)
Montgomery Daily Advertiser (Montgomery, Ala.)
Muscatine Weekly Journal (Muscatine, Iowa)
National Tribune (Washington, D.C.)
New York Herald (New York, N.Y)
New York Times (New York, N.Y.)
Richmond Enquirer (Richmond, Va.)
Richmond Examiner (Richmond, Va.)
Rochester Daily Union and Advertiser (Rochester, N.Y.)

Published Primary Sources

Abbott, Allen O. *Prison Life in the South: At Richmond, Macon, Savannah, Charleston, Columbia, Charlotte, Raleigh, Goldsborough, and Andersonville, during the Years 1864 and 1865*. New York: Harper, 1865.

Allen, Robert D., and Cheryl A. Allen, eds. *A "Guest" of the Confederacy: The Civil War Letters & Diaries of Alonzo M. Keeler, Captain Company B., Twenty-Second Michigan Infantry Including Letters & Diaries Written while a Prisoner of War*. Nashville: Cold Tree Press, 2008.

Ames, Amos W. "A Diary of Life in Southern Prisons." *Annals of Iowa* 40, no. 1 (Summer 1969): 1–19.

Andrews, Eliza Frances. *The War-Time Journal of a Georgia Girl, 1864–1865*. Edited by Spencer Bidwell King Jr. Macon, Ga.: Ardivan Press, 1960.

Armstrong, William M. "Cahaba to Charleston: The Prison Odyssey of Lt. Edmund E. Ryan." In *Civil War Prisons*, edited by William B. Hesseltine, 114–23. Kent, Ohio: Kent State University Press, 1997 [1962].

[Atwater, Dorence, and Clara Barton]. *A List of the Union Soldiers Buried at Andersonville. . . .* New York: Tribune Association, 1866.

Barrett, John G., ed. *Yankee Rebel: The Civil War Journal of Edmund DeWitt Patterson*. Chapel Hill: University of North Carolina Press, 1966.

Basile, Leon, ed. *The Civil War Diary of Amos E. Stearns, a Prisoner at Andersonville*. Rutherford, N.J.: Fairleigh Dickinson University Press, 1981.

Beaudry, Louis N., ed. *The Libby Chronicle: Devoted to Facts and Fun. A True Copy of the Libby Chronicle as Written by the Prisoners of Libby in 1863. V. 1, no. 1–7; Aug. 21– Oct. 2, 1863*. Albany, N.Y.: p.p., 1889.

Bell, Whitfield J., Jr., ed. "Notes and Documents: Diary of George Bell, A Record of Captivity in a Federal Military Prison, 1862." *Georgia Historical Quarterly* 22, no. 2 (1938): 169–84.

Bierce, Ambrose. *Tales of Soldiers and Civilians*. Edited by Donald T. Blume. Kent, Ohio: Kent State University Press, 2011.

Browne, Junius Henri. *Four Years in Secessia: Adventures within and beyond the Union Lines: Embracing a Great Variety of Facts, Incidents, and Romance of the War. . . .* Hartford, Conn.: O. D. Case, 1865.

Brumgardt, John R., ed. *Civil War Nurse: The Diary and Letters of Hannah Ropes*. Knoxville: University of Tennessee Press, 1980.

Bryan, Charles F., Jr., and Nelson D. Lankford, eds. *Eye of the Storm: A Civil War Odyssey. Written and Illustrated by Private Robert Knox Sneden*. New York: Free Press, 2000.

Buck, Martina. "A Louisiana Prisoner-of-War on Johnson's Island, 1863–65." *Louisiana History* 4, no. 3 (Summer 1963): 233–42.

Burson, William. *A Race for Liberty; or, My Capture, Imprisonment, and Escape*. Wellsville, Ohio: W. G. Foster, 1867.

Byers, Samuel Hawkins Marshall. *What I Saw in Dixie; or, Sixteen Months in Rebel Prisons*. Danville, N.Y.: Robbins & Poore, 1868.

Byrne, Frank L., ed. "A General behind Bars: Neal Dow in Libby Prison." In *Civil War Prisons*, edited by William B. Hesseltine, 60–79. Kent, Ohio: Kent State University Press, 1997 [1962].

Campbell, Andrew Jackson. *The Civil War Diary*. Edited by Jill Knight Garrett. Columbia, Tenn.: p.p., 1965.

Cavada, Federico Fernández. *Libby Life: Experiences of a Prisoner of War in Richmond, Va., 1863-64*. Philadelphia: King and Baird, 1864.

Confederate States of America Congress. *Report on the Joint Select Committee Appointed to Investigate the Condition and Treatment of Prisoners of War*. Richmond: C.S.A. Congress, 1865.

Confederate States of America, War Department. *Articles of War, for the Government of the Army of the Confederate States*. Montgomery, Ala: Barrett, Wimbish & Co., 1861.

Coulter, Merton, ed. "From Spotsylvania Courthouse to Andersonville: A Diary of Darius Starr." *Georgia Historical Quarterly* 41, no. 2 (June 1957): 176–90.

Curran, Robert Emmett, ed. *John Dooley's Civil War: An Irish American's Journey in the First Virginia Infantry Regiment*. Knoxville: University of Tennessee Press, 2012.

Curtis, Orson Blair. *History of the Twenty-Fourth Michigan of the Iron Brigade*. . . . Detroit: Winn & Hammond, 1891.

Day, W. W. *Fifteen Months in Dixie; or My Personal Experience in Rebel Prisons*. . . . Owatonna, Minn.: People's Press, 1889.

Dennison, James H. *Dennison's Andersonville Diary*. Edited by Jack Klasey. Kankakee, Ill.: Lindsay Publications, 1987.

de Wolfe, Mark, ed. *Touched by Fire: Civil War Letters and Diary of Oliver Wendell Holmes, Jr., 1861-1864*. Cambridge, Mass.: Harvard University Press, 1947.

Domschcke, Bernhard. *Twenty Months in Captivity: Memoirs of a Union Officer in Confederate Prisons*. Edited and translated by Frederic Trautmann. Madison, N.J.: Fairleigh Dickinson University Press, 1987.

Dougherty, Michael. *Prison Diary of Michael Dougherty*. . . . Bristol, Pa.: C. A. Dougherty, 1908.

Durham, Roger S., ed. *A Confederate Yankee: The Journal of Edward William Drummond, a Confederate Soldier from Maine*. Knoxville: University of Tennessee Press, 2004.

Fairchild, Charles Bryant. *History of the 27th Regiment N.Y. Vols*. . . . Binghamton, N.Y.: Carl & Matthews, 1888.

Flint, Austin, ed. *Contributions Relating to the Causation and Prevention of Disease, and to Camp Diseases; Together with a Report of the Diseases, etc., among the Prisoners at Andersonville, Ga.* New York: Published for the U.S. Sanitary Commission, by Hurd and Houghton, 1867.

Foner, Philip S., ed. *The Life and Writings of Frederick Douglass, Vol. 2, Pre-Civil War Decade, 1850–1860.* New York: International Publishers, 1950.

Forbes, Stephen Alfred. *The Insect, the Farmer, the Teacher, the Citizen, and the State.* Urbana: Illinois State Laboratory of Natural History, 1915.

Frost, Griffin. *Camp and Prison Journal, Embracing Scenes in Camp, on the March, and in Prisons. . . .* Quincey, Ill.: Quincey Herald Book and Job Office, 1867.

Genoways, Ted, and Hugh H. Genoways. *A Perfect Picture of Hell: Eyewitness Accounts by Civil War Prisoners from the 12th Iowa.* Iowa City: University of Iowa Press, 2001.

Glazier, Willard W. *The Capture, the Prison Pen, and the Escape. . . .* New York: H. E. Goodwin, 1869.

Gould, Benjamin Apthorp. *Investigations in the Military and Anthropological Statistics of American Soldiers.* New York: Published for the U.S. Sanitary Commission by Hurd and Houghton, 1869.

Gower, Herschel, and Jack Allen, eds. *Pen and Sword: The Life and Journals of Randal W. McGavock.* Nashville: Tennessee Historical Commission, 1959.

[Gunn, John C.] *Gunn's Domestic Medicine; or, Poor Man's Friend, in the Hours of Affliction, Pain and Sickness. . . .* Springfield, Ohio: John M. Gallagher, 1836.

Harrold, John. *Libby, Andersonville, Florence. The Capture, Imprisonment, Escape and Rescue of John Harrold, A Union Soldier in the War of the Rebellion. . . .* Philadelphia, Pa.: Wm B. Selheimer, 1870.

Hartmann, Fred J., ed. "My Libby Prison Diary August 12 to September 26th 1862." *Detroit in Perspective: A Journal of Regional History* 3, no. 2 (Winter 1979): 77–113.

Helmreich, Paul C., ed. "The Diary of Charles G. Lee in Andersonville and Florence Prison Camps, 1864." *Connecticut Historical Society Bulletin* 41, no. 1 (January 1976): 12–26.

Heslin, James J., ed. "The Diary of a Union Soldier in Confederate Prisons." *New York Historical Society Quarterly* 41, no. 3 (July 1957): 233–78.

House Special Committee on the Treatment of Prisoners of War and Union Citizens. *Report on the Treatment of Prisoners of War, by the Rebel Authorities, during the War of the Rebellion. . . .* 40th Cong., 3rd sess., House Report 45. Washington: GPO, 1869.

[Ingraham, Joseph Holt]. *The South-West, By a Yankee.* 2 vols. New York: Harper & Brothers, 1835.

Jennings, Warren A., ed. "Prisoner of the Confederacy: Diary of a Union Artilleryman." *West Virginia History* 36, no. 4 (July 1975): 309–23.

Jones, J. B. *A Rebel War Clerk's Diary at the Confederate States Capital.* Philadelphia, Pa.: J. B. Lippincott, 1866.

Keiley, Anthony M. *In Vinculis; or, The Prisoner of War. . . .* New York: Blelock, 1866.

Kelley, Daniel G. *What I Saw and Suffered in Rebel Prisons.* Buffalo, N.Y.: Matthews & Warren, 1866.

King, John R. *My Experience in the Confederate Army and in Northern Prisons.* Clarksburg, W.Va.: United Daughters of the Confederacy, 1917.

Kirby, William. *On the Power, Wisdom and Goodness of God as Manifested in the Creation of Animals and in Their History, Habits, and Instincts.* Vol. 2. London: William Pickering, 1835.

Lincoln, Abraham. *Collected Works of Abraham Lincoln.* Vol. 4. Ann Arbor: University of Michigan Digital Library Production Services, 2001.

Livermore, Mary A. *My Story of the War: A Woman's Narrative of Four Years Personal Experience.* . . . Hartford, Conn.: A. D. Worthington, 1889.

Mahood, Wayne, ed. *Charlie Mosher's Civil War.* . . . Hightstown, N.J.: Longstreet House, 1994.

McCord, David J., ed. *The Statutes at Large of South Carolina, Vol. 7, Containing the Acts Relating to Charleston, Courts, Slaves, and Rivers.* Columbia, S.C.: A. S. Johnston, 1840.

McLaughlin, Florence C., ed. "Diary of Salisbury Prison by James W. Eberhart." *Western Pennsylvania Historical Magazine* 56, no. 3 (July 1973): 211–51.

Meissner, Frances Taylor, and Charles William Meissner Jr., eds. *I Had Rather Lose a Limb and Be Free.* Seaford, Va.: p.p., 2005.

Mettam, Henry C. "Civil War Memoirs of the 1st Maryland Cavalry, C.S.A." *Maryland Historical Magazine* 58, no. 2 (June 1963): 137–70.

Moore, Hugh. "Illinois Commentary: A Reminiscence of Confederate Prison Life." Edited by Clifford H. Haka. *Journal of the Illinois State Historical Society* 65, no. 4 (Winter 1972): 451–61.

Niccum, Norman, ed. "Documents: Diary of Lieutenant Frank Hughes." *Indiana Magazine of History* 45, no. 3 (September 1949): 275–84.

Nightingale, Florence. *Notes on Nursing: What It Is, and What It Is Not.* New York: D. Appleton and Company, 1860.

Northup, Solomon. *Twelve Years a Slave.* . . . Auburn, N.Y.: Derby and Miller, 1853.

O'Brien, Michael, ed. *An Evening When Alone: Four Journals of Single Women in the South, 1827-67.* Charlottesville: University Press of Virginia, 1993.

Osborn, George C., ed. "Writings of a Confederate Prisoner of War." *Tennessee Historical Quarterly* 10, no. 1 (March 1951): 74–90.

Pierson, William Whatley, Jr., ed. *Diary of Bartlett Yancey Malone.* Chapel Hill: University of North Carolina Press, 1919.

Pollan, Howard O., and Randal B. Gilbert, eds. "The Camp Ford Diary of Captain William Fortunatus McKinney." *Chronicles of Smith County, Texas* 25 (Summer 1996): 15–25.

Ransom, John L. *John Ransom's Diary.* Introduction by Bruce Catton. New York: Paul S. Ericksson, 1963.

Rawick, George P. ed. *The American Slave: A Composite Autobiography.* 14 vols. Westport, Conn.: Greenwood, 1972.

Reynolds, Mary Elizabeth, and Rosemary Wiseman Seal, eds. *All for the Flag: The Civil War Diaries of Eugene Forbes.* N.p.: p.p., 2014.

Ripple, Ezra Hoyt. *Dancing along the Deadline: The Andersonville Memoir of a Prisoner of the Confederacy.* Edited by Mark A. Snell. Novato, Calif.: Presidio Press, 1996.

Robins, Glenn, ed. *They Have Left Us Here to Die: The Civil War Prison Diary of Sgt. Lyle Adair, 111th U.S. Colored Infantry.* Kent, Ohio: Kent State University Press, 2011.

Roe, Alfred S. *The Melvin Memorial: Sleepy Hollow Cemetery, Concord, Massachusetts, A Brother's Tribute; Exercises at Dedication June 16, 1909.* Cambridge, Mass.: Riverside Press, 1910.

Root, George Frederick. *Tramp! Tramp! Tramp! Or, the Prisoners Hope.* Chicago: n.p., 1864.

Sabre, Gilbert E. *Nineteen Months a Prisoner of War. Narrative of Lieutenant G. E. Sabre, Second Rhode Island Cavalry.* . . . New York: American News Company, 1865.

Sanderson, James M. *Camp Fires and Camp Cooking; or Culinary Hints for the Soldier: Including Receipt for Making Bread in the "Portable Field Oven" Furnished by the Subsistence Department.* Washington, D.C.: Government Printing Office, 1862.

———. *My Record in Rebeldom: As Written by Friend and Foe.* New York: W. E. Sibell, 1865.

Sanitary Commission. *Report of the Sanitary Commission of New Orleans on the Epidemic Yellow Fever of 1853.* New Orleans: Picayune, 1854.

Savarin, Brillat. *The Physiology of Taste, or, Transcendental Gastronomy.* Translated by Fayette Robinson. Waiheke Island: The Floating Press, 2008 [1825].

Schiller, Herbert M., ed. *A Captain's War: The Letters and Diaries of William H. S. Burgwyn, 1861-1865.* Shippensburg, Pa.: White Mane Publishing Company, 1994.

Sims, J. Marion. *The Story of My Life.* New York: D. Appleton and Company, 1884.

Southall, John. *A Treatise on Buggs.* . . . London: J. Roberts, 1730.

Sprague, Homer B. *Lights and Shadows in Confederate Prisons: A Personal Experience, 1864-5.* New York: G. P. Putnam's Sons, 1915.

State of New York. *Annual Report of the Adjutant-General of the State of New York for the Year 1893.* . . . Vol. 2. Albany: James B. Lyon, State Printer, 1894.

Stephenson, Wendell Holmes, and Edwin Adams Davis, eds. "The Civil War Diary of William Micajah Barrow September 23, 1861–July 13, 1862." *Louisiana Historical Quarterly* 17 (October 1934): 712–31.

Stillé, Charles J. *History of the United States Sanitary Commission Being the General Report of Its Work during the War of the Rebellion.* New York: Hurd and Houghton, 1868.

Swedberg, Claire E., ed. *Three Years with the 92nd Illinois: The Civil War Diary of John M. King.* Mechanicsburg, Pa.: Stackpole Books, 1999.

Thornton, Mary Lindsay, ed. "The Prison Diary of Adjutant Francis Atherton Boyle, C.S.A." *North Carolina Historical Review* 39, no. 1 (Winter 1962): 58–84.

Tocqueville, Alexis de. *Democracy in America: A New Translation by George Lawrence.* Edited by J. P. Mayer. New York, Anchor Books, 1969 [1835].

Toney, Marcus B. *Privations of a Private.* . . . Nashville: M. E. Church, 1905.

United States Congress. House. *The Trial of Henry Wirz: A Congressionally Mandated Report Summarizing the Military Commission's Proceedings.* 40th Cong., 2nd sess., House Executive Document 23, December 7, 1867.

———. Joint Committee on the Conduct of the War. *Returned Prisoners.* 38th Cong., 1st sess., 1864, Report No. 67.

United States Sanitary Commission. *Narrative of Privations and Sufferings of United States Officers and Soldiers while Prisoners of War in the Hands of the Rebel Authorities.* Philadelphia: King and Baird, 1864.

[United States Sanitary Commission]. *Sanitary Memoirs of the War of the Rebellion. Collected and Published by the United States Sanitary Commission.* Vol. 1. New York: Hurd and Houghton, 1867.

[United States War Department]. *An Act, Establishing Rules and Articles for the Government of the Armies of the United States. . . .* Albany, N.Y.: Websters and Skinners, 1812.

―――――. *Revised United States Army Regulations of 1861: With an Appendix Containing the Changes and Laws Affecting Army Regulations and Articles of War to June 25, 1863.* Washington, D.C.: Government Printing Office, 1863.

United States War Department. *The War of the Rebellion: A Compilation of the Official Records of the Union and Confederate Armies.* 128 vols. Washington, D.C.: Government Printing Office, 1880–1901.

Urban, John W. *My Experiences Mid Shot and Shell and In Rebel Den.* Lancaster, Pa.: Hubbard Brothers, 1882.

Vaughter, John B. *Prison Life in Dixie: Giving a Short History of the Inhuman and Barbarous Treatment of Our Soldiers by Rebel Authorities.* Chicago: Central Book Concern, 1881.

Wesley, John. *The Works of John Wesley.* 14 vols. Grand Rapids, Mich.: Zondervan, 1872.

Whitman, Walt. *Specimen Days & Collect.* Philadelphia: David McKay, 1882.

Wilkeson, Frank. *Turned Inside Out: Recollections of a Private Soldier in the Army of the Potomac.* Lincoln: University of Nebraska Press, 1997 [1886].

[Wood, Samuel]. *The History of Insects.* New York: Samuel Wood, 1813.

Woodward, C. Vann, ed. *Mary Chesnut's Civil War.* New Haven, Conn.: Yale University Press, 1981.

Secondary Sources

Books and Articles

Ackerman, Diane. *A Natural History of the Senses.* New York: Vintage, 1991.

Adam, Barbara. *Timewatch: The Social Analysis of Time.* Cambridge: Polity Press, 1995.

Adams, Michael C. C. *Living Hell: The Dark Side of the Civil War.* Baltimore: Johns Hopkins University Press, 2014.

Aley, Ginette, and J. L. Anderson, eds. *Union Heartland: The Midwestern Home Front during the Civil War.* Carbondale: Southern Illinois University Press, 2013.

Baldwin, Peter C. "How Night Air Became Good Air, 1776–1930." *Environmental History* 8, no. 3 (July 2013): 412–29.

―――――. *In the Watches of the Night: Life in the Nocturnal City, 1820–1930.* Chicago: University of Chicago Press, 2012.

Beitzell, Edwin W. *Point Lookout Prison Camp for Confederates.* Abell, Md.: Author, 1972.

Bell, Andrew McIlwaine. *Mosquito Soldiers: Malaria, Yellow Fever, and the Course of the American Civil War.* Baton Rouge: Louisiana State University Press, 2010.

Berger, Martin A. *Sight Unseen: Whiteness and American Visual Culture*. Berkeley: University of California Press, 2005.

Berry, Stephen. *All That Makes a Man: Love and Ambition in the Civil War South*. New York: Oxford University Press, 2003.

———, ed. *Weirding the War: Stories from the Civil War's Ragged Edges*. Athens: University of Georgia Press, 2011.

———. "When Metal Meets Mettle: The Hard Realities of Civil War Soldiering." *North & South* 9, no. 4 (August 2006): 12–21.

Blight, David W. *Race and Reunion: The Civil War in American Memory*. Cambridge, Mass.: Belknap Press of Harvard University Press, 2001.

Bouman, Mark J. "Luxury and Control: The Urbanity of Street Lighting in Nineteenth-Century Cities." *Journal of Urban History* 14, no. 1 (November 1987): 7–37.

Boynton, L. O. J. "The Bed-Bug and the 'Age of Elegance.'" *Furniture History* 1 (1965): 15–31.

Brady, Lisa M. "From Battlefield to Fertile Ground: The Development of Civil War Environmental History." *Civil War History* 58, no. 3 (September 2012): 305–21.

———. *War upon the Land: Military Strategy and the Transformation of Southern Landscapes during the American Civil War*. Athens: University of Georgia Press, 2012.

Brown, Kathleen M. *Foul Bodies: Cleanliness in Early America*. New Haven, Conn.: Yale University Press, 2009.

Brumberg, Joan Jacobs. *Fasting Girls: The History of Anorexia Nervosa*. New York: Vintage, 2000 [1988].

Brundage, W. Fitzhugh. *The Southern Past: A Clash of Race and Memory*. Cambridge, Mass.: Belknap Press of Harvard University Press, 2005.

Bryant, William O. *Cahaba Prison and the Sultana Disaster*. Tuscaloosa: University of Alabama Press, 1990.

Burnham, Philip. *So Far from Dixie: Confederates in Yankee Prisons*. Lanham, Md.: Taylor Trade Publishing, 2003.

Bush, David R. *I Fear I Shall Never Leave This Island: Life in a Civil War Prison*. Gainesville: University of Florida Press, 2011.

———. "Interpreting the Latrines of the Johnson's Island Civil War Military Prison." *Historical Archaeology* 34, no. 1 (2000): 62–78.

Bynum, W. F., and Roy Porter, eds. *Medicine and the Five Senses*. New York: Cambridge University Press, 1993.

Byrne, Frank L. "Libby Prison: A Study in Emotions." *Journal of Southern History* 24, no. 4 (November 1958): 430–44.

Camp, Stephanie M. H. *Closer to Freedom: Enslaved Women and Everyday Resistance in the Plantation South*. Chapel Hill: University of North Carolina Press, 2004.

Cashin, Joan E. "Hungry People in the Wartime South: Civilians, Armies, and the Food Supply." In *Weirding the War: Stories from the Civil War's Ragged Edges*, edited by Stephen Berry, 160–75. Athens: University of Georgia Press, 2011.

———, ed. *The War Was You and Me: Civilians in the American Civil War*. Princeton, N.J.: Princeton University Press, 2002.

Classen, Constance, ed. *A Cultural History of the Senses in the Age of Empire*. London: Bloomsbury, 2014.

―――. *The Deepest Sense: A Cultural History of Touch*. Urbana: University of Illinois Press, 2012.

―――. "Foundations for an Anthropology of the Senses." *International Social Science Journal* 153 (September 1997): 401–12.

―――. "The Witches' Senses: Sensory Ideologies and Transgressive Femininities from the Renaissance to Modernity." In *Empire of the Senses: The Sensual Culture Reader*, edited by David Howes, 70–84. Oxford: Berg, 2005.

Classen, Constance, David Howes, and Anthony Synnott, eds. *Aroma: The Cultural History of Smell*. London: Routledge, 1994.

Cloyd, Benjamin G. *Haunted by Atrocity: Civil War Prisons in American Memory*. Baton Rouge: Louisiana State University Press, 2010.

Corbin, Alain. *The Foul and the Fragrant: Odor and the French Social Imagination*. Cambridge, Mass.: Harvard University Press, 1986.

―――. "Urban Sensations: The Shifting Sensescape of the City." In *A Cultural History of the Senses in the Age of Empire*, edited by Constance Classen, 47–68. London: Bloomsbury, 2014.

Cornelius, Steven H. *Music of the Civil War Era*. Westport, Conn.: Greenwood, 2004.

Costa, Dora L., and Matthew E. Kahn. "Surviving Andersonville: The Benefits of Social Networks in POW Camps." *American Economic Review* 97, no. 4 (September 2007): 1467–87.

Covey, Herbert C., and Dwight Eisnach. *What the Slaves Ate: Recollections of African American Foods and Foodways from the Slave Narratives*. Santa Barbara, Calif.: Greenwood Press, 2009.

Cowan, Alexander, and Jill Steward, eds. *The City and the Senses: Urban Culture since 1500*. Aldershot, U.K.: Ashgate, 2007.

Crawford, Dorothy H. *Deadly Companions: How Microbes Shaped Our History*. Oxford: Oxford University Press, 2007.

Daniel, Larry J. *Soldiering in the Army of Tennessee: A Portrait of Life in a Confederate Army*. Chapel Hill: University of North Carolina Press, 1991.

Davis, Robert Scott. *Ghosts and Shadows of Andersonville: Essays on the Secret Social Histories of America's Deadliest Prison*. Macon, Ga.: Mercer University Press, 2006.

―――. "'Near Andersonville': An Historical Note on Civil War Legend and Reality." *Journal of African American History* 92, no. 1 (Winter 2007): 96–105.

Davis, William C. *A Taste for War: The Culinary History of the Blue and the Gray*. Mechanicsburg, Pa.: Stackpole Books, 2003.

Drake, Brian Allen, ed. *The Blue, the Gray, and the Green: Toward an Environmental History of the Civil War*. Athens: University of Georgia Press, 2015.

Ekirch, A. Roger. *At Day's Close: Night in Times Past*. New York: Norton, 2005.

―――. "Sleep We Have Lost: Pre-Industrial Slumber in the British Isles." *American Historical Review* 106, no. 2 (April 2001): 343–86.

Elias, Norbert. *The History of Manners*. Translated by Edmund Jephcott. New York: Pantheon Books, 1978 [1939].

Ellinger, Esther Parker. *The Southern War Poetry of the Civil War*. Hershey, Pa.: Hershey Press, 1918.

Ellis, Meredith A. B., Christopher W. Merritt, Shannon A. Novak, and Kelley J. Dixon. "The Signature of Starvation: A Comparison of Bone Processing at a Chinese Encampment in Montana and the Donner Party Camp in California." *Historical Archaeology* 45, no. 2 (June 2011): 97–112.

Estabrook, Charles E., ed. *Wisconsin Losses in the Civil War*. Madison, Wis.: Democrat Printing Company, 1915.

Fabian, Ann. *The Unvarnished Truth: Personal Narratives in Nineteenth-Century America*. Berkeley: University of California Press, 2000.

Faust, Drew Gilpin. *This Republic of Suffering: Death and the American Civil War*. New York: Vintage, 2009.

Fetzer, Dale, and Bruce Mowday. *Unlikely Allies: Fort Delaware's Prison Community in the Civil War*. Mechanicsburg, Pa.: Stackpole Books, 2000.

Fiege, Mark. "Gettysburg and the Organic Nature of the American Civil War." In *Natural Enemy, Natural Ally: Toward an Environmental History of War*, edited by Richard P. Tucker and Edmund Russell, 93–109. Corvallis: Oregon State University Press, 2004.

———. *The Republic of Nature: An Environmental History of the United States*. Seattle: University of Washington Press, 2012.

Flammang, Janet A. *The Taste for Civilization: Food, Politics, and Civil Society*. Urbana: University of Illinois Press, 2009.

Foner, Eric. *Reconstruction: America's Unfinished Revolution, 1863–1877*. New York: Harper & Row, 1988.

Foote, Lorien. *The Gentlemen and the Roughs: Violence, Honor, and Manhood in the Union Army*. New York: New York University Press, 2010.

Frank, Joseph A., and George A. Reaves. *"Seeing the Elephant": Raw Recruits at the Battle of Shiloh*. Westport, Conn.: Greenwood, 1989.

Frohman, Charles E. *Rebels on Lake Erie*. Columbus: Ohio Historical Society, 1965.

Futch, Ovid L. *History of Andersonville Prison*. Gainesville: University of Florida Press, 2011 [1968].

Geier, Clarence R., David G. Orr, and Matthew B. Reeves, eds. *Huts and History: The Historical Archaeology of Military Encampment during the American Civil War*. Gainesville: University of Florida Press, 2006.

Gillispie, James M. *Andersonvilles of the North: The Myths and Realities of Northern Treatment of Civil War Confederate Prisoners*. Denton: University of North Texas Press, 2008.

Gilman, Sander. "Touch, Sexuality, and Disease." In *Medicine and the Five Senses*, edited by W. F. Bynum and Roy Porter, 198–224. Cambridge: Cambridge University Press, 1993.

Glatthaar, Joseph T. *The March to the Sea and Beyond: Sherman's Troops in the Savannah and Carolinas Campaigns*. New York: New York University Press, 1985.

Grant, Susan-Mary. *North over South: Northern Nationalism and American Identity in the Antebellum Era*. Lawrence: University Press of Kansas, 2000.

Gray, Michael P. *The Business of Captivity: Elmira and Its Civil War Prison*. Kent, Ohio: Kent State University Press, 2001.

———. "Captivating Captives: An Excursion to Johnson's Island Civil War Prison." In *Union Heartland: The Midwestern Home Front during the Civil War*, edited by Ginette Aley and J. L. Anderson, 16–32. Carbondale: Southern Illinois University Press, 2013.

Green, Fletcher Melvin. *Democracy in the Old South and Other Essays by Fletcher Melvin Green*. Edited by J. Isaac Copeland. Nashville: Vanderbilt University Press, 1969.

Hall, James R. *Den of Misery: Indiana's Civil War Prison*. Gretna, La.: Pelican Publishing, 2006.

Harris, Marvin. *Good to Eat: Riddles of Food and Culture*. Long Grove, Ill.: Waveland Press, 1998 [1985].

Hess, Earl J. *The Union Soldier in Battle: Enduring the Ordeal of Combat*. Lawrence: University Press of Kansas, 1997.

Hesseltine, William B., ed. *Civil War Prisons*. Kent, Ohio: Kent State University Press, 1997 [1962].

———. *Civil War Prisons: A Study in War Psychology*. New York: Frederick Ungar Publishing, 1964 [1930].

Hilliard, Sam Bowers. *Hog Meat and Hoecake: Food Supply in the Old South, 1840–1860*. Carbondale: Southern Illinois University Press, 1972.

Hindus, Michael Stephen. *Prison and Plantation: Crime, Justice, and Authority in Massachusetts and South Carolina, 1767–1878*. Chapel Hill: University of North Carolina Press, 1980.

Hoffer, Peter Charles. *Sensory Worlds in Early America*. Baltimore: Johns Hopkins University Press, 2003.

Hoock, Holger. *Scars of Independence: America's Violent Birth*. New York: Crown, 2017.

Hooker, Richard James. *Food and Drink in America: A History*. Indianapolis, Ind.: Bobbs-Merrill, 1981.

Horigan, Michael. *Elmira: Death Camp of the North*. Mechanicsburg, Pa.: Stackpole Books, 2002.

Horwitz, Tony. *Confederates in the Attic: Dispatches from the Unfinished Civil War*. New York: Vintage, 1999.

Howes, David. "Can These Dry Bones Live? An Anthropological Approach to the History of the Senses." *Journal of American History* 95, no. 2 (September 2008): 442–51.

———, ed. *Empire of the Senses: The Sensual Culture Reader*. Oxford: Berg, 2005.

———. *Sensual Relations: Engaging the Senses in Culture and Social Theory*. Ann Arbor: University of Michigan Press, 2003.

———. *The Varieties of Sensory Experience: A Sourcebook in the Anthropology of the Senses*. Toronto: University of Toronto Press, 1991.

Humphreys, Margaret. *Marrow of Tragedy: The Health Crisis of the American Civil War*. Baltimore: Johns Hopkins University Press, 2013.

Ignatieff, Michael. *A Just Measure of Pain: The Penitentiary in the Industrial Revolution, 1750–1850*. New York: Pantheon Books, 1978.

Inglis, David. "Sewers and Sensibilities: The Bourgeois Faecal Experience in the Nineteenth-Century City." In *The City and the Senses: Urban Culture since 1500*, edited by Alexander Cowan and Jill Steward, 105–30. Aldershot, U.K.: Ashgate, 2007.

Jenner, Mark S. R. "Tasting Lichfield, Touching China: Sir John Floyer's Senses." *The Historical Journal* 53, no. 3 (September 2010): 647–70.

Johnson, Walter. *River of Dark Dreams: Slavery and Empire in the Cotton Kingdom*. Cambridge, Mass.: Belknap Press of Harvard University Press, 2013.

Joslyn, Mauriel P. *Immortal Captives: The Story of 600 Confederate Officers and the United States Prisoner of War Policy*. Shippensburg, Pa.: White Mane Publishing, 1996.

Jütte, Robert. "The Senses in Philosophy and Science: From the Senses to Sensations." In *A Cultural History of the Senses in the Age of Empire*, edited by Constance Classen, 113–36. London: Bloomsbury, 2014.

Kantor, MacKinlay. *Andersonville*. Cleveland: World Publishing Company, 1955.

———. "The Last Full Measure of Devotion: The Author Tells How He Relived the Tragedy." *New York Times Book Review*, October 30, 1955, 1, 32–33.

Keys, Ancel, Josef Brozek, Austin Henschel, Olaf Mickelsen, and Henry Longstreet Taylor. *The Biology of Human Starvation*. 2 vols. Minneapolis: University of Minnesota Press, 1950.

Korsmeyer, Carolyn. *Making Sense of Taste: Food and Philosophy*. Ithaca, N.Y.: Cornell University Press, 1999.

———, ed. *The Taste Culture Reader: Experiencing Food and Drink*. Oxford: Berg, 2005.

Kytle, Ethan J., and Blain Roberts. *Denmark Vesey's Garden: Slavery and Memory in the Cradle of the Confederacy*. New York: New Press, 2018.

Levin, Kevin M. *Remembering the Battle of the Crater: War as Murder*. Lexington: University Press of Kentucky, 2012.

Levy, George. *To Die in Chicago: Confederate Prisoners at Camp Douglas, 1862–1865*. Evanston, Ill.: Evanston Publishing, 1994.

Linderman, Gerald F. *Embattled Courage: The Experience of Combat in the American Civil War*. New York: Free Press, 1987.

Logue, Larry M. *To Appomattox and Beyond: The Civil War Soldier in War and Peace*. Chicago: Ivan R. Dee, 1996.

Manning, Chandra. *Troubled Refuge: Struggling for Freedom in the Civil War*. New York: Knopf, 2016.

———. *What This Cruel War Was Over: Soldiers, Slavery, and the Civil War*. New York: Vintage, 2008.

Marks, Stuart A. *Southern Hunting in Black and White: Nature, History, and Ritual in a Carolina Community*. Princeton, N.J.: Princeton University Press, 1991.

Marvel, William. *Andersonville: The Last Depot*. Chapel Hill: University of North Carolina Press, 1994.

Massey, Mary Elizabeth. *Ersatz in the Confederacy: Shortages and Substitutes on the Southern Homefront*. Columbia: University of South Carolina Press, 1993.

McAdams, Benton. *Rebels at Rock Island: The Story of a Civil War Prison*. DeKalb: Northern Illinois University Press, 2000.

McLuhan, Marshall. *The Gutenberg Galaxy: The Making of Typographic Man*. Toronto: University of Toronto Press, 1962.

———. "Inside the Five Sense Sensorium." In *Empire of the Senses: The Sensual Culture Reader*, edited by David Howes, 43–52. Oxford: Berg, 2005.

McPherson, James M. *Battle Cry of Freedom: The Civil War Era*. Oxford: Oxford University Press, 1988.

———. *For Cause and Comrades: Why Men Fought in the Civil War*. New York: Oxford University Press, 1997.

———. *What They Fought For, 1861–1865*. Baton Rouge: Louisiana State University Press, 1994.

McPherson, James M., and William J. Cooper Jr. *Writing the Civil War: The Quest to Understand*. Columbia: University of South Carolina Press, 1998.

McWhirter, Christian. *Battle Hymns: The Power and Popularity of Music in the Civil War*. Chapel Hill: University of North Carolina Press, 2012.

Meier, Kathryn Shively. "The Man Who Has Nothing to Lose." In *The Blue, the Gray, and the Green: Toward an Environmental History of the Civil War*, edited by Brian Allen Drake, 67–95. Athens: University of Georgia Press, 2015.

———. *Nature's Civil War: Common Soldiers and the Environment in 1862 Virginia*. Chapel Hill: University of North Carolina Press, 2013.

Melbin, Murray. *Night as Frontier: Colonizing the World after Dark*. London: Free Press, 1987.

Melosi, Martin V. *The Sanitary City: Urban Infrastructure in American from Colonial Times to the Present*. Baltimore: Johns Hopkins University Press, 2000.

Mitchell, Reid. "'Not the General but the Soldier': The Study of Civil War Soldiers." In *Writing the Civil War: The Quest to Understand*, edited by James M. McPherson and William J. Cooper, 81–95. Columbia: University of South Carolina Press, 1998.

Mitman, Gregg. "In Search of Health: Landscape and Disease in American Environmental History." *Environmental History* 10, no. 2 (April 2005): 184–210.

Nead, Lynda. *Victorian Babylon: People, Streets and Images in Nineteenth-Century London*. New Haven, Conn.: Yale University Press, 2000.

Nelson, Megan Kate. *Ruin Nation: Destruction and the American Civil War*. Athens: University of Georgia Press, 2012.

Ong, Walter J. *Orality and Literacy: The Technologizing of the World*. London: Routledge, 1988 [1982].

Orwell, George. *The Collected Essays, Journalism, and Letters of George Orwell, Vol. 4, In Front of Your Nose, 1945–1950*. Edited by Sonia Orwell and Ian Angus. London: Secker & Warburg, 1968.

Ouchley, Kelby. *Flora and Fauna of the Civil War: An Environmental Reference Guide*. Baton Rouge: Louisiana State University Press, 2010.

Palmer, Bryan D. *Cultures of Darkness: Night Travels in the Histories of Transgression*. New York: Monthly Review Press, 2000.

Phillips, Jason. "Battling Stereotypes: A Taxonomy of Common Soldiers in Civil War History." *History Compass* 6, no. 6 (2008): 1407–25.

———. *Diehard Rebels: The Confederate Culture of Invincibility*. Athens: University of Georgia Press, 2007.

———. "The Grape Vine Telegraph: Rumors and Confederate Persistence." *Journal of Southern History* 72, no. 4 (November 2006): 753–88.

Pickenpaugh, Roger. *Camp Chase and the Evolution of Union Prison Policy*. Tuscaloosa: University of Alabama Press, 2007.

———. *Captives in Blue: The Civil War Prisons of the Confederacy*. Tuscaloosa: University of Alabama Press, 2013.

———. *Captives in Gray: The Civil War Prisons of the Union*. Tuscaloosa: University of Alabama Press, 2009.

———. *Johnson's Island: A Prison for Confederate Officers*. Kent, Ohio: Kent State University Press, 2016.

Rable, George C. *Civil Wars: Women and the Crisis of Southern Nationalism*. Urbana: University of Illinois Press, 1989.

———. *God's Almost Chosen Peoples: A Religious History of the American Civil War*. Chapel Hill: University of North Carolina Press, 2010.

Rath, Richard Cullen. "Hearing American History." *Journal of American History* 95, no. 2 (September 2008): 417–31.

———. *How Early America Sounded*. Ithaca, N.Y.: Cornell University Press, 2003.

Reed, David L., Jessica E. Light, Julie M. Allen, and Jeremy J. Kirchman. "Pair of Lice Lost or Parasites Regained: The Evolutionary History of Anthropoid Primate Lice." *BMC Biology* 5, no. 7 (March 2007): 1–11.

Roberts, Lissa. "The Death of the Sensuous Chemist: The 'New' Chemistry and the Transformation of Sensuous Technology." In *Empire of the Senses: The Sensual Culture Reader*, edited by David Howes, 106–27. Oxford: Berg, 2005.

Robins, Glenn. "Race, Repatriation, and Galvanized Rebels: Union Prisoners and the Exchange Question in Deep South Prison Camps." *Civil War History* 53, no. 2 (June 2007): 117–40.

Rosen, Christine Meisner. "'Knowing' Industrial Pollution: Nuisance Law and the Power of Tradition in a Time of Rapid Economic Change, 1840–1864." *Environmental History* 8, no. 4 (October 2003): 565–97.

———. "Noisome, Noxious, and Offensive Vapors, Fumes and Stenches in American Towns and Cities, 1840–1865." *Historical Geography* 25 (1997): 49–82.

Russell, Edmund. *War and Nature: Fighting Humans and Insects with Chemicals from World War I to Silent Spring*. Cambridge: Cambridge University Press, 2001.

Sanders, Charles W., Jr. *While in the Hands of the Enemy: Military Prisons of the Civil War*. Baton Rouge: Louisiana State University Press, 2005.

Sarasohn, Lisa T. "'That Nauseous Venomous Insect': Bedbugs in Early Modern England." *Eighteenth-Century Studies* 46, no. 4 (Summer 2013): 513–30.

Scarry, Elaine. *The Body in Pain: The Making and Unmaking of the World*. New York: Oxford University Press, 1985.

Scott, James C. *Domination and the Arts of Resistance: Hidden Transcripts*. New Haven, Conn.: Yale University Press, 1990.

Silber, Irwin, ed. *Songs of the Civil War*. New York: Dover, 1995 [1960].

Smilor, Raymond W. "Personal Boundaries in the Urban Environment: The Legal Attack on Noise, 1865–1930." *Environmental Review* 3, no. 1 (March 1979): 24–36.

Smith, Mark M. "Getting in Touch with Slavery and Freedom." *Journal of American History* 95, no. 2 (September 2008): 381–91.

———, ed. *Hearing History: A Reader*. Athens: University of Georgia Press, 2004.

———. *How Race Is Made: Slavery, Segregation, and the Senses*. Chapel Hill: University of North Carolina Press, 2006.

———. *Listening to Nineteenth-Century America*. Chapel Hill: University of North Carolina Press, 2001.

———. *Mastered by the Clock: Time, Slavery, and Freedom in the American South*. Chapel Hill: University of North Carolina Press, 1997.

———. "Of Bells, Booms, Sounds, and Silences: Listening to the Civil War South." In *The War Was You and Me: Civilians in the American Civil War*, edited by Joan E. Cashin, 9–34. Princeton, N.J.: Princeton University Press, 2002.

———. "Producing Sense, Consuming Sense, Making Sense: Perils and Prospects for Sensory History." *Journal of Social History* 40, no. 4 (Summer 2007): 841–58.

———. *Sensing the Past: Seeing, Hearing, Smelling, Tasting, and Touching in History*. Berkeley: University of California Press, 2007.

———. *The Smell of Battle, the Taste of Siege: A Sensory History of the Civil War*. Oxford: Oxford University Press, 2015.

Smith, Shawn Michelle. *American Archives: Gender, Race, and Class in Visual Culture*. Princeton, N.J.: Princeton University Press, 1999.

Speer, Lonnie R. *Portals to Hell: Military Prisons of the Civil War*. Mechanicsburg, Pa.: Stackpole Books, 1997.

Springer, Paul J., and Glenn Robins. *Transforming Civil War Prisons: Lincoln, Lieber, and the Politics of Captivity*. New York: Routledge, 2015.

Stansell, Christine. *City of Women: Sex and Class in New York, 1789–1860*. Urbana: University of Illinois Press, 1987.

Stauffer, John. *Black Hearts of Men: Radical Abolitionists and the Transformation of Race*. Cambridge, Mass.: Harvard University Press, 2002.

Sternhell, Yael A. "The Afterlives of a Confederate Archive: Civil War Documents and the Making of Sectional Reconciliation." *Journal of American History* 102, no. 4 (March 2016): 1025–50.

———. *Routes of War: The World of Movement in the Confederate South*. Cambridge, Mass.: Harvard University Press, 2012.

Stewart, Susan. "Remembering the Senses." In *Empire of the Senses: The Sensual Cultural Reader*, edited by David Howes, 59–69. Oxford: Berg, 2005.

Sutherland, Daniel E. "The Rise and Fall of Esther B. Cheesborough: The Battles of a Literary Lady." *South Carolina Historical Magazine* 84, no. 1 (January 1983): 22–34.

Tarr, Joel A. *The Search for the Ultimate Sink: Urban Pollution in Historical Perspective*. Akron, Ohio: University of Akron Press, 1996.

———. "Urban Pollution: Many Long Years Ago." *American Heritage Magazine* 22, no. 6 (October 1971): 64–69.

Taylor, Joe Gray. *Eating, Drinking, and Visiting in the South: An Informal History*. Baton Rouge: Louisiana State University Press, 1982.

Thelen, David. "Memory and American History." *Journal of American History* 75, no. 4 (March 1989): 1117–29.

Thomas, Keith. *Man and the Natural World: A History of the Modern Sensibility*. New York: Pantheon Books, 1983.

Thompson, Tommy. "'Dying Like Rotten Sheepe': Camp Randall as a Prisoner of War Facility during the Civil War." *Wisconsin Magazine of History* 92, no. 1 (Autumn 2008): 2–15.

Tucker, Richard P., and Edmund Russell, eds. *Natural Enemy, Natural Ally: Toward an Environmental History of War*. Corvallis: Oregon State University Press, 2004.

Urry, John. "Time, Leisure and Social Identity." *Time and Society* 3, no. 2 (June 1994): 131–49.

Valenčius, Conevery Bolton. *The Health of the Country: How American Settlers Understood Themselves and Their Land*. New York: Basic Books, 2002.

Varon, Elizabeth R. *Southern Lady, Yankee Spy: The True Story of Elizabeth Van Lew, a Union Agent in the Heart of the Confederacy*. New York: Oxford University Press, 2003.

A Voice from Rebel Prisons; Giving an Account of Some of the Horrors of the Stockades at Andersonville, Milan, and Other Prisons. Boston: Geo. C. Rand and Avery, and Cornhill, 1865.

Waldstreicher, David. *In the Midst of Perpetual Fetes: The Making of American Nationalism, 1776–1820*. Chapel Hill: University of North Carolina Press, 1997.

Warren, Craig A. *The Rebel Yell: A Cultural History*. Tuscaloosa: University of Alabama Press, 2014.

Watson, Harry L. "The Man with the Dirty Black Beard: Race, Class, and Schools in the Antebellum South." *Journal of the Early Republic* 2, no. 1 (Spring 2012): 1–26.

Wells, Cheryl A. *Civil War Time: Temporality and Identity in America, 1861–1865*. Athens: University of Georgia Press, 2005.

White, Deborah Gray. *Ar'n't I a Woman? Female Slaves in the Plantation South*, rev. ed. New York: Norton, 1999.

White, Jonathan W. *Midnight in America: Darkness, Sleep, and Dreams during the Civil War*. Chapel Hill: University of North Carolina Press, 2017.

White, Shane, and Graham White. "Listening to Southern Slavery." In *Hearing History: A Reader*, edited by Mark M. Smith, 247–66. Athens: University of Georgia Press, 2004.

———. *The Sounds of Slavery: Discovering African American History through Songs, Sermons, and Speech*. Boston: Beacon, 2005.

Wiley, Bell Ivrin. *The Life of Johnny Reb: The Common Soldier of the Confederacy*. Cincinnati: Bobbs-Merrill, 1943.

Williams, Timothy J. *Intellectual Manhood: University, Self, and Society in the Antebellum South*. Chapel Hill: University of North Carolina Press, 2015.

Williams, Timothy J., and Evan A. Kutzler. *Prison Pens: Gender, Memory, and Imprisonment in the Writings of Mollie Scollay and Wash Nelson, 1863–1866*. Athens: University of Georgia Press, 2018.

Winslow, Hattie Lou, and Joseph R. H. Moore. *Camp Morton, 1861–1865: Indianapolis Prison Camp*. Indianapolis: Indiana Historical Society, 1995 [1940].

Witt, John Fabian. *Lincoln's Code: The Laws of War in American History*. New York: Free Press, 2012.

Wood, Peter H. *Near Andersonville: Winslow Homer's Civil War*. Cambridge, Mass.: Harvard University Press, 2010.

Zinsser, Hans. *Rats, Lice, and History*. Boston: Little, Brown and Company, 1963 [1965].

Zombek, Angela M. *Penitentiaries, Punishment, and Military Prisons: Familiar Responses to an Extraordinary Crisis during the American Civil War*. Kent, Ohio: Kent State University Press, 2018.

Dissertations and M.A. Theses

Gardner, Douglas G. "Andersonville and American Memory: Civil War Prisons and Narratives of Suffering and Redemption." Ph.D. diss., Miami University, 1998.

Hunter, Leslie Gene. "Warden for the Union: General William Hoffman (1807–1884)." Ph.D. diss., Arizona State University, 1971.

Lane, Lea Catherine. "'A Marvel of Taste and Skill': Carved Pipes of the American Civil War." M.A. thesis: University of Delaware, 2015.

Newhall, Caroline Wood. "'This Is the Point on Which the Whole Matter Hinges': Locating Black Voices in Civil War Prisons." M.A. thesis: University of North Carolina, 2016.

Plaag, Eric William. "Strangers in a Strange Land: Northern Travelers and the Coming of the American Civil War." Ph.D. diss., University of South Carolina, 2006.

Smithpeters, Jeffrey Neal. "'To the Latest Generation': Cold War and Post–Cold War U.S. Civil War Novels in their Social Contexts." Ph.D. diss., Louisiana State, 2005.

Index

128, 130; rat meat, 117, 161n54; rye (grain), 124, 125; soup, 24, 109, 115, 116, 118, 121; sugar, 105, 119, 120, 122, 123, 126; sweet potatoes, 121, 122, 126, 127; tea, 105, 120, 121, 133; tomatoes, 121, 122; turkey, 104, 119

Dillard, William, 60

dishonor, 6, 63, 75, 78

Dix, Dorothea, 111

Dix, John A., 11, 12

Dolphin, William, 24, 108–9, 126, 127–28

Dooley, John, 65, 117

Dougherty, Michael, 22

Douglass, Frederick, 110

Downes, William, 128

drainage systems, 41, 43, 50, 51, 52, 53, 55, 56–57, 60, 71

dreams/dreaming, 2, 5, 17, 22, 33–34, 35, 94, 115–16, 144n88, 158n101

Drummond, Edward, 119, 120, 123

drums, 18, 19, 27, 90, 109

drunkenness, 19, 32, 90

dysentery, 1

Eberhart, James, 74, 142n36

Eddy, Hiram, 9, 10, 12, 42, 98–99, 126

Eldridge, E. J., 56

Ellis, E. John, 25–26, 116–17

Elmira (NY) Prison, 6, 12, 28, 29, 117, 124, 131, 161n54; and prisoner deaths, 5, 48, 55; and sanitation, 53–54, 72; and tobacco use, 125, 126

escape fantasies/escapes, 2, 14, 30–31, 33, 36, 45, 55

Fabian, Ann, 14, 140n39

Farinholt, Benjamin, 123

Faucette, Lindsey, 65

Fisher, Louis, 80

fleas, 19, 25, 64, 68

flies, 59, 63, 64

Flinn, John, 27, 28

Flowers, William, 75

Follett, John, 19

food foraging, 8, 64, 108, 141n23

Foote, Lorien, 61, 91

Forbes, Eugene, 75, 97, 140n39

Forbes, Stephen, 81

Forrest, Nathan Bedford, 45

Fort Delaware (DE), 12, 27, 89, 91, 155n51; diets in, 105, 106, 115, 116, 117, 122, 123; and disease, 23; and hygiene/sanitation, 52, 72, 73; soundscapes of, 88; and vermin, 70, 117

Fort Donelson (KY), 11, 30, 120

Fort McHenry (MD), 11, 42, 70

Fort Pulaski (GA), 12, 34

Fort Warren (MA), 11, 42, 44, 95, 97, 99, 105, 119, 120, 125

Forty-Sixth Article of War, 17

Foster, John, 1, 2

Foust, Samuel, 23, 133

Franklin, Benjamin, 26

Franklin, James, 26–27, 87, 116

frogs, 19, 129, 135

Frost, Griffin, 27, 31, 45

fumigation, 42, 55

gangrene, 47

Garfield, James, 71

gender/gendering, 15, 38, 73, 75, 76

General Orders No. 100, 12, 112

Gibson, John, 117

Gibson, Rachel, 13, 14

Gibson, Samuel, 1–2, 3, 13, 14, 15, 23, 43, 98, 134, 136

Gill, George, 25

Gillespie, James, 140n39

Gillette, James, 121

Grant, Ulysses S., 12, 30, 85, 88, 96

graybacks. See lice

Grosvenor, Samuel, 27, 45

guards, 10, 28, 29, 67, 71, 81, 83, 94, 109, 120, 121, 122–23; and gunfire, 30, 44; at nighttime, 17, 28–29; and noise, 32, 34, 36, 85, 87, 89, 96, 97, 98; and odor, 43, 59–60; and prisoner escapes, 5, 30–31, 33